A PROJECT GUIDE TO

UX DESIGN

FOR USER EXPERIENCE DESIGNERS IN THE FIELD OR IN THE MAKING

SECOND EDITION

RUSS UNGER AND **CAROLYN CHANDLER**

New Riders VOICES THAT MATTER™

A Project Guide to UX Design, Second Edition
Russ Unger and Carolyn Chandler

New Riders
1249 Eighth Street
Berkeley, CA 94710
(510) 524-2178
(510) 524-2221 (fax)

Find us on the Web at: www.newriders.com
To report errors, please send a note to errata@peachpit.com

New Riders is an imprint of Peachpit, a division of Pearson Education.

Copyright © 2012 by Russ Unger and Carolyn Chandler

Project Editor: Michael J. Nolan
Development Editor: Jeff Riley/Box Twelve Communications
Production Editor: Tracey Croom
Copyeditor: Jeff Riley/Box Twelve Communications
Proofreader: Rose Weisburd
Interior and Cover Designer: Mimi Heft
Indexer: Rebecca Plunkett

Notice of Rights

Notice of Liability

Trademarks

ISBN 13: 978-0-321-81538-5
ISBN 10:   0-321-81538-6

9 8 7 6 5 4 3

Printed and bound in the United States of America

Praise for *A Project Guide to UX Design*

If Russ Unger and Carolyn Chandler were magicians, the Alliance would be after them for revealing their best secrets. Fortunately for you, they're not. Russ and Carolyn have collected up sage wisdom previously only known to the most experienced UX project leaders and codified it for all to see. Now you can learn the secrets necessary to running great user experience projects.

Jared M. Spool, CEO and founding principal of User Interface Engineering

Is there one book that can tell you everything you need to know about designing user experiences? No. Is there a book that can get you most of the way there? There is now. Carolyn and Russ have laid a solid foundation for planning and managing design projects. This is an essential handbook for anyone mired in the competing methodologies, the endless meetings, and all the moving parts of user experience design.

Dan Brown, author of *Communicating Design*

This book is a fantastic introduction to how to design great products for real people. But it covers much more than just design—it also includes all the things around design: managing projects, working with people, and communicating ideas. A great all-rounder.

Donna Spencer, author of "Card Sorting: Designing Usable Categories"

This is a practical, accessible, and very human guide to a very human activity: working together with people to make great things for other people.

Steve Portigal, Portigal Consulting

If you've heard of Wil Wheaton the author, you understand why I hold Russ Unger in such high regard. Russ's experience and guidance was fundamental to the construction and design of Monolith Press, and he's been one of the most valuable collaborators I've ever worked with.

Wil Wheaton, actor and author of *Dancing Barefoot*, *Just a Geek*, and *The Happiest Days of Our Lives*

Acknowledgments

Russ Unger

When you agree to write a second edition of a book, it seems it should be a breeze. Then you start to review the tasks ahead of you, and you realize that it can be every bit as challenging as the first edition. Fortunately, as with the first edition, there was a lot of help in creating this.

My family allowed me to do this. Again. I'm eternally grateful. Thank you for keeping me in smiles and laughter at times when I've been in short supply. Thank you for laughing at jokes no one else would ever find funny.

My friends chimed in, threw in support at the last minute, and stepped up to bat to provide content and confidence, both of which were definitely needed at points during this endeavor. In no specific order, the stars of the second edition are: Brad Nunnally, Kim Nunnally, Jonathan "Yoni" Knoll, Brad Simpson, Gabby Hon, Laura Creekmore, Tim Frick, Margot Bloomstein, Dr. Arthur Doederlein, Sarah Krznarich, Matthew Grocki, Dave Gray, and Todd Zaki Warfel. I'm blessed to know such amazing people, who have offered their time and resources.

Carolyn and our counterparts at New Riders, who are always a blessing to get to work with: Michael Nolan, Jeff Riley, Tracey Croom, and Mimi Heft pulled together to help us really nail this down. It is a pleasure to get to work with you all.

Everyone who helped out with the first edition, and offered continued support: Linda Laflamme, Becca Freed, Steve "Doc" Baty, Brad Simpson, Mark Brooks, Jonathan Ashton, Jono Kane, Lou Rosenfeld, Christina Wodtke, Todd Zaki Warfel, Will Evans, David Armano, Livia Labate, Matthew Milan, Troy Lucht, Ross Kimbarovsky, Wil Wheaton, Tonia M. Bartz, Leah Buley, Dave Carlson, Christopher Fahey, Nick Finck, Jesse James Garrett, Austin Govella, Jon Hadden, Whitney Hess, Andrew Hinton, Gabby Hon, Kaleem Khan, James Melzer, Chris Miller, Maciej Piwowarczyk, Stephanie Sansoucie, Kit Seeborg, Josh Seiden, Jonathan Snook, Joe Sokohl, Samantha Soma, Jared M. Spool, Keith Tatum, Tim Bruns, Peter Ina, Jean Marc Favreau, Steve Portigal, Andrew Boyd, Dan Brown, Christian Crumlish, Alec Kalner, Hugh Forrest, and all of the UX Book Clubs (http://uxbookclub.org) across the world that continue to support the authors crazy enough to put it down in writing.

Finally, it is important to note that without organizations like the Information Architecture Institute, Interaction Design Association, and others, it would have been impossible for me to make the connections with many of the people mentioned. If you're at all curious about the field of UX design, go explore these organizations, join them, and get involved!

Carolyn Chandler

Every worthy challenge brings its own set of lessons, and writing a book is certainly that kind of challenge. In writing the first edition, I learned how difficult it is to step away from what you do day to day, and to tell that story of a user-centered project approach from beginning to end. I kept jumping to the middle, but thankfully Linda Laflamme kept Russ and me focused on the overall flow and clarity.

In working on this edition, I finally realized how closely the book-writing process resembles the design process. You need to research, immerse, talk to users, talk to experts, generate concepts and create structure before you can really get into the details.

The experts in this edition helped me immerse in some of the most recent and relevant changes in the field. Nate Bolt shared his expertise in remote research tools, which have had an unbelievable growth in both number and effectiveness since the first edition. Jeff Gothelf brought his experience in Lean UX, an approach that has helped entrepreneurs focus on bringing user-centered products to light quickly and inexpensively. Brian Henkel, Chris Ina, and Jim Jacoby provided invaluable information on considerations when designing for mobile devices. And Brandy Taylor brought the new information on design principles to a higher level by sharing her philosophy and process in working with the visual, emotional elements of a design.

A hearty "thanks!" to these experts, and to all the folks at Manifest Digital who gave me extra time and space to write this edition, including Jennifer Conklin, Sue Hardek, and Michael Latiner. And of course, I'd like to thank Jim Jacoby for talking me off the ledge when I wasn't sure how to balance everything. It all turned out fine, just like you said, Jim!

In addition to the people Russ has already acknowledged, I'm continually grateful for the people who contributed to the first edition, with support, expertise, and time: Steve Baty, John Geletka, Linda Laflamme, Christine

Mortensen, Brett Gilbert, Jen O'Brien, Jason Ulaszek, Haley Ebeling, Meredith Payne, Jenn Berzansky, Santiago Ruiz—and for Danyell Jones, for helping me get set up on delightside.com.

Last but not least, I want to thank my family and friends, who once again patiently dealt with my random appearances, and my occasional hermit-like retreats to the writing cave. I'm coming out now—see you in the sunlight!

Contents

INTRODUCTION xiii

CHAPTER 1: The Tao of UXD 1

    What Is User Experience Design? 3

      The Broad Definition 3

      Don't Forget the Tangible 4

      Our Focus 5

    About UX Designers 6

    Where UX Designers Live 7

    Let's Get Started! 8

CHAPTER 2: The Project Ecosystem 9

    Identify the Type of Site 10

      Brand Presence 11

      Marketing Campaign 14

      Content Source 16

      Task-Based Applications 18

      E-Commerce Sites 19

      E-Learning Applications 20

      Social Networking Applications 21

      Mobile Sites and Applications 21

    Choose Your Hats 30

      Information Architect 30

      Interaction Designer 31

      User Researcher 32

      Other Roles You May Play or May Need 35

      Building a Network of User Advocacy 41

    Understand the Company Culture 42

      History 43

      Hierarchy 45

      Logistics 46

    Pulling It Together 47

CHAPTER 3: Proposals for Consultants and Freelancers 49

Proposals 50

Creating the Proposal. 51

Title Page. 52

Revision History 53

Project Overview 54

Project Approach 55

Scope of Work 57

Assumptions 57

Deliverables. 58

Ownership and Rights 59

Additional Costs and Fees. 60

Project Pricing. 61

Payment Schedule 62

Acknowledgment and Sign-Off 63

Statements of Work 65

CHAPTER 4: Project Objectives and Approach 67

Solidify Project Objectives. 68

How Can a UX Designer Help? 71

Understand the Project Approach 73

Waterfall Approach. 74

Agile Approaches 75

Modified Approaches. 80

How Does the Approach Affect Me?. 81

CHAPTER 5: Business Requirements 83

Understand the Current State. 86

Heuristic Analysis 86

Gather Ideas from Stakeholders 90

Outline Responsibilities 91

Gather the Right Stakeholders 92

Create a Plan for the Meetings. 94

Sales: Requirements-Gathering Meeting. 94

Run the Meetings Effectively. 96

Coalescing Requirements. 98

CHAPTER 6: User Research 101

Basic Steps of User Research 102

Define Your User Groups 102

Create a List of Attributes 103

Prioritize and Define 105

Choosing Research Techniques 107

How Many Research Activities Can I Include? 110

User Interviews 111

Contextual Inquiry 114

Surveys 118

Focus Groups 121

Card Sorting 124

Usability Testing 127

After the Research 128

CHAPTER 7: Personas 129

What Are Personas? 130

Why Create Personas? 130

Finding Information for Personas 131

Creating Personas 131

Minimum Content Requirements 134

Optional Content 137

Advanced Personas 139

Guerrilla Personas: The Empathy Map 141

Final Thoughts on Personas 143

CHAPTER 8: Content Strategy 145

Why Do You Need Content Strategy? 146

When Do You Need Content Strategy? 147

Who Does Content Strategy? 149

How Long Does Content Strategy Last? 149

This Sounds Familiar… 150

Tools of the Trade 152

The Artifacts 152

What is the One Artifact You Need? 156

Additional Resources 156

Things to Look Out For 160

CHAPTER 9: Transition: From Defining to Designing 163

    Ideate and Visualize Features 165

    The Basic Process of Storyboarding 166

    Facilitate the Prioritization Process. 169

    Maintain a Good Tension 173

    The Development Advocate 175

    Managing Conflict During Prioritization 177

    Plan Your Activities and Documentation 181

CHAPTER 10: Design Principles. 185

    Visual Design 186

    Unity and Variety. 187

    Hierarchy and Dominance 189

    Economy of Elements. 191

    Proportion and Balance. 193

    Interaction 196

    Associations and Affordance 197

    Economy of Motion. 200

    Response. 202

    Psychology 205

    The Effect of Attractive Design. 205

    Flow & Game Design. 207

    Social Proof. 212

    Creating Your Own Guiding Principles 215

CHAPTER 11: Site Maps and Task Flows. 219

    Tools of the Trade 221

    Basic Elements of Site Maps and Task Flows. 222

    Page. 222

    Pagestack 222

    Decision Point. 223

    Connectors and Arrows 223

    Conditions. 224

    Common Mistakes 224

    Sloppy Connections. 225

    Misaligned and Unevenly Spaced Objects 225

    Poorly Placed Text 226

Lack of Page Numbering. 226

The Simple Site Map 228

Advanced Site Maps 228

Breaking the Site Map Mold. 230

Task Flows 231

Taking Task Flows to the Next Level. 234

Swimlanes 234

CHAPTER 12: Wireframes and Annotations. 237

What Are Annotations?. 239

Who Uses Wireframes? 239

Creating Wireframes 240

Tools of the Trade. 241

Start Simply:
Design a Basic Wireframe 244

Getting Started 245

The Wireframes and Annotations. 246

Creating Wireframes: A Sample Process 249

What is This Sketching You Mention? 250

Into the Digital: Wireframes 251

Into the Digital: Visual Design. 253

Hey, What About This Responsive Design Stuff I Hear About? 254

Wireframes Vs. Prototypes 256

Which Design Is Right? 256

A Final Note on Presenting Wireframes. 257

CHAPTER 13: Prototyping. 259

How Much Prototype Do I Need? 260

Paper Prototyping. 261

Digital Prototyping 262

Wireframe vs. Realistic Prototypes. 263

HTML vs. WYSIWYG Editors 264

Additional Tools for Prototyping. 274

Working with a Developer. 275

Prototype Examples 276

What Happens After Prototyping? 278

CHAPTER 14: Design Testing with Users 279

Exploring Visual Design Mock-Ups. 283

Choosing a Design Testing Approach 284

Qualitative Research vs. Quantitative Research 285

In-Person Research vs. Remote Research 286

Remote Research Considerations 287

Moderated Techniques vs. Automated Techniques. 288

Usability Testing. 292

Planning the Research. 295

Recruiting and Logistics 299

Writing Discussion Guides. 304

Facilitating 306

Analyzing and Presenting Results. 308

Creating Recommendations. 310

CHAPTER 15: Transition: From Design to Development and Beyond 311

Almost Done.... 312

Visual Design, Development, and Quality Assurance 312

Design Testing with Users (Again). 315

10, 9, 8, 7, 6, 5, 4, 3, 2, 1 ... Launch!. 315

Personal Advantage 316

Support 316

Network Opinion 317

Postlaunch Activities. 317

Postlaunch Analytics 318

Postlaunch Design Testing with Users (Again, Again) 319

CHAPTER 16: A Brief Guide to Meetings 321

The Agenda 323

Meeting Rules 325

After the Meeting 328

Dealing with Nonconformers 330

A Final Note on Meetings. 331

All Done, Right?. 332

Just Like Starting Over.... 332

INDEX 321

333

Introduction

Why We Wrote This Book

Welcome to the second edition of *A Project Guide to UX Design*.

Somewhere there's a student in user experience design losing sleep because he doesn't know what it will be like to work on a real project at his new company. Across town, there's a visual designer with plenty of project experience who yearns to take on new responsibilities in defining her site's user experience. These are two people at different points in their lives but with a similar need: to understand how to integrate user experience practices within the context of a living, breathing project.

Our goal with this book is to give you the basic tools and context that will help you use UX tools and techniques with working teams. As you'll see in many of these chapters, we're not trying to be everything to all people, but we're trying to provide you with the core information and knowledge that you should have to perform many of the duties you'll be assigned as a UX designer. Beyond our own examples, we provide you with examples that help you identify ways to jumpstart the basic materials and allow you to mash up the information and create something newer, better, or even more suited to your own purposes.

We hope we've done a decent job of articulating that this is a pretty good approach to UX design projects.

We're nothing if not constantly trying to learn and improve *(whatever we do)* with each iteration. That's why, to a degree, we're in this field.

A Word from Russ

A lot has changed since the first edition, but fundamentals still exist. As UX roles start to expand to encompass more responsibility (content strategy, research, kick-off meetings, design, prototyping, testing with users, and so on), it is sometimes difficult to find for a good place to start. We like to think we have offered up a good place to start in UX. It will not encompass everything, and it will not go as deep as everyone needs—we have done our best to supply additional resources to help you take the deeper dives where it is important to you, while providing you a foundation that helps you get started.

I was at the Information Architecture Summit (www.iasummit.org) in 2008 when the idea for this book first began to take shape. I started planning and plotting an outline of the topics I wish someone would have covered with me when I was getting started, and luckily, I found Carolyn a willing and capable co-author who helped sand the corners off of the ideas and inject her own. That start, and the back-and-forth iterations on the content, eventually became this book.

A Word from Carolyn

For many years now, I've been in the lucky position of building and managing UX teams. I say "lucky" because I find that UX designers in general have a great balance of characteristics that make them plain fun to work with, mixing right-brain intuition and left-brain logic.

As I've conducted interviews to build these teams, one thing has really stuck out: A related educational background, like human factors or communication design, is a great indicator that someone is committed to the field of UX design, but it's not the number one indicator of whether someone would be a good fit within the team or on a project. Just as important—if not more so—is the person's ability to have a consultant's mind-set. This means a positive attitude, a drive to understand and include others throughout a project, and—above all—a focus on making a real impact for users and clients.

This mind-set means taking the time to understand the perspectives of other roles on the project, making cases, and making compromises where necessary. It takes experience and effort to get this mind-set down really well, but having an open mind, a strong foundation, and a good set of questions (with the courage to ask them) can take you a long way. This book may not supply all "the answers," but it will give you the questions to ask to help you find them.

Who Should Read This Book

A Project Guide to UX Design provides a broad, introductory overview to UX design within the context of a project. Anyone with an interest in UX design should find something useful here. We focused on the following groups in particular:

Students taking UX design courses (such as human-computer interaction or interaction design) who want to supplement their coursework with information on how to apply their learning to real-life situations, where communication and collaboration are vital.

Practitioners who would like to deepen their knowledge of the basic tools and techniques of UX design and improve team communication about the roles involved. Chapter 3 is also particularly geared toward freelancers who need to create their own proposals.

Leaders of UX design groups who are looking for a book that will help their teams integrate project best practices with UX design activities.

Leaders of any project teams who are interested in learning more about how UX design integrates into their projects, what the value is, and what to expect from UX designers.

IF YOU NEED TO...	THEN YOU SHOULD READ...
Define user experience design and understand what draws people to the field	Chapter 1: The Tao of UXD
Ask the questions that are important to have answered before the project begins (or at least before you start to work on it)	Chapter 2: The Project Ecosystem Chapter 3: Proposals for Consultants and Freelancers
Start things off right with efficient meetings, clear objectives, and well-understood approval points	Chapter 16: A Brief Guide to Meetings Chapter 4: Project Objectives and Approach
Define project requirements for content and functionality that are unambiguous and easy to prioritize, drawn from business stakeholders and users	Chapter 5: Business Requirements Chapter 6: User Research Chapter 8: Content Strategy Chapter 9: Transition: From Defining to Designing
Learn about your users and represent their needs throughout the project	Chapter 6: User Research Chapter 7: Personas Chapter 14: Design Testing with Users
Choose and utilize the tools and techniques that enable you to bring visual ideas to your project team quickly	Chapter 10: Design Principles Chapter 11: Site Maps and Task Flows Chapter 12: Wireframes and Annotations Chapter 13: Prototyping
Ensure your site is easily found and searched by users and by search engines	Online chapter: User Experience Design and Search Engine Optimization
Communicate and evolve your design with the project team once development begins	Chapter 15: Transition: From Design to Development and Beyond

Be sure to visit www.projectuxd.com to read the bonus chapter "User Experience Design and Search Engine Optimization" and to download other bonus materials such as templates.

What's New in the Second Edition

Most of the information from the first edition is still relevant three years later and is still present here, refreshed with some new examples.

In addition, you'll find updates and new chapters based on the following reader suggestions and new developments in the field.

Mobile and gestural design considerations have been added to Chapter 2: The Project Ecosystem. The number of mobile devices, and frequency of their use, has outpaced that of desktops. They form a crucial part of your users' ecosystem and should be a part of any digital product strategy.

Lean UX makes a new appearance in Chapter 4: Project Objectives and Approach. This approach has helped entrepreneurs bring a user-centered focus to developing new businesses in the face of high uncertainty.

Content strategy finds itself as a new topic in the book at Chapter 8. The content strategy field is blowing up and the information is timely, relevant, and a good springboard into the topic.

Design principles make their debut in the new Chapter 10. In response to reader requests for additional information on the elements of design, you'll find some of the prevalent principles in visual design, interaction design, and psychology to ground your design decisions, as well as tips on creating unique design principles for your own products.

Prototyping got an overhaul in Chapter 13. Jonathan "Yoni" Knoll lent a hand (and by "lent a hand," I mean "guided the process, wrote the code, made the examples available, and was an all-around good friend") and guided the chapter to being closer to a primer for those interested in finding out if they want to be "designers who code."

Chapter 12: Wireframes and Annotations was updated to include sketching and to show more of the process of creating wireframes. The change was minor and significant at the same time.

Remote research techniques and automated research tools get a deeper dive in Chapter 14: Design Testing with Users. You'll find information on balancing the choice between remote and in-person research, as well as an overview of the types of results you might expect from some of the popular automated tools.

A Note on Methodology

There are a variety of approaches and methodologies out there. We aren't proponents of one approach over another. Our goal for this book is to focus on the steps that are common to most projects: defining the project needs, designing the experience, and developing and deploying the solution. The amount of overlap between these steps will vary greatly depending on the project approach you use (see Chapter 4 for more detail). For the most part, our framework is a loose, linear approach, where the definition step comes first—but in each step we take advantage of facilitation and design techniques where they're most helpful.

What This Book Is *Not*

An encyclopedia of all techniques. The UX field has an enormous number of creative people, and they're always trying new approaches to design problems. Including all of those approaches here would make a much larger book—and one that would quickly be outdated. What we've included here are the most commonly used techniques, the nuts and bolts of UX design. We've tried to provide enough information to both intrigue you and allow you to communicate the activities to other project members—including the basic process for each technique and additional references to books or sites that will help you implement it once you choose your path.

A guide to being a project manager. Good project management (including setting and tracking project objectives, timelines, and budgets) is key to any project's success. We don't cover specifics on how to be a project manager or how to choose a particular project methodology. We do discuss the skills that a UX designer brings to a project that allow it to run effectively, such as facilitation and communication, as well as the ability to clarify and maintain focus on project objectives. These skills will help you become a partner in project management.

The only or the perfect process or methodology for *you* to follow. We don't have all the answers—no one does, today. The UX design field is relatively young, and we're all working to improve upon where we are. You will probably find that trial and error, enhancements and improvements, and feedback from others will help you tailor a process to fit your needs. When you find something that works for you—share it! Let us know!

How to Use This Book

There are many excellent resources out there for UX designers. We cover topics broadly here but point you to references that will allow you to explore topics at a deeper level depending on how much time you want to dedicate to them. To help you understand the amount of time generally needed for each reference, we've split them out into three major categories:

Surfing
References called out with the surfboard are shorter features (usually online) that will take 5 to 30 minutes to read.

Snorkeling
Those called out with the snorkel are longer online articles, white papers, or short books that take anywhere from an hour to a weekend to read.

Deep Diving
Those called out with the diver's helmet are longer books that will probably take more than one weekend to read; they give you in-depth coverage of the topic.

1 The Tao of UXD
Curiosity Meets Passion Meets Empathy

The important thing is not to stop questioning. Curiosity has its own reason for existing. One cannot help but be in awe when he contemplates the mysteries of eternity, of life, of the marvelous structure of reality. It is enough if one tries merely to comprehend a little of this mystery every day.

Albert Einstein

A sense of curiosity is nature's original school of education.

Smiley Blanton

Passion and purpose go hand-in-hand. When you discover your purpose, you will normally find it's something you're tremendously passionate about.

Steve Pavlina

The great gift of human beings is that we have the power of empathy.

Meryl Streep

Quite simply, this chapter is about you—and about others who are drawn to the field of user experience design (or UX design, for short).

If you're reading this sentence, you're a curious person.

You want to know how things work—anything from doorknobs to airplanes to that thing in the back of your throat. Most of all, you want to know what makes people tick.

You don't see things as black and white; there are a whole lot of shades of gray to explore! Sure, sometimes you may drive your peers a little crazy by always volunteering to play the devil's advocate, but it's not like you can stop yourself from trying to look at the other side of the coin.

Lucky you!

The user experience design field attracts curious folk who are comfortable working with many shades of gray.

We seek out patterns and thrive for organization and structure. We connect the dots. We relentlessly pursue the next piece of the puzzle, and when the puzzle is solved, we look for ways to improve it!

We can be analog or digital. We are at home with pencil and paper, whiteboards and dry erase markers, Post-it notes, and Sharpie pens. We talk in terms of Axure and 'Graffle, wireframes and prototypes, and we live in a world of boxes and arrows connected on the multiple screens of our computers.

We are not only curious. We are passionate!

We have a passion for brainstorming ideas and facilitating discussions. We have a passion for creating things that make a difference for those who use them—and those who create them. Oddly enough, we're most proud when something we create is so good that people don't realize how good it is!

And, of course, we have empathy.

We can feel it deep within the core of the fabric of our being when we encounter a bad experience. Even worse, we instantly try to find solutions to solve the problems.

We know what it's like to have an unexpected response to what seems like a simple request—and we don't like it! We don't want users—people just like us—to have to endure the confusion and feelings of inadequacy that often go hand-in-hand with a poor experience.

When you combine that almost constant, childlike curiosity with an unrivaled passion for "doing what we do" and a sense for how others feel, you end up with a lively community of professionals who are comfortable speaking their minds, asking questions, sharing solutions, and being wrong—all in the name of getting to what is right.

Welcome to the UX design community.

What Is User Experience Design?

There are many definitions for user experience design. After all, it's a field that thrives on defining things. Admittedly, sometimes we don't do such a good job of "defining the damn thing" when it comes to the various parts of the whole, but we at least know what the whole is.

In this book we'll be focusing on two definitions in particular: the broadest sense of the term *UX design* and the definition we will use in the context of this book.

The Broad Definition

User experience design is

> The creation and synchronization of the elements that affect users' experience with a particular company, with the intent of influencing their perceptions and behavior.

These elements include the things a user can touch (such as tangible products and packaging), hear (commercials and audio signatures), and even smell (the aroma of freshly baked bread in a sandwich shop).

It includes the things that users can interact with in ways beyond the physical, such as digital interfaces (websites and mobile phone applications), and, of course, people (customer service representatives, salespeople, and friends and family).

One of the most exciting developments of the past few years has been the ability to merge the elements affecting these different senses into a richer, integrated experience. Smell-o-vision is still far in the future, but otherwise products continue to blur the traditional lines.

Don't Forget the Tangible

Although we're focusing on the digital aspects of the user experience, these types of interactions don't occur in a vacuum. Be sure to consider the effects of the tangible experience when designing your digital products. The environment your users are working within matters, as do the physical products (screens, keyboards, and other input devices) that affect the way your users will interact with your design. Chapter 6 offers techniques to help you understand the impact of context.

Also, don't forget the other touchpoints a product or company has with those who interact with it. After all, the brand of the company is affected by many things, and the brand experience doesn't end at the screen of a computer or a mobile phone. The best possible website design can't make up for a reputation for poor customer service or provide the satisfaction of well-designed packaging when a product gets delivered.

Tangible experiences, such as learning in a classroom (**Figure 1.1**), are increasingly being influenced by digital applications.

Figure 1.1 *A modern classroom experience blends the analog and the digital.*

Likewise, experiences that used to be individual, such as choosing which at-home karaoke machine to buy, are increasingly becoming enhanced through social interaction, such as online reviews (**Figure 1.2**).

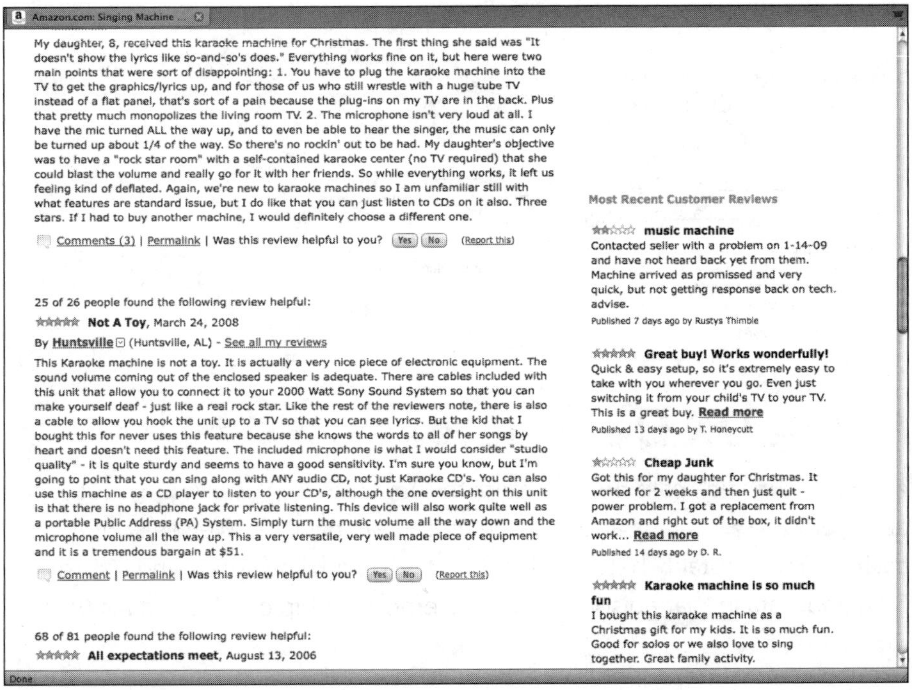

Figure 1.2 Online reviews are a major influencer of consumers.

Our Focus

As you can see, the scope of UX design is large, and growing. For the purposes of this book, we'll be focusing on projects centered on the *design of digital experiences*—in particular, such interactive media as websites and software applications (**Figure 1.3**). To be successful, the user experience design of these products must take into account the business objectives of the project, the needs of the product's users, and any limitations that will affect the viability of product features (such as technical limitations or constraints around project budget or time frame).

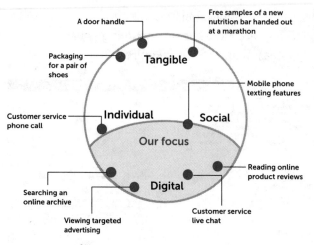

Figure 1.3 This book focuses on the digital aspects of user experience design.

About UX Designers

Although curiosity, passion, and empathy are traits that user experience designers share, there is also a desire to achieve balance. We seek out a balance, most notably between logic and emotion, like Spock and Kirk, or Data and Data in that episode where his emotion chip overloaded his positronic relays.

You get the idea.

To create truly memorable and satisfying experiences, a UX designer needs to understand how to create a logical and viable structure for the experience *and* needs to understand the elements that are important to creating an emotional connection with the product's users.

The exact balance may shift according to the product. An ad campaign for a child's toy will have a different balance than an application for tracking patient information at a hospital. A product designed without understanding the need for both is likely to miss opportunities for a truly memorable experience—and the resulting benefits to the company behind the product.

Note For additional information about emotional design, read about design principles in Chapter 10 and check out Donald Norman's Emotional Design: Why We Love (or Hate) Everyday Things (Basic Books, 2005).

Achieving that balance requires a heightened sense of empathy: the ability to immerse yourself in the worlds of potential product users to understand their needs and motivations. User experience designers perform research to reach this understanding (see Chapter 6) and create such tools as personas (see Chapter 7) to help the rest of the project team focus their efforts.

Remember, emotion is just a part of the overall picture. Use the logical side to bring you back from the edge and keep your mind on the tasks at hand. In most cases, you will be working against a budget that is based on the time and materials required to complete the project. You'll need to understand that sometimes you need to fish or cut bait.

Where UX Designers Live

You're not alone in this. Look around and you'll find a number of organizations and communities that can foster your development as a user experience designer. In addition to offering mailing lists, online resources, and a whole slew of really smart people, many of these organizations sponsor events or conferences that can help you broaden your horizons and narrow your career focus all at the same time.

A number of companies host events geared to providing continuing education, including User Interface Engineering's Web User Interface Conference, Adaptive Path's UX Intensive and UX Week, and the Nielsen Norman Group's Usability Week. In addition to these organizations, there are other conferences that you can attend, often at a very reasonable rate, such as Midwest UX (http://midwestux.com), Big Design (http://bigdesignevents.com), and WebVisions (http:/webvisionsevent.com/) and plenty of meetup groups (http://meetup.com) that will allow you to meet with like-minded individuals, see talented speakers, and learn from people in your area.

There has also been a growth in the number of longer UX courses, like Robert Hoekman Jr.'s online course (https://learnable.com/courses/user-experience-tools-tricks-techniques-183) and in-person courses like those offered at Code Academy.

Several professional organizations sponsor yearly conferences, as well. **Table 1.1** provides a short list of some of the more well-known organizations, their websites, and events that they host.

TABLE 1.1 A Sampling of UX Organizations

ORGANIZATION	WEBSITE	MAJOR CONFERENCE (TYPICALLY HELD)
Interaction Design Association (IxDA)	www.ixda.org	Interaction (early February)
The Information Architecture Institute (IAI)	www.iainstitute.org	World IA Day (February/Early spring)
American Society for Information Science and Technology (ASIS&T)	www.asis.org	IA Summit (March)
ACM Special Interest Group on Computer-Human Interaction (SIGCHI)	www.sigchi.org	CHI (early April)

Let's Get Started!

You've made it this far. It's time to get into the reason you picked up this book in the first place. Turn the page and take a dive into how user experience design exists within the realm of projects.

But don't stop there—this book is a guide to get you started. It has a lot of examples that can help you deliver on many of the activities you will be tasked with. We've also tried to provide additional examples to help you expand and find your own best approach for creating deliverables that are useful to your team and your clients.

Keep your curiosity, passion, and empathy alive! Challenge yourself to find new ways to inspire others to build that ideal user experience.

That is, of course, before you set out to improve upon it.

2 The Project Ecosystem

Planning for Project Needs, Roles, and Culture

Are you about to start a brand new project? Or are you in the middle of one? Either way, take a moment to consider the dynamics and context of the project—the issues that will affect you and the rest of the project team. What type of sites or applications are involved? Which roles and skills are needed? What is the company culture? Answering these questions will help you define the project and ultimately determine the tools and skills you need to bring to the table to be successful.

Carolyn Chandler

E ach project has its own unique challenges. If you're designing websites or applications, many of those challenges will involve specific features and functionality, such as building a method for a user to share photos with friends and family online or restructuring the information in an intranet so that content can be more easily found and shared.

Around those specific design goals, however, all projects have a larger context that you need to understand and integrate into your planning. This context is the project's *ecosystem,* and it includes the environment you're working within (the company culture), the general type of work you will all be engaged in (such as the type of site you're designing), and the people you'll be interacting with (including their roles and responsibilities).

If you take the time to understand the project ecosystem, you'll have knowledge that will help you throughout the project. You can communicate your responsibilities and ideas more effectively, and you can help others on the team anticipate project needs they may not have considered.

To help you, this chapter identifies different types of projects you may work on, as well as the roles you may play, the people you may depend on and how their involvement tends to vary by the type of site or application being designed. Finally, the chapter discusses some elements of company culture that may affect how you work during the project.

Note *Depending on how your client company structures its projects, a particular project may involve the design of more than one site or application. For the sake of simplicity, this book assumes that a project involves the design of a single type of site. If you have more than one site, consider each separately to make sure you have the right roles represented on the project team.*

Identify the Type of Site

Although no black-and-white distinctions exist between one type of site and another, some relative differences in site focus and characteristics are identifiable. Understanding these similarities and differences can help you:

▶ Set design goals for yourself. These are the general problems that need to be solved (such as "explain the company's business model") or the attributes that need to represented (such as "demonstrate the company's responsiveness to its customers") within the site's visual design and interaction design.

- ▶ Solidify the primary objectives of the project (see Chapter 4).
- ▶ Understand which departments or business units may (or should) be involved as you gather business requirements (see Chapter 5).
- ▶ Determine the best methods for incorporating user research (see Chapter 6).
- ▶ Ask questions about which systems and technologies may be involved.

Your site will probably associate strongly with one of four types:

 Brand presence—a constantly present online platform that facilitates the relationship between the company and a general audience (anyone interested in its products or services)

 Marketing campaign—a targeted site or application meant to elicit a specific and measurable response from a particular audience or from a general audience over a limited period of time

Content source—a store of information, potentially composed of several types of media (articles, documents, video, photos, tutorials) meant to inform, engage, or entertain users

 Task-based application—a tool or collection of tools meant to allow users to accomplish a set of key tasks or workflows

The next sections take a closer look at each of these types, discussing their characteristics and the impact they'll have on your challenges during the design of the site or application. We'll also discuss the most common *cross-over projects*—e-commerce, e-learning, social networking, and mobile projects—which have characteristics of more than one type.

Brand Presence

What do you think of when someone says the word *brand*? Often the first thing that comes to mind is a company's logo, such as the Nike Swoosh or the Coca-Cola script emblem. A company's brand is much more than their logo, however; it's the entire series of impressions that a particular person has about the company.

Dirk Knemeyer presents some excellent definitions of brand in his article "Brand Experience and the Web":

> *Brand* represents the intellectual and emotional associations that people make with a company, product, or person. That is to say, brand is something that actually lies inside each of us....

> The science of *branding* is about designing for and influencing the minds of people—in other words, building the brand.

Surfing

For more information on the distinctions between a customer's *experience* of a company's brand and a company's efforts to *build* their brand, read Dirk Knemeyer's explanation in "Brand Experience and the Web": www.digital-web.com/articles/brand_experience_and_the_web.

For an excellent discussion of how a site's UX design can influence an individual's brand experience, read Steve Baty's article "Brand Experience in User Experience Design": http://www.uxmatters.com/mt/archives/2006/07/brand-experience-in-user-experience-design.php.

A company can do a lot to influence the associations made with its brand, from running memorable advertising campaigns to expressing brand traits (such as "responsiveness" or "value") through the features and design of its websites.

All sites within a company are likely to have some impact on a company's brand, either directly (by presenting a site that customers can visit) or indirectly (by enabling a key service that customers rely on, such as customer support). Brand presence sites, however, are the most focused on presenting the company's brand messages and values. They provide channels that interface directly with customers and serve as a broad online funnel for those interested in finding out more about the company or its offerings.

A brand presence site is often the company's primary .com or .org site, such as GE.com. For larger and more distributed companies, they are the primary sites for business units of varying sizes, such as GEhealthcare.com. Distinct product lines also often have their own unique brand presence online. For instance, Pepsico.com has one brand presence; while Pepsi.com has its own distinct presence.

If you're working on a brand presence site, you'll probably be designing for a variety of user groups, including current and potential customers, investors, partners, the media (such as news organizations and authors of prominent blogs), and job seekers.

Common Brand Presence Sites

▶ A company's main home site (company.com, company.org, company.net, etc.)

▶ A site for a primary business unit of the company (often a unique site for a particular industry, region, or large suite of products)

▶ Sites for prominent sub-brands within a company

Brand Presence Design Goals

The design goals that are often of most importance in a brand presence project are these:

▶ Communicate the brand values and brand messages of the company, either explicitly (perhaps a statement about the importance placed on being responsive to customer needs) or through the overall experience upon entering the site (such as ensuring it performs well and prominently offers features that encourage customers to communicate with the company).

▶ Provide quick and easy access to company information. You want to answer the questions "What does the company do?" and "How do I contact someone for more information?"

▶ Present or explain the business model and value proposition of the company: "What can the company do for me?" and "How does the company do it?"

▶ Engage a set of primary user groups and guide them to relevant interactions, functionality, or content.

▶ Help the company attain goals being set against key metrics, such as the number of unique visitors. Often this is one part of an overall marketing strategy.

Later, in the section "Choose Your Hats," you'll learn the various roles that may be involved in designing a brand presence site. For now, let's take a look at the other types of sites you may work on, including one that has a close relationship with brand presence sites: the marketing campaign site.

Marketing Campaign

Marketing campaign sites are similar to brand presence sites, as both are focused on engaging users with an experience that influences their perception of the company's brand. Marketing campaign sites, however, tend to be evaluated on their ability to achieve very specific actions within a set focus (such as within a particular time frame or with a targeted audience). Rather than serving as a funnel for channeling interest, they are meant to be the engines that *generate* interest. From an online standpoint this generally means they are aligned with an overall marketing strategy and may be run in conjunction with other marketing efforts using different channels, such as TV or radio commercials, print ads, and other promotions.

Common Marketing Campaign Sites

▶ A landing page that promotes a specific offer. The page is reached via a banner ad from another page.

▶ A small site (or microsite) promoting a particular event

▶ A game or tool that has been created for the purpose of generating buzz or traffic

The primary purpose of a marketing campaign site is to create a narrowly *focused campaign* usually targeting a specific set of *metrics*. The focus is often narrowed by one or more of the following:

▶ **Time**—for example, a campaign centered around an event (such as a conference) or a season (such as the Christmas shopping season)

▶ **User group**—such as a campaign targeted to teenagers or teachers

▶ **Product, product suite, and/or a specific use for that product**— for example, a site that highlights kitchen appliances by showing virtual kitchens with matching ovens, dishwashers, and stoves

A campaign using a mix of these strategies would be a spring campaign targeted to selling patio equipment, combining time and product suite. **Figure 2.1** shows an example of product suite and user group.

A marketing campaign site may be as simple as a banner ad leading to a landing page in the company's .com site, or it could be a *microsite*, a small site that often veers away from the branding apparent on the .com site to provide a tailored experience according to one or more of the areas of focus. "Small" is relative here—some microsites have only one page and others have many, but either way the microsite is smaller and more focused than the company's main brand presence site.

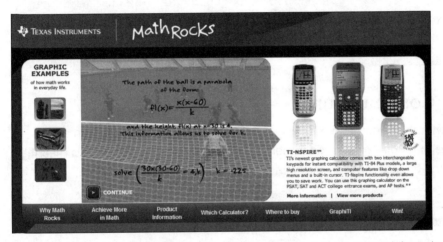

Figure 2.1 *Texas Instruments used this education-focused microsite to present information on the company's graphing calculators. The product suite is used primarily by high school and college students in algebra classes. The microsite maintained general ties to the Texas Instruments brand but was intentionally distinct in order to attract a younger audience and organize content and features according to their needs.*

Marketing Campaign Design Goals

For the person or team responsible for designing and implementing a marketing campaign site, the design goals that are often of most importance are these:

▶ Generate interest and excitement, often by presenting a clear and immediate *value proposition* (the value that a product or service brings to the user, such as the possibility of quick loan qualification) or some kind of incentive (a special offer, entry in a contest, or entertainment such as an online game).

► Engage a set of primary user groups in order to elicit a particular action, such as clicking through to a specific location on a brand presence site, signing up for a newsletter, or applying for a loan. When this action is performed by a user, it's called a *conversion*.

► Help the company attain goals being set against key metrics, such as number of unique visitors. Often this is one part of an overall marketing strategy.

Deep Diving

For more on designing pages to support marketing campaigns, see *Landing Page Optimization: The Definitive Guide for Testing and Tuning for Conversion*, by Tim Ash (Sybex, 2008).

Content Source

A content source site contains a store of information, potentially in several types of media (articles, documents, video, photos, tutorials), and is meant to inform, engage, and/or entertain users.

Common Content Source Sites

► A company's intranet

► An online library or resource center for members of an organization

► Sites or areas of sites that are focused on providing news or frequently updated posts (large commercial blogs may fall into this category)

► Customer support centers

All sites and applications have some content, of course, but some sites place a particular emphasis on the presentation and structure of their content. The emphasis may come about because the site has such a large amount of content that it poses its own challenge or because specific types of content carry a high degree of importance; they might, for instance, support critical decisions or draw users back to the site frequently.

The primary purpose of a content source site is to increase user knowledge and self-sufficiency by providing relevant content (an intranet, for example). They often also encourage some kind of action, such as sharing information or purchasing a product after reviewing its description.

Content Source Design Goals

A content source site often has to do one or more of the following:

▶ Present content that is the primary draw for first and repeat visits to the site.

▶ Demonstrate a company's thought leadership capabilities, for example, by providing access to ideas and perspectives held by the CEO or other subject matter experts within the company.

▶ Support critical decisions among the user base.

▶ Increase a company's enterprise knowledge, by bringing out ideas that may be buried within individual departments. This may be part of a larger goal to identify more opportunities for innovation.

▶ Support users who are seeking information in different ways. For example, some don't know what specific product they need yet (and are more likely to browse), while others may know exactly what they're looking for (and are more likely to use a search field).

 Deep Diving

Kristina Halvorson and Melissa Rach provide guidance in content strategy, including case studies and clear recommendations, in their book *Content Strategy for the Web* (New Riders, 2012).

With regard to UX design, some of the tasks that are most common in a content source project are

▶ Creating a categorization structure that fits the mental models of your users

▶ Determining how to incorporate a system for organic growth of content (for example, functions such as tagging and filtering)

▶ Designing an effective search tool

Surfing

For more information on the different ways users tend to seek information, read "Four Modes of Seeking Information and How to Design for Them," by Donna Spencer: http://boxesandarrows.com/view/four_modes_of_seeking_information_and_how_to_design_for_them

See Chapter 8 for more on content strategy—the planning of content creation, delivery, and management.

Task-Based Applications

Task-based applications can vary from a simple calculator embedded in a mortgage site to a full system handling multiple critical workflows. If your project involves the latter, there will be more roles involved and, most likely, a substantial requirements-gathering process (for more on this process, see Chapter 5).

Common Task-Based Applications

▶ A software application that supports the creation of a particular type of item (such as a spreadsheet or print piece)

▶ A web tool or application that supports a critical workflow within a company (such as a ticket-management application for an IT support group or a customer tracking application for a call center)

▶ A website that allows for access to, and management of, personal data (such as Flickr)

The primary objective of a task-based application is to allow users to perform a set of tasks that are aligned with their needs and, ultimately, with the client's business goals.

Task-Based Application Design Goals

Most task-based applications need to

▶ Enable users to do something they couldn't do elsewhere—or if they can, to do it better ("better" can mean more efficiently, more effectively, with a higher degree of satisfaction, or more conveniently)

▶ Support novice users with easy-to-access instructions and visual prioritization of key tasks

▶ Support intermediate and advanced users with access to shortcut features and deeper functionality

▶ Reduce the load on the user and make the best use of system resources (for example, reusing data versus requiring duplicate entries)

▶ Be designed and deployed with attention to the degree of change required of the application's users—ideally, with a design that facilitates learning and a communication plan that demonstrates the value to the user

One of the biggest challenges of designing a task-based application is to keep "feature creep" under control. As a project is being developed it's very common for great ideas to come up at later stages of the design, or even during development. User experience design is well suited to guarding against feature creep because user models such as personas can be used to identify high-value features and to keep focus throughout the project.

If a truly great idea does come up later in the process, *and* it meets the needs of a high-priority user group, *and* it aligns with the business goals of the site, your team may be able to build a case for changing direction. If an idea can't make it through that wringer, it may not be worth the delay and cost.

E-Commerce Sites

E-commerce sites can include elements of all four project types, because a site that is primarily intended for e-commerce needs to have its own brand presence, provide content (usually product specs or descriptions of product usage), and facilitate tasks (searching, comparing, writing reviews, checkout). Marketing campaigns are often closely tied into these sites as well and may involve multiple marketing groups within the organization.

Common additional design goals for e-commerce sites are

▶ Explain the model for the site, if it's nonstandard. As online marketplaces are constantly being reconceived, this explanation will help set expectations (for example, eBay, Amazon, and Craigslist have very different models).

▶ Support decision making as the user moves from learning to consideration to comparison to purchase, with helpful content and features.

▶ Make use of points in the experience where cross-selling and upselling is possible, and place those suggestions in a way that is eye-catching without being disruptive.

▶ Create a communication flow from the point of purchase through the point of delivery. Communication needs to happen not just within the site but also with other channels, such as integration with delivery tracking systems and e-mailed communications about order status.

E-Learning Applications

E-learning applications are crossovers between a content source and a task-based application. Content for lessons must be generated, which often requires that the team add the roles of learning specialist and subject matter expert (SME) for the topic being covered. The product is task-based in that the user usually follows a flow through the lesson and may also need to track progress or explore related topics. Some hands-on lessons may also require tasks to be completed.

Common design goals are

▶ Set an understanding of the baseline knowledge needed to start a course and who it is targeted to.

▶ Provide content in manageable chunks that are paced for comprehension.

▶ Engage the learner in activities that simulate hands-on learning.

▶ Communicate performance and progress and, if applicable, suggest next steps for continuing the educational process, such as more advanced courses.

Social Networking Applications

A social networking application is primarily a task-based application, because users need to be able to find and add friends, manage their profile, connect, post, and search. They also contain challenges associated with content sources, however, especially the need for an organic framework that can handle a potentially very large amount of user-generated content. If the site is essentially given its own identity, it will also have the characteristics of a brand presence site.

> ### Snorkeling
>
> If you're working on a social networking application or trying to integrate social features into another type of site, this book will help you on your way: *Designing for the Social Web*, by Joshua Porter (New Riders, 2008).

Common design goals for social networking applications are

▶ Focus potential users on the purpose and the values of the network.

▶ Facilitate meaningful user interactions that support, and are supported by, the features presented (such as image sharing, video sharing, and discussions).

▶ Protect the integrity of the site by ensuring those within the network understand how to control their information and respond to inappropriate behavior.

▶ Harness and display the power of the community to bring forward features that are only possible with active members, such as popular features and reviews.

Mobile Sites and Applications

On February 7th, 2011, International Data Corporation (IDC) announced that vendors had shipped over 100 million smartphones globally during the previous quarter. For the first time, smartphone sales had surpassed global PC sales, which came in at 92 million.

The explosion of availability and usage of mobile devices like smartphones and tablets has made them an increasingly essential part of company strategy and product planning, and an extremely important skillset for designers to develop.

Unfortunately, many companies still consider mobile an afterthought. More than one company has concluded a list of requirements for a larger web design project with three "simple" words: "make it mobile."

When to Think Mobile

Thinking about mobile should occur at the same time it does for any digital project: when a user need or problem has been identified and can be addressed via digital means, or when the company wants to build a relationship with their customers. Perhaps the situation calls for a mobile solution and a PC-oriented solution won't be as effective, leading the team down the mobile channel from the beginning.

If you are already planning a larger website project and know that a mobile channel will be an important aspect of it, consider designing the mobile experience first. Luke Wroblewski began the "Mobile First" rallying cry, based on these key points:

▶ **The *growth* of mobile usage is explosive.** This includes the number of people who have access to mobile devices, as well as the amount of time and number of activities performed on mobile platforms instead of desktops. Your user base may be much larger with a mobile device than with a desktop.

▶ **Starting with mobile design creates *constraints* that make you focus on the essential data and actions in your product.** With the availability of larger monitors for displaying desktop browsers, it's all too easy to add *cruft* to your pages (advertisements, "helpful" tagging features, and other elements that can distract users from the actual content or functionality they're looking for). The limited real estate of a mobile device forces you to consider the primary actions and make those actions stand out. This will help you design a better, larger view later when you have more real estate.

▶ **There are exciting *capabilities* that mobile devices provide which aren't as available or effective in PCs.** This includes location-based services using precise locations determined from GPS, the greater availability of multi-touch, gestural interfaces, and accelerometer features that are sensitive to device orientation and allow for tracking a user's movements (a great area for the healthcare industry to develop). Mobile devices also tend to be more deeply integrated with the user's digital ecosystem, tying together common tasks with communication tools like phones and text messages, as well as scheduling tools. If project planning starts with a PC-based solution, these amazing capabilities are likely to be ignored or under-utilized during the "mobile optimization" process.

Mobile Planning

Once you decide to make a mobile audience a priority, you have another choice to make. Should you

▶ Build one website that looks good on multiple devices?

▶ Build a unique mobile website experience, in addition to (or instead of) a desktop site experience?

▶ Build a mobile application (for example, an iPhone app)?

Let's look at each of these choices in more detail.

Let's say you decide that you'd like to focus on creating one site that can adapt to multiple displays. You can do this by focusing on techniques in *responsive design* (similar terms you may hear are *progressive enhancement* or *adaptive layout*), which support the creation of flexible interfaces that expand or contract to make the best use of the real estate available (see **Figure 10.6** in the chapter on Design Principles for an excellent example, or visit www.bostonglobe.com yourself to see it in action).

Ethan Marcotte, author of *Responsive Web Design*, provides an excellent walk-through of responsive design techniques, utilizing

▶ **Flexible grids** that expand or contract content based on screen resolution

▶ **Flexible images** that decrease in size on smaller screens or increase to a set maximum size on larger screens

▶ **Media queries**, which are elements of code that can be placed in a site's HTML and stylesheet. These queries gather information about a device's display capabilities and use them to serve up different styles accordingly.

Using these techniques can help you take one common site and adapt the layout to multiple devices, providing a flexibility that covers a variety of resolutions from smartphone, to tablet, to desktop browser.

 Deep Diving

If you'd like to try your own hand at building a responsive website, follow Ethan Marcotte's excellent walkthrough, available in *Responsive Web Design* (A Book Apart, 2011).

Dive deeper into the code—and improve your skills in designing for accessibility as well—using *Designing for Progressive Enhancement: Building the Web That Works for Everyone* by Todd Parker, Patty Toland, Scott Jehl, and Maggie Costello Wachs (New Riders, 2010).

However, a responsive design approach using a single site may not solve a key issue. Your users may actually have different needs when they're using a mobile device—or, a mobile device may have capabilities that address their needs more effectively. For example, as mentioned in the previous section, mobile devices will have valuable information about a user's location that may affect their ability or desire to use functions like maps. You could design one site that plans for both, and hide the code that doesn't apply, but this can lead to slower-loading pages as unnecessary data downloads.

An alternative approach is to plan for and design a unique mobile experience for your users, focusing on the strengths of a mobile platform from the beginning and removing non-essential content (see **Figures 2.2–2.4**).

If this is the direction you choose, you'll need to make a choice of designing a mobile-optimized website, or a mobile application. Mobile apps, like those native to iPhones, Androids, and Blackberrys, have

▶ **Currently, a better user experience than mobile websites (in general).** With the constraint of devices, app designers have a greater degree of control over how their products are viewed and the interactions that result. The common app platforms (iPhone and Android, for example) have guidelines that help ensure a greater degree of consistency in interaction. As HTML5

Figure 2.2 *Cisco, the official network infrastructure provider for the 2012 Summer Olympic Games in London, created a series of digital products for the games. Here's their mobile-optimized website. Notice the simple navigation and focus on a single, interactive piece of content (the "Game Readiness" quiz).*

Figure 2.3 *With the larger real estate available on a tablet, the tablet-friendly version of Cisco's site provides additional navigation and content features, while maintaining a balanced use of space and avoiding clutter.*

Figure 2.4 *Cisco's desktop browser version has the full view, with an additional column for sharing features on the left. Attempting to put all these elements in an iPhone version, or even a tablet version, would have been overwhelming—but these stages show a nice progression for each device's real estate (http://www.ciscolondon2012.co.uk/).*

and other web development tools close the gap, however, the differences between app and web experiences may become less pronounced.

▶ **An easier method for monetizing the product (if that's your goal).** Purchasing an app is generally easy when it's part of a store like iTunes. Providing users with the ability to purchase a web-based mobile site involves more involved integration, which you may need to take on yourself.

Mobile-optimized websites bring

▶ **A greater degree of reach.** Those developing apps are limited to specific platforms, like Apple's iOS, and need to build multiple versions if they want to provide access via other platforms. A mobile website, on the other hand, can be viewed on any device with the appropriate web browser.

▶ **In most cases, a more cost-effective solution.** Because one mobile-optimized website can reach many more people, the cost may be substantially lower. In his excellent article, "Is Developing a Mobile App Worth the Cost?" Aaron Maxwell estimates that you can reach nearly five times the number of people per dollar invested, by going with a mobile-optimized website instead of multiple mobile apps (www.mashable.com/2011/02/24/mobile-app-dev-cost). There are companies that provide software that promises to help you build one app and deploy it to multiple devices (see www.verivo.com, for example). Tools like this come with their own constraints, so be sure to explore them before going down the path of an app.

Whichever path you choose, be sure to pick your target devices and platforms before you begin to walk down it. Those choices will constrain your design and impact your testing plans.

Mobile Design Principles

The great number of mobile devices can make design decisions somewhat daunting. However, the very fact of their mobility gives them some common principles that can help you focus. Julie A. Ask, VP at Forrester Research, has spoken often of these aspects of mobile solutions that give them such importance and convenience for users:

▶ **Immediacy**. Mobile devices are readily available and ideally provide immediate access to information that meets user needs. Following scores, looking for breaking news, and searching for answers to questions that come up in dinner conversation are all common activities that benefit from a focus on immediacy in product design. Consider the content or features that your users will need quickly, and then be sure to provide clear access and fast retrieval. Alerts, when used in a way that's respectful of users (and can be turned on or off by them), are particularly effective when tied to location-based information (like nearby places or friends), or schedules.

▶ **Simplicity**. As mentioned previously, the smaller screens of mobile devices force a focus on a small set of clear options. They also lend themselves well to quick, linear tasks. Designing for simplicity allows users to treat their mobile device like a toolkit, fitting their unique needs when they need them. Ensure tasks completed on your mobile solution are simple, short, and effective.

▶ **Context**. Mobile devices have context on a user's location, communication history, and past behavior. These elements can work together powerfully to anticipate user needs and provide relevant information, just-in-time. Solutions that take advantage of this are connecting people to their environment in ways that can feel like magic.

Context in particular is one of the most exciting ways that mobile devices differ from desktop experiences. Mobile devices literally go out in the world with their users—where they work, where they play, where they commute, and where they wait.

People who would never bring their laptop out when standing at a bus stop kill the time by using their phones or reading on tablets. These golden opportunities to provide useful, delightful, and engaging experiences will be missed by companies who do not consider the real-world context of their users. When designing for mobile, consider these in-between times, and explore your mobile devices users' differences in need, attention, concentration, and physical interaction as their context of use changes.

Snorkeling

For more on mobile strategy, and tips on designing for mobile interfaces, pick up the quick-read *Mobile First* by Luke Wroblewski (A Book Apart, 2011).

Gestural Interactions

Gestural interactions are those that use natural user movements, like swiping and pinching with the hand, instead of (or in addition to) traditional interactions with mouse and keyboard. They require a touchscreen interface, and other hardware and software that can interpret one or more user touches and specific actions users will make.

Gestural interactions aren't limited to mobile devices, and there are amazing interactions possible with full-body gestures, such as those with the Xbox Kinect or Nintendo Wii. However, the most common use of gestural interfaces can be found on mobile devices like smartphones and tablets, and should be a part of your considerations when designing a mobile solution.

Gestures are their own type of language and it's still a bit like the Wild West out there when it comes to which gestures should have which responses. It's exciting when you can create gestures that mean something to your users, but if you're looking for guidelines that provide the beginnings of a standard, there are gestural patterns that are emerging with a good deal of weight and momentum behind them (**Figure 2.5**).

When designing gestural interfaces, make sure your interactive elements, like buttons and anything else that can be manipulated, are large enough for the digits needed to use them (one finger for pushing, two fingers for pinching, multiple fingers for a swipe, and so on). Testing is essential to understanding if your product responds in the natural way expected by users.

Deep Diving

Dan Saffer provides an in-depth look at designing for touchscreens and other interactive devices, in *Designing Gestural Interfaces* (O'Reilly, 2008). He includes a background in the technology involved, and new interface patterns for designers to consider.

Identifying the type of site or application you may be working on during a project is only the first step. Next, you should consider the different roles that are often needed and how their involvement may vary based on the type of project.

Touch Gesture Reference Guide

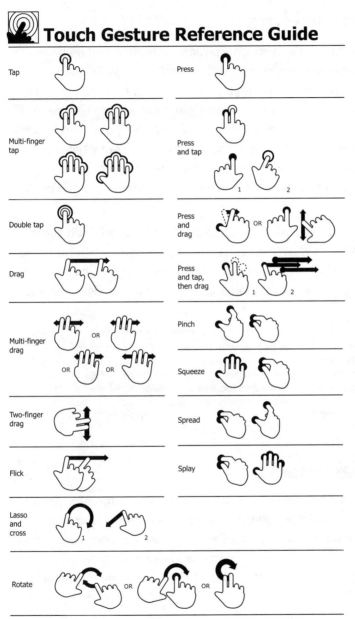

Tap		Press	
Multi-finger tap		Press and tap	
Double tap		Press and drag	
Drag		Press and tap, then drag	
Multi-finger drag		Pinch	
		Squeeze	
Two-finger drag		Spread	
Flick		Splay	
Lasso and cross			
Rotate			

Supporting materials for this guide can be found online at: http://www.lukew.com/touch/

Figure 2.5 *The simply beautiful Touch Gesture Reference Guide (created by Craig Villamor, Dan Willis, and Luke Wroblewski) provides a visual catalog of some of the most commonly used gestures for touch commands. The guide also features an outline that shows how popular software programs support touch gestures. Additionally, the guide is available in the form of handy flash cards. (www.lukew.com/ff/entry.asp?1071)*

Choose Your Hats

When you become the UX designer on a project, you often end up having to play several roles. Whether they're formally defined within your client organization or not, the roles you will play depend on the type of project and the makeup of the rest of the team, as well as a client's experience with each. It's good to know which roles you're already comfortable taking on and which you think you can learn on the job. It's also helpful to find out what expectations others may have about the responsibilities covered by these roles. With this understanding, you can represent yourself more clearly from the beginning of the project.

What are the most common roles expected of a UX designer? Each client company you work for may have different titles for those roles (or no name at all, if it's not a formal job in the organization). In general, you can expect to encounter the big three: information architect, interaction designer, and user researcher.

> **Note** *Few companies have the size or budget to split these common roles among different individuals. Keep the role names in your mind when defining a project, but speak in terms of needs and responsibilities when talking to the client—otherwise they may think you're building a very large team! This focus on responsibilities rather than titles will also help keep you sane: If you're performing several of these roles, it doesn't necessarily mean you're doing the job of many people, because responsibilities ebb and flow through different parts of the project.*

Information Architect

An information architect is responsible for creating models for information *structure* and using them to design user-friendly navigation and content categorization. During the design of sites and applications, common responsibilities include creating detailed site maps (discussed in Chapter 11) and ensuring that categories and subcategories of information are distinct and user-friendly.

Understanding Expectations

Within the UX field, distinctions are made between the roles of the information architect and the interaction designer (discussed next). At a particular company, however, there is seldom a common distinction between the two roles, at least when it comes to what is stated as a need for a particular project. For example, you may end up on a team with the title of information architect because that's the historical term for the role, whether or not that truly fits your responsibilities.

Should you correct the project team if the title you're given doesn't match the main role you're taking on? If this is a shorter term project (say, four months or less) and the title you have is widely accepted within the organization, with clear responsibilities outlined, it may not be worth the potential confusion you'd be introducing to try to change it. If there is no widely accepted title, however, and you think there's a chance you'll need both roles to be represented—potentially by different people—then it's worth making a distinction early in the project when you're planning your involvement and communicating your responsibilities.

Essentially, for more task-based applications it makes sense to emphasize the role of interaction designer, and for more content-based projects it makes sense to emphasize the role of information architect. But what may make the most sense of all is to use the term familiar to the client organization and ensure the team understands how you're defining the role with regard to the responsibilities you're taking on. This definition is something you'll want to make clear in the statement of work (see Chapter 3).

The responsibilities of an information architect can also blur with those of a content strategist (see below, under "Other Roles"). If these roles are represented by different people on the project team, be sure to discuss how you'll be collaborating at the beginning of the project.

Interaction Designer

An interaction designer is responsible for defining the *behavior* of a site or application in accordance with user actions. This includes flows in the site across multiple views and interactivity within a particular view. During the design of sites or applications, common activities are to create task flows showing interaction across pages or components within the site (see Chapter 11) and to create wireframes showing in-page interactions such as dynamic menus and expandable areas of content (see Chapter 12).

Understanding Expectations

If you're working on a small team or on a project that isn't highly focused on creating new task-based functionality (for example, if you're working on a brand presence site that mainly includes some content categories, a contact form, and a sign-up form for a newsletter) interaction designer may be the main role responsible for capturing the project requirements (see Chapter 5).

If you're working as the interaction designer on a project with a high level of new functionality, most likely you'll have a separate person on the team in charge of outlining detailed requirements (for example, a business analyst or product manager). The process of gathering and detailing functional requirements can be helped greatly by the skills of a UX designer, and documents such as functional specifications and use cases are affected by experience design. Be sure to sit down with the person in charge of gathering requirements to discuss how you can best work together.

User Researcher

A user researcher is responsible for providing *insights* regarding the needs of end users, based on information that is generated from, or validated with, the research that person conducts with users. There are many types of activities that can fall into the category of user research, and they can occur at several points in the project timeline. (See Chapter 6 for a description of common techniques, such as user interviews, surveys, and usability testing.)

Understanding Expectations

The client company's appetite for user research can vary immensely, based on the importance placed on it by the project team or the project sponsor. The fact that you're talking to a project sponsor about UX design before a project starts shows that someone on the client team knows it's a priority to ensure that user needs are represented. But as those who have worked on their share of computer-based projects know, introducing research can also introduce anxiety among project team members—sparked by concerns that user research will create a bottleneck, increase risk (What if we find something wrong, and need to make big changes to fix it?), or disprove the value of a particular idea that has gained a lot of momentum. The expectations for user research can vary between business stakeholders and the project team, so be sure to clarify expectations for the role with both groups.

The client may also expect the user researcher to provide insights based on site analytics—tools and reports that communicate patterns of use on the site, such as frequently visited pages and common points where users leave the site. Some of the most common analytics tools are from Google (www. google.com/analytics), WebTrends (www.webtrends.com), and Omniture (www.omniture.com/en/products/analytics).

You may find yourself taking on all three of these roles: information architect, interaction designer, and user researcher. Can you balance all three, or are you biting off more than you can chew? In part that depends on the size and timeline of the project, but the type of project also has an impact on how much involvement each role is likely to have. **Table 2.1** (on the next page) describes how UX design roles can vary by project type.

Surfing

Need to make the case for UX design? These articles offer approaches that can help:

"User Experience as Corporate Imperative," by Mir Haynes:
http://www.hesketh.com/thought-leadership/our-publications/user-experience -corporate-imperative

"Evangelizing User Experience Design on Ten Dollars a Day," by Louis Rosenfeld:
http://louisrosenfeld.com/home/bloug_archive/000131.html

TABLE 2.1 Common Responsibilities of the UX Design Role

ROLE	BRAND PRESENCE	MARKETING CAMPAIGN	CONTENT SOURCE	TASK-BASED APPLICATION
Information Architect	Medium involvement. The greater the content challenge, the more like a content source the project will become.	Low involvement for smaller sites (like a single landing page). Medium involvement if working with larger microsites.	Very high involvement. Content sources require an information architecture that has an appropriate balance of structure and flexibility, to give users a solid base to stand on and allow for planned growth.	Medium to high involvement, mainly focused on creating the navigational framework, unless there are larger content areas that need to be referenced during some workflows.
Interaction Designer	Medium involvement. The greater the number of tasks, the more like a task-based application the project will become.	Low involvement for smaller sites, medium to high involvement for larger microsites or *advergames* (sponsored online games meant to generate play and buzz).	Medium to high involvement. Search, tagging, and filtering features cross the line between information architecture and interaction design. Content sources may also have workflows involving content creation and management.	Very high involvement. This kind of project often requires the heaviest lifting, as interaction design deliverables (such as user process flows and wireframes) are key to communicating requirements visually.
User Researcher *Involvement will vary based on budget and access to users. Listed here are common techniques for each project type. For more on each of these techniques, see Chapter 6.*	Research efforts may focus on understanding needs of priority user groups (through surveys or interviews) or design research testing the effectiveness of a particular visual design in conveying the right brand message.	Due to the often temporary nature of campaigns, user involvement is often light. More permanent solutions may use research similar to brand presence sites. It's also common to use analytics tools to present two or more variations of a particular page to see which one leads to the most conversions. This is called *A/B testing*.	Field research such as contextual inquiry can help the team understand how different users currently work with information. Card sorting is an excellent way to understand how your users may group information and common patterns and mental models. Once a framework has been set, usability testing can validate the structure.	Field research such as contextual inquiry can be done to understand tasks as users are currently completing them. The most frequently used and best understood technique for involving users in the design of a task-based application, however, is usability testing.

Other Roles You May Play or May Need

Several roles don't typically fall under the role of UX designer, but their responsibilities often overlap with the UX design role—especially if you're working on a project where no one is officially playing the role and you have skills to bring to the table.

Some of the more common overlapping roles include

▶ Brand strategist or steward

▶ Business analyst

▶ Content strategist

▶ Copywriter

▶ Visual designer

▶ Front-end developer

The following sections look at each of these roles in more detail and discuss how they may vary depending on the type of site being designed.

Brand Strategist and Brand Steward

A *brand strategist* is responsible for building a relationship with key markets through the definition and consistent representation of the company's branding elements, which can include anything from brand values (such as "responsiveness") to guidelines for copy and messaging to specifications for logo treatments, colors, and layout. This role often entails creating or representing branding guidelines and understanding how they apply to different projects. It may also involve knowing or defining the target audiences of importance on the project you're working on. For the most part, you'll probably work with a brand strategist but won't be taking the responsibility on yourself.

The *brand steward* doesn't necessarily set the guidelines but is responsible for ensuring that they are followed appropriately during the project. This responsibility may be given to the UX designer or visual designer on a project.

If the company's brand attributes, values, and guidelines have already been well defined and the site is expected to follow them, your role as the project's brand steward will mainly be to ensure the result is in line with those guidelines. Your touchpoint outside the project would most likely be a member of the marketing department who is available on a consultative or review basis but is not on the team full time.

The brand steward role may be more active if the site is meant to extend the brand somehow—targeting a new market, for example. It's most involved when a completely new brand presence is being created or when the company is making a dramatic change in its brand, effectively rebranding itself. For example, CellularOne rebranded itself completely to become Cingular, a major effort for an established company. In that situation you should either be very experienced in brand development or establish a clear and close relationship with the person at the company who is.

Key questions that will help you understand expectations around a brand-related role are these:

▶ Do brand guidelines exist already?

▶ If so, how closely do they need to be adhered to for this project?

▶ Who is responsible for setting or maintaining brand messaging, brand look-and-feel, and tone of content (such as casual or professional)?

▶ Are new audiences going to be targeted that aren't covered by previous brand definitions? If so, who is responsible for ensuring the brand guidelines are still appropriate to those audiences?

▶ Will there be naming or renaming activities? If so, how should I plan to be involved? (An example would be creating a name for a new tool that will be heavily promoted.)

For projects that don't have a large potential impact on customers' perception of the brand, such as the development of an internal application, brand steward involvement may be as light as an occasional check-in to ensure the brand is being well represented.

Business Analyst

A *business analyst* (sometimes referred to as a business *systems* analyst on IT projects) is responsible for identifying key business stakeholders, driving the requirements-gathering process (see Chapter 5), and serving as the primary liaison between business stakeholders and the technology team. He or she is also the primary owner of detailed requirements documentation, such as functional specifications and use cases, if needed.

The role of business analyst or product manager may not exist on your project at all or it may be one of the most important roles through the design process. Task-based applications and content sources often have this kind of role; brand presence projects and marketing campaigns may not. A task-based application is most likely to need this role. The more features and the greater the complexity of the project, the greater the needs will be for a dedicated person and for documentation of functionality.

Although a business analyst is not typically considered a member of the UX team, small UX teams are often asked to fill the role, so it's important to understand where these responsibilities lie. Business analysts drive the capture of business requirements, serving as the liaison between the technology team and the key business stakeholders. If there is a business analyst on a project, that person and the interaction designer are often joined at the hip. If it's the same role, the person responsible may have a lot of documentation to keep up with!

To understand expectations in this area, ask who will be responsible for outlining the scope of the project, facilitating the discussions around requirements, and documenting requirements throughout the project. For small projects or those that are not heavy in functionality, the project manager sometimes will take on these responsibilities. Either way, if it's not you, you'll still know who you need to stay close to in order to ensure your deliverables are in sync.

Content Strategist

A content strategist is responsible for understanding business and user requirements for content in various media (articles, documents, photos, and video), identifying gaps in existing content, and facilitating the workflow and development of new content.

Content-related efforts are often underestimated. A client may have a large amount of content that's wonderful in one medium (such as print brochures or videos), but that content may not be appropriate for the project you're working on. Also, there are sometimes unspoken expectations that people within the client organization will generate content—expectations that may come as a surprise to those people when the time comes to populate your product with descriptions, news, and help topics! If high-quality content is a key business driver in your project, make sure you know who is responsible for the following:

▶ Setting content guidelines for the new product (type of content, tone, amount)

▶ Assessing the appropriateness of existing content against those guidelines

▶ Developing new content. This will vary based on general project type. For task-based applications, it may include instructional copy, error messages, and help topics. For content sources, it may include articles, news items, and blog posts.

▶ Serving as the stakeholder–technical team liaison to communicate the limitations and possibilities of the content management system

▶ Defining different content types as well as each one's *metadata* (the information that ultimately makes searching and cross-referencing more effective)

▶ Planning for the *migration* of content, which involves creating templates for different content types and making sure content is tagged and loaded properly when it's moved into the site's content management system. (This is another area where the effort required is often underestimated.)

Copywriter

A *copywriter* is responsible for writing the text on the site that frames the overall experience. In some cases, this copy remains fairly unchanged from day to day. It typically includes site and page introductions or in-page instructions. A copywriter may also be involved in the ongoing creation of dynamic content, such as news stories or copy for marketing campaigns.

Copywriting is one of those gray areas that often falls to a UX designer, especially if wireframes are being created (see Chapter 12). You may initially put in sample text to serve as placeholder for copy such as a site description or in-page instructions, but someone eventually needs to populate it with the final text that will be seen by users—and because many projects don't have a dedicated copywriter, this task may default to you.

You're less likely to be asked to take on the copywriter role for high-profile areas of brand presence sites or marketing campaigns; in those situations each word may be given close scrutiny. But if you're working on a task-based application that needs short instructional messages, error messages, or other types of information that don't necessarily fall into a clear content bucket, you may end up inheriting that writing task (or it will fall to the developer by default). Ask upfront if a copywriter will be available, and ask again when you're wireframing if one hasn't been found. If the job does fall to you, be sure to include that effort when you're planning your activities during the project. And be forewarned: This is a responsibility that's often left out or underestimated.

Visual Designer

A *visual designer* is responsible for the elements of the site or application that the user sees. This effort includes designing a look and feel that creates an emotional connection with the user that's in line with the brand guidelines. For example, a banking site often needs to appear stable, trustworthy, and accessible. The visual design can give this assurance through visual elements such as colors and imagery. That promise will then be kept (or broken) by the interaction design of the site and other touchpoints with the company (such as a call center).

Let's be frank: A lot of people out there call themselves visual designers, web designers, or graphic designers, and a lot of sites have poor or only passable visual designs. There is a big difference between creating an effective, immersive, and emotional visual design and just getting by. Sometimes getting by is enough to meet the project objectives, and sometimes it leads to project frustrations and delays when the project sponsor is unhappy, or early users are not engaged with the design.

On the other hand, it can also be easy to focus too strongly on creating an impact with the visual design, allowing the usability of the design to suffer. If you're being asked to take on this role and are unsure of your abilities to create the right impact for the client, take a look at the company's current site and the sites or products the clients admire from a visual standpoint to assess your comfort level.

Visual designers often take a very central role in brand presence projects and marketing campaigns, having the primary role responsible for communicating the company's brand effectively.

For content source projects, they may focus on creating content templates that can be applied to many pages (for example, a template for an article). For task-based applications, they may provide a style guide that can be applied to common interaction elements, such as navigation areas and tools (which calls for a high degree of collaboration with the interaction designer).

Front-End Developer

A *front-end developer* is responsible for building the technical structure behind the page designs and flows, as well as interactive elements within the site, such as rollover menus, expandable areas of content, and interactions with multimedia elements like video. This work often uses technologies such as XHTML, CSS, Flash, JavaScript, Ajax, and Silverlight. Front-end development focuses on the elements of the site that tie directly to what the user sees, as opposed to the systems on the back end that provide the underlying platform (such as databases, content management systems, and the code needed to build the functionality behind complex features).

If you or members of your team are taking on the role of front-end developer, close collaboration with the rest of the development team is important to understanding expectations and responsibilities. Other important questions include which back-end systems will need to be integrated with, the method used for generating HTML, the need for flexibility in page structure to accommodate customized "skins," and the expectations concerning technologies such as Flash. If a prototype is being planned (see Chapter 13), ask who is responsible for developing the prototype and what level of functionality is expected. A prototype meant to simply communicate possibilities can be created quickly in an application such as Flash, but a fully functioning prototype that needs to pull real data (for example the account information a user just entered in a form) will need to be done in close collaboration with members of the back-end development team.

Worried about taking on all these roles? Unless you're working on a very small project—or at a very small company—you most likely won't be taking them all on yourself. The key is to understand which of the roles you are able and willing to take on, as needed, for the particular project you're working on. For the rest, you can get the support you need on the project team by building a network within the client company or by recommending additional people to fill the needs. Let's take a moment to talk about ways you can do this.

Building a Network of User Advocacy

For those areas that you're not sure you can or want to take on, it's time to start looking for help. There are three main ways you can go about doing this:

▶ Recommend additional team members be added, if the need is apparent enough.

▶ Educate yourself in key areas where there are gaps—if the new responsibilities are manageable and you have the time to dedicate to them.

▶ Build a support network within the company to help you at key junctures.

Let's take a closer look at how you can build a support network.

There are most likely some key resources in other departments within the company that can help you be successful. You'll need to gauge how much time you can rely on from these people, because requesting outsiders' time can be tricky with projects that are primarily owned by one department. If you don't want to ask for a large amount of their time out of the gate, just ask if you can partner with (or consult with) them to ensure the best result for the major responsibilities for that role. Once you've done some partnering you'll have a better understanding of the amount of interaction you may need and whether you need to make a more formal request for his or her time.

Each company will have a different structure and different names for its departments, but here are some common places to look for partners:

▶ For the brand strategist role, ask if there's anyone within the marketing department who can serve as your touchpoint. This may also be a source for visual designers and content strategists.

▶ Visual design and content strategy partners may also be found in program or product management or in the research and development, operations, or corporate strategy department, where you can often find business analysts and product managers.

▶ The IT or engineering department is often your best bet for front-end developers and others who can help you get access to and insight into tools for site analytics.

If you have recently been hired by a new company and expect to be working across departments, one of the best things you can do out of the gate is to identify key people who could be partners and schedule some interview time with them to understand their roles and experience. It starts you off with a network that you can often rely on for a long time and gives you the opportunity to explain your responsibilities (and user experience design in general). You can also ask a great question at the end of the interview: "Who else do you think I should talk to?" The answer can help you find people who may not be apparent to your main project manager or client contact.

If you've been at a company for a while, you can still initiate an interview schedule like this. In that situation it's best to tie it to a particular milestone (such as the start of a new project) or a corporate objective that has some urgency behind it, to ensure high participation.

Make sure that your manager knows what you're doing to avoid looking like you're going around him or her. Good communication is key to understanding expectations about roles and building trust.

Another key to gaining trust within the company is to understand its *culture*, the often unspoken expectations of how a company works, such as those created by past project experiences (positive or negative), etiquette regarding organizational hierarchy, and acceptable work logistics (such as working from home).

Understand the Company Culture

Culture is a little like dropping an Alka-Seltzer into a glass—you don't see it, but somehow it does something.

—Hans Magnus Enzensberger

A company's culture may not be consistent across all of its regions, business units, or departments, but you can usually identify key characteristics that will affect you and the project or projects you're undertaking. The following are some aspects that are good to keep in mind as you scope projects and navigate potentially tricky political situations.

History

We all know the quote that those who cannot remember the past are condemned to repeat it, and project work is no exception. Understanding how a project or team has gotten to its current state of need can help you understand the challenges you may face during the project.

Let's cover some of the questions you can ask to understand the history that may affect a project. Although some of the answers to these questions may seem dire, keep in mind that something has triggered the need to bring you in on the project, so a project can have a rocky history and still be successful. Perhaps you'll be a key component of that success! However, if many of the problems discussed below seem to apply, and you don't feel you'll be able to help address them, it may be a red flag. In that case, consider an overall evaluation of whether this project is positioned to succeed.

▶ **What is an example of a past project that seems to have been considered a success, and what seems to have made it so? What is a past project that seems to have been a failure (or particularly painful), and why did it fail?**

Asking these questions (either directly or in a more subtle, conversational manner) can help you understand a couple of things: how the person answering defines success, potential risks to your project, and any biases or expectations that will be carried through to this project, as well as approaches that worked well.

▶ **Has the company worked with and released a designer on the same project or team?**

If so, try to find out what didn't seem to be working and how the client expects your approach to be different. If you can ask more than one person at the company this question, it will help you understand a lot about unspoken expectations. If you get two very different answers, it could mean the designer's responsibilities weren't well defined and you may need to ensure there's a lot of communication about your responsibilities throughout the project.

▶ **Has the project team been working on the project (or related materials) for what seems like an unusually long time without finishing?**

If so, this could be a sign that key client stakeholders are not on the same page or are not being involved at appropriate times, causing multiple stalls, direction changes, or lost time due to multiple iterations. It may also mean there is not a clear leader, someone who can say no (or at least effectively prioritize) to keep the focus on business objectives. If you're in a position to influence the communication on the project, it may help to create guidelines for participation to help move the project forward.

▶ **Has the company created designs without the previous participation of a UX designer?**

This can be a mixed blessing. On one hand, you're dealing with a team that understands the need for design and has attempted to fill the gap. On the other, you may be given a design that you feel does not meet the project goals for the user experience. This can be a delicate situation to navigate. It's often best to approach the creator of those designs with the tone of a respectful mentor or helpful consultant, pointing out the good aspects of the design first, then discussing user experience goals and how they may be better achieved with a different approach. The creator is likely to be a valuable member of your support network, so it's important not to burn the bridge here, but to redefine your roles in a collaborative way to keep the enthusiasm alive.

▶ **Does the main sponsor or project manager seem particularly anxious about the project?**

There are many reasons this could occur, especially if some of the factors above are in play. Anxiety could also be due to market pressures that it would be helpful for you to understand. For example, has the company stock price been dropping? Has a particular competitor made recent alarming strides? Is the business operating in the red? Again, these situations do not necessarily mean you shouldn't take the project on; after all, they're the kind of situations that often get a project funded in the first place. But if you have a significant concern that the company won't be able to pay its invoices, that's a risk you'll want to weigh.

Hierarchy

Geert Hofstede has an excellent model outlining differences in culture, what he calls "cultural dimensions," that often affect the way people interact and communicate. One of them is the concept of *power distance*, which is the extent to which members of a society (in our case, a company) understand and accept the distance between people of different levels of power. For example, if members of a company's executive team are viewed as particularly powerful and potentially unapproachable, a company may have a large power distance and its employees may be more focused on the hierarchy. If the company encourages a democratic sharing of ideas and questioning of vision, it may have a relatively small power distance.

Power Distance Is

"... the extent to which the less powerful members of organizations and institutions (like the family) accept and expect that power is distributed unequally. This represents inequality (more versus less), but defined from below, not from above. It suggests that a society's level of inequality is endorsed by the followers as much as by the leaders."

Geert Hofstede
Cultural Dimensions
www.geert-hofstede.com

Neither extreme can be considered good or bad in itself, although generally in the United States most employees seem to prefer the appearance of a small power distance in their workplace. What's interesting to note is that this isn't necessarily an indicator of how successful a company is. Apple has a relatively large power distance (if you consider the aura around Steve Jobs), and Google has a relatively small power distance as part of its culture, but both companies are known for being innovative leaders.

What is important to note is that the power distance within the client company will have an impact on how you successfully navigate the political waters during the project. This aspect will become particularly important at key points in the project: during requirements gathering (discussed in Chapter 5) and at key milestones such as sign-off points (discussed in Chapter 4).

If you're working at a company with a large power distance, take some extra time to understand reporting relationships before scheduling meetings such as stakeholder interviews and reviews, and consider involving more people at intermediate levels during your communications.

Logistics

In addition to the larger aspects of culture mentioned above, it's also helpful to understand some of the elements that are more logistical in nature, so you can better integrate with current work methods or introduce change in a thoughtful way.

For example, it's helpful to understand the general pace expected within the company, including key release dates or deadlines that will affect the project (creating a software application on a yearly release schedule would probably have a different pace than a microsite supporting a seasonal campaign, for instance). Will your team be expected to work late hours to meet looming deadlines?

Expectations regarding remote work versus on-site work are good to understand as well. If heavy on-site time is expected, you'll need to plan for travel and resource setup there. If remote work is acceptable (or encouraged, which is common when working with global companies), it's important to understand methods and tools of communication. For example, is use of instant messaging applications acceptable? What web conferencing tools are in use? Are there methods of including international stakeholders that have proven effective in the past?

It's also interesting to understand the "paper culture" at a company. Some companies favor electronic media for most things, in which case a good projector and a consistent Ethernet connection is important. Others are very paper-centric, in which case you'll need to make sure you bring enough copies to a meeting to make it productive. You may be able to change the culture of the project if you think another way is more effective. But it's good to know that you're asking people to change so that you can smooth the transition—and potentially understand why a particular approach isn't working as you expected.

Pulling It Together

Now that you've explored the terrain of the project, you should have a better understanding of the project ecosystem: the environment you're working within (the company culture), the general type of work you will all be engaged in (such as the types of sites you're designing), and the people who you'll be interacting with (including their roles and responsibilities).

This information will be valuable as you outline your role in the project and get ready to begin in earnest. If you're working as a freelancer or subcontractor, it will provide a base for writing a proposal covering your work on the project (see the next chapter, which discusses UX proposals). If you're working as a member of a larger team and are not directly involved in writing the proposal, you can take your new knowledge into the project kickoff—the first meeting of your team. For a basic guide to running a good meeting, see the chapter, "A Brief Guide to Meetings," available on the companion website. Or if you want to get straight into the kinds of questions to ask when the project gets started, see Chapter 4, "Project Objectives and Approach."

3 Proposals for Consultants and Freelancers

A Guide for Those in the Business Who Also Manage Their Own Business

It can be challenging enough to manage projects and client expectations, but if you don't have an appropriate agreement in place, you can find yourself on the losing end of any project you take on. Proposals and statements of work are essential to protecting your business—and yourself—from financial and legal troubles. After you accept a project and shake hands, make sure you spend the right amount of time composing an agreement that details the terms of your relationship and the payment schedule for your client.

Russ Unger

Proposals

There is an old saying that "no good deed goes unpunished," and the same generally goes for getting invited to pitch a potential client on a new project—the high-fives and feel-good moments are quickly replaced with "Oh, crap! It's time to write the proposal!"

The biggest challenge in writing the proposal is writing your very first one. It's nearly impossible to know where to begin if you've never had to author one yourself, and that's where this chapter should come in handy.

Every type of project you encounter will have varying flavors that will keep you on your toes when it comes time to author the proposal. Fortunately, there's something of a core that is common to all proposals and can be reused from project to project. (For a detailed discussion of project types, see Chapter 2.)

When should you write a proposal? Always.

Why should you write a proposal? Throughout the history of working on projects, the ones that have put people in the most uncomfortable situations have been those where there was no agreement in place between the client and the vendor.

You may be very tempted to skip this step when you make the first connection with a potential client and things seem to click. Even though you have an apparent understanding about the client's needs and are able to articulate it in a way that they understand, you really are not quite yet ready to start working.

In fact, this is exactly the point where you need to slow down and take a breath.

Instead of getting right to work, take the time to define your professional relationship and the rules of engagement with your new client. Jean Marc Favreau of the law firm Peer, Gan & Gisler, LLP, in Washington D.C., says,

> All too often contractors and their clients believe there is a meeting of the minds at the beginning of their relationship, when in fact ambiguities are just lying in wait. While it is almost impossible to prepare for all possible contingencies, a comprehensive written contract is your best defense and the smartest way to ensure that you do not later find yourself in a courtroom arguing about the terms of your relationship. The more clearly you define the terms and parameters of your relationship with a client in a written contract up front, the less likely you will end up fighting over each party's obligations down the line.

New projects and new people are exciting. There is often a desire not to "kill the deal" by throwing a proposal into the mix, but, as in any relationship, the honeymoon feeling can eventually subside.

Promises can be broken on both sides of the relationship.

A client can fail to provide you with timely access to content. (I know that this is almost unheard of, but believe it or not, it happens! That's sarcasm, in case you missed it.) Funding that was once available for the project may be shifted elsewhere—and then you, the one who is engaged in the work, may be left holding the bag.

Companies also realize that they are taking risks working with external vendors—especially those who are very small businesses or independent contractors. Well-written proposals provide clients with a sense of stability and protection, which can help alleviate many of the concerns that might arise.

A proposal also allows you to define terms that protect both sides in the event that something changes. If the client does not provide you with timely access to their resources, your timeline may slip; you need to make them aware of their obligations to the project's success. If a client loses funding and kills the project—and you do not have a proposal or other form of contract in place—then you may run the risk of not getting paid for work you have already completed.

The point should be crystal clear: Always write a proposal.

Creating the Proposal

After you land the project, it's time to get the proposal done. The sooner a proposal is approved and signed, the sooner you can begin work and—most importantly—begin to get paid for the work.

The core components of a good proposal are these:

- ▶ Title page
- ▶ Revision history
- ▶ Project overview
- ▶ Project approach
- ▶ Scope of work
- ▶ Assumptions
- ▶ Deliverables
- ▶ Ownership and rights

- ▶ Additional costs and fees
- ▶ Project pricing
- ▶ Payment schedule
- ▶ Acknowledgement and sign-off

Let's take a deeper dive into each part of the proposal.

Title Page

The title page is the simple page that introduces your document. Title pages are an interesting beast: there are a number of ways you can create them from a style and information perspective. How you do it is up to you.

A typical title page consists of the following elements:

- ▶ Client company name
- ▶ Client company logo (if you have permission to use it)
- ▶ Project title
- ▶ Document type (proposal)
- ▶ Version of proposal
- ▶ Submission date
- ▶ Your company name
- ▶ Proposal authors
- ▶ Project reference number
- ▶ Cost
- ▶ Confidentiality

For your first proposal, include everything—except the client's company logo, the cost, and (potentially) the project reference number.

Why not include these elements on the title page?

Your client knows who they are. It's probably not worth the time and effort to request permission to use the company logo, nor is it worth the possible unpleasantness if you inadvertently misuse it. The cost is best placed after you have identified the various components of the project in the body, and the cost information leads nicely into the payment schedule. The project reference number is something to be aware of. A lot of companies will not use one at all; however, some government agencies are known to rely upon this particular item, and if it is not found on your title page (**Figure 3.1**), your proposal may be rejected.

In Figure 3.1, the (fictional) client logo was used. In the event that permission was not given or a relationship was not established, it is best not to display the logo of the client company.

Figure 3.1 *Sample proposal title page*

Revision History

The revision history is its own section of the proposal and is used to identify how many times you have updated the proposal since the original version. In general, it is best to provide the version number, date, author, and any comments associated with the version, such as what was modified, in order to provide the reader with context as to the modifications (**Table 3.1**).

TABLE 3.1 Sample Revision History Table

REVISION	SECTION	DESCRIPTION	EDITOR	DATE
1.0		Original Document	REU	8-Jan-12
1.1	Assumptions	Updated to reflect software requirements	REU	11-Jan-12

Occasionally, clients will sign off on a proposal and then ask you for further revisions. If you choose to move forward with the client and make these changes, you should take the opportunity to update your document from version 1.x to 2.0.

In essence, when a client approves a proposal and both parties agree upon the terms, you are ready to begin working. So when additional modifications are requested, you need to review them very carefully. This ensures your costs still make sense and that there is a clear understanding on both sides about the modifications and at what stage the project is restarting (if necessary). You should also always provide an appropriate explanation of why the revision constitutes a full new version in the revision history.

Project Overview

The overview section is a description of the project you will be working on—in your own words. This description should provide your client with a clear picture of what you envision their product will entail, as well as an explanation of what they can expect to find in the rest of the proposal.

Here is an example of the beginning of an overview:

> [Client Company Name] is seeking to create a new online web presence. This web presence provides [Client Company Name] customers with an ability to research and purchase products online, as well as other services and benefits available through the company. The goals of the online web presence are to...

You should be able to give a solid overview in one or two paragraphs, providing a very high-level amount of detail as to what the client should expect from you. It is a good idea to conclude the overview with a sound explanation of your recommendations and proposed approach to completing the project:

> This proposal will detail [Your Company Name]'s recommendations and approach for the design and development of [Client Company Name]'s online web presence. Given the deadline of [deadline date], it is proposed that...

Project Approach

The approach to the project will vary depending on what type of project you are undertaking. This is your opportunity to identify to your client how you plan on working on the project with them. You get to define your rules of engagement and set expectations for the work that is ahead of you.

Many individuals and companies operate with very similar methodologies—but use different names or clever acronyms that dovetail with their overall branding.

The PURITE Process™

Once upon a time, a mythological methodology was created to show to (potential) clients, and it found its way into many proposals. The process was called The PURITE Process™ (pronounced "purity"), and in sharing this with you, a mythological being has just died a little on the inside, so please take care to read this as a piece of fiction. The name of the process is slightly cheesy, and the process is clearly somewhat incomplete. Post-launch analysis was omitted from this methodology (an oversight), but it should be included for all clients, of course. Without further delay, here's the PURITE approach:

[Your Company Name] has identified a standard process for project success with our clients. Although each of these phases may not be applicable to [Project Title], the entire process is defined as follows:

The PURITE Process™ is [Your Company Name]'s in-house methodology for ensuring success across the board for all initiatives. By utilizing PURITE, [Your Company Name] has a proven set of guidelines for working closely with clients and users/audiences to reliably maintain and exceed delivery expectations.

P — Prepare. We dedicate a portion of every initiative to understanding your industry and your competitors and how they do business in order to be as informed as possible prior to beginning requirements gathering.

U — Understand. We work closely with your subject matter experts and/or users to define the requirements for building the project correctly.

R — Render. Through the Render phase we create and develop all the pieces of the project/product. In our experience, any development phase requires a lot of heads-down, focused work effort but also timely, open communication with your team(s). It also requires that we...

I — Iterate. The Iterate phase is repeated throughout the entire lifecycle of the project. We move as quickly as possible to bring the project to life, and this often requires creating multiple iterations in rapid timelines. This requires direct and timely involvement from you and your dedicated resources. The end result is the product you've specified—and helped to create.

T – Test. We test every project throughout the course of our Render phase; however, we also require an extra set of eyes—from our own testing team and from your designated user group/audience group to perform goal-based testing. This additional round of testing helps ensure that as few stones as possible are left unturned in order to deliver a project that has been rigorously evaluated from multiple levels.

E – Enable. Upon successful completion of the five previous phases and your signed approval, we will enable the solution and take it live.

The PURITE Process™ doesn't end there. After project completion, we regularly communicate with our clients. We will continue to gauge your satisfaction levels, understand your changing goals or project enhancements, and assist you in defining the best approach for the future development of your project.

You are welcome to use as little or as much of this as is applicable or useful to you. The mythological author who created the process does not mind if you do not credit the source, either.

Defining your process can be as detailed as above or as simple as the following:

Plan, Define, Develop, Extend

- ▶ Plan the overall strategy
- ▶ Define the detailed project requirements
- ▶ Develop, test, refine, and launch the work product
- ▶ Extend the project by recommending enhancements and improvements based on information learned during development, testing, and post-launch

After you define your process, you have the opportunity to detail the various efforts that will take place in each phase of your approach, as well as what each of those efforts means to you and your client.

The approach section of your proposal will vary in length depending upon the project, your process, and the activities that take place within each step of your process. Try to keep it to two to three pages maximum, though, and ensure that you include only the outputs that you will be able to deliver to your client—to prevent further updating of the document or revisiting the project pricing.

Scope of Work

The scope of work section is where you identify the division of labor for the project. That is, you identify which components of the project you are responsible for and which the client is responsible for.

Reread that. Think about it for a moment. Let it sink in. There we go.

That's right. This is the part of the proposal where you tell the client, in writing, *we* are going to do this and *you* are going to do that. Then later, when the client signs your proposal, they are agreeing to this arrangement, and you have a paper trail to back you up in the event of any misunderstandings.

The intention here is to clearly identify who is going to be handling what aspects of the project, as well as what aspects of the project are included within your proposal and for the price that you have estimated.

If you can find no other really compelling reason to write a proposal, this should be reason enough.

Here is a very brief example of a scope of work:

> We were approached by [Client Company Name] to provide all services required to build [Project Type].

> [Your Company Name] will focus solely on the [User Experience Design Aspect(s)] of the [Client Company Name]'s website.

> [Client Company Name] will provide detailed feedback on all aspects of [Project Type] in accordance to the Project Plan.

> [Client Company Name] will provide any required assets for use in the project, including fonts, color schemes, brand standards, etc.

Assumptions

The assumptions section of the proposal is a good place to spell out, without leaving room for debate, what is needed from your client to ensure your success. That is, these are the things that you are assuming—and communicating to the client—that you will have access to or that will be delivered to you to make the project a success.

What you're calling *assumptions* in this section are really *expectations*. It's just a lot more polite to assume.

You can create as many project plans as you would like, but if neither you nor the client commit to meeting milestones and objectives, both sides are committing to certain project failure. In general, the assumptions are an expectation of resources and assets, as well as timely (translation: prompt, immediate) access to both of these.

Here is an example of how to write assumptions:

Assumptions

It is necessary that [Client Company Name] provide the following assets and resources. An inability to provide these assets and resources in a timely and complete manner may contribute to the unsuccessful or delayed delivery of this project.

The following assets and resources are expected:

Timely access to all required [Client Company Name] employees.

Timely access to all required assets of the [Project] in current state, including any source files, if available.

Content, as required and including but not limited to copy, imagery, audio, etc. for any aspect of [Project].

Deliverables

Deliverables are the work product that you will create and turn over to the client. This section is your opportunity to detail to the client what type of work product they can expect from you during the course of the project. It is recommended that you handle status reporting separately, closer to the end of the project, but feel free to add it to this part of the project.

Do provide descriptions of any work product that you might include, even if the work product does not get produced. This might seem as if it could be overkill or has the potential to open the "I read about [deliverable type] in the proposal, but I don't see it here" can of worms, but one little word, *may*, can make the difference.

Deliverables

[Your Company Name] provides a variety of deliverables throughout the course of a project. For [Client Company Name], we have identified the following deliverables:

Creative Brief

The Creative Brief is the first step of the project. This document will help us to create a quick and effective, high-level overview of the project. The purpose of the Creative Brief is to clarify the goals and needs of the users and to define any of the special resources and/or constraints related to the project.

And so on...

Ownership and Rights

It is important to consider the extent to which you will allow your client to use the work product that you produce. These rights can be defined in many different ways, but the majority of your work will fall into two categories:

▶ Work for hire

▶ Licensed work

Work for hire (known in the legal world as "work made for hire") projects are considered to be created by and under copyright to the party who pays for the work—not the party responsible for doing the actual work.

This means that when performing work on a project that is work for hire, you have absolutely no rights to the work and everything you create related to the project is owned by the client. This situation is difficult for many companies and individuals to contend with: It often means there is no downstream "maintenance" work (with its additional revenue), as clients may decide to maintain the project on their own once it has been completed.

Do not be swayed from a project where a client forces the stipulation; it is not uncommon. When you put work for hire projects in the context of full-time employment with a company, this is pretty standard for an employer-employee relationship. It is also an opportunity to visit your pricing model—many projects are billed at a somewhat increased rate to compensate for the potentially lost revenue in the future.

Remember, this all depends upon the relationship you have with your client and how you choose to do business. Time and experience will help you make the right determination for the types of work you do and the pricing models you choose.

Licensed work projects enable you to retain the copyright to the work but grant other parties the right to copy and/or distribute it. You can build any number of stipulations into the licensing agreement. You will most likely take advantage of licensing your work when you retain ownership of all of the source material of your work and deliver only limited-use work product to your clients (such as PDFs instead of original, editable Word, Visio, Axure, OmniGraffle, or other documents).

You can take many different approaches to licensing your work, including licensing work to be used without modification, noncommercially, or a number of other ways that may fit your situation.

> **Note** *Creative Commons (http://creativecommons.org/about/licenses) provides easy-to-understand explanations of a variety of license types that you might make use of, but those are only a small subset of the licensing world. If you find yourself in a situation where you are getting into very detailed and specific needs, it is always best to contact a copyright attorney to assist you in creating the best possible solution.*

Additional Costs and Fees

It is important that your client understand whether the project pricing you will provide for them does (or does not) account for external resources.

For example, some projects may require the purchase of stock photography from a vendor. You can either purchase the imagery (with the appropriate usage rights) and include that as a part of your fee, or you can clearly identify the purchase of imagery as an additional cost that will be passed along to your client. You may also offer services that you want to make your client aware of—this is a good opportunity to promote those services.

Here is an example of how to explain how additional costs and fees will be handled:

Additional Costs and Fees

In the event that outside resources are required (such as content, imagery, fonts, etc.), these shall be identified, approved by and billed to [Client Company Name].

In addition, [Your Company Name] can provide hosting services to our clients with very low overhead. We provide hosting services—including configurable, web-based e-mail—starting as low as $25 per month, with a $25 setup fee. In the event that [Client Company Name] would like to purchase a "maintenance" package, [Your Company Name] will work to create a package that is mutually agreeable and beneficial to both parties.

If you anticipate any travel and travel-related fees including hotels, car rentals, per diem, etc.), you need to get very specific as to where the financial responsibility falls for each party and how this will be invoiced.

Project Pricing

After you document the details of how you're going to perform the work for the project, it's a pretty good idea to let the client know the cost.

How you arrive at the price is largely up to you, but here's a tip: Estimate how long you think it will take *you* to do the project—including a specific number of revisions, estimate a reasonable amount of time for project management, which could be around 25 percent; then determine the hourly billable rate you want to charge, and calculate it all out. There are a variety of formulas to help you with this, such as applying degrees of difficulty to each portion of the project, to help you come up with a cost range to provide to your client.

In most cases, experience is going to be the key to helping you appropriately estimate your projects—from a time-and-materials perspective.

How do you determine your billing rate? Research what others are charging, for comparison, by locating salary surveys and contractor rates. For example, organizations such as the Information Architecture Institute (www.iainstitute. org), AIGA (www.aiga.com), Coroflot (www.coroflot.com), and the talent agency Aquent (www.aquent.com) perform salary and contractor rate surveys. You can get a decent idea of the rates you could charge by taking into account your experience, what others in your market are charging, and what you feel is somewhat fair.

Remember: You can always lower your rate. It's a lot more difficult to ask your client to pay you more money once they've seen numbers on a page!

There are many different ways to structure the pricing for your project. Depending on the nature of your project, you may want or need to provide multiple estimates that allow for a variety of pricing options. Suppose, for example, you provide a client with two options: a static HTML website or a website with a content management system (CMS) that would allow for dynamic content (which the client could then administer without dedicated resources). Here's how you could phrase the project estimates:

Project Estimate

[Your Company Name] has proposed multiple estimates for [Client Company Name], in order to provide the best possible options for your immediate and/or future needs. [Your Company Name] makes the assumption that all content will be provided by [Client Company Name]. In the event that [Your Company Name] is requested to provide content services, the estimates will need to be redefined.

[Your Company Name]'s estimates allow for flexibility from a cost and needs perspective. The estimates are as follows:

Estimate 1

[Your Company Name] estimates that the [Project] for [Client Company Name], without any interactive content...

Remember, there is no real wrong way to put together your project estimate—unless you put yourself into a negative cash flow position!

Payment Schedule

There is a myth floating around that all freelance projects are paid 50 percent up front, before the work begins, and 50 percent upon completion, when the project ends.

This myth needs to be dispelled—*right now*! This is no way to do business, and it is no way to ensure timely, consistent income while you perform the work. You don't want to put yourself in a position where you have to make change after change for a client simply because you want to get the project done and get paid, instead of working through a change order process.

You can price projects a number of ways—from submitted invoices in a predetermined time frame to milestone-based payments. A wiser approach is to steer your projects to a recurring payment schedule with regular, detailed invoices. This approach should also provide clients with a clear understanding of what has been accomplished and what work is remaining on the project.

The following example is one way to structure payments for your work:

Payment Schedule

[Your Company Name]'s typical payment schedule is to receive a retainer fee of XX% of the total estimated price of the project prior to commencement.

[Your Company Name] shall submit invoices on the 1st and 15th of every month; payment is due in full within 14 days.

Upon completion of the project, [Your Company Name] shall deliver all work product to [Client Company Name]. Once the materials are satisfactorily approved, [Your Company Name] shall refund any payment excess remaining from the retainer or [Your Company Name] shall submit a final invoice for amounts not covered by the retainer.

Note: If [Project] is placed on hold for a period of more than 14 days with no work progress made, [Your Company Name] shall submit a final invoice for any fees not covered by the retainer and shall be provided with the right of first refusal in the event that the project is reopened.

Although it's not required, it is helpful to include a note about how the project will be handled if it is put on hold for an extensive period of time. This stipulation can help you keep your project on track and moving forward—and it gives you a discussion point with your clients. If you will not be doing additional work for them for a long time, you want to be able to move on and look for work to fill the void.

Acknowledgment and Sign-Off

While it is very important to ensure that you have a proposal in place, by itself it's not enough. The proposal really doesn't mean much until the right person at your client company has approved and signed it.

It's vital to make sure that everyone has a clear understanding of what is going to be taking place and how much is expected from each side. It is equally important that you protect yourself from the "iteration superhighway" and reduce your risk of allowing a client to engage you in "feature creep": continually requesting "just one more thing" that needs to be included.

Sign-offs are pretty simple and clear. Once you have created the proposal document, you will provide your client with an acknowledgment and sign-off that will approve the agreement between your two companies. Always prepare two copies—one for each party—and ensure that both copies are signed.

Here is an example of an acknowledgment you can use:

Acknowledgment

This proposal is acknowledged and agreed in its entirety by [Client Company Name]. This proposal must be signed and dated by an authorized representative of [Client Company Name] in order to be in effect. Alternately, a signed purchase order referencing this proposal will constitute acceptance in place of this signed document (provided, however, that any preprinted terms on such purchase order shall be considered null and void and of no effect).

This proposal constitutes the entire agreement between the parties with respect to the subject matter of this proposal. This proposal merges and supersedes all prior oral or written agreements, discussions, negotiations, commitments, writings, or understandings. This includes without limitation any representations contained in any sales literature, brochures, or other written descriptive or advertising material and is the complete and exclusive statement of the terms of the parties' agreement. Each of the parties acknowledges and agrees that in executing this proposal it has not relied upon, and it expressly disclaims any reliance upon, any representation or statement not set forth herein or in the Agreement.

Accepted by the authorized representatives of:

[Your Company Name]	[Client Company Name]
By: _____	By: _____
Name: _____	Name: _____
Title: _____	Title: _____
Date: _____	Date: _____

Make all checks payable to: [Your Company Name]

Ask the Experts: Laura Creekmore

Laura Creekmore is President of Creek Content (http://creekcontent. com), a content strategy and information architecture consultancy based in Nashville and Austin focusing on healthcare and other highly regulated industries.

When you are a small shop working with a behemoth client, it is INCREDIBLY likely that they will have their own agreements they want to use, and their own army of lawyers that want to cross every t and dot every i. However, I have found on more than one occasion that it is MORE THAN WORTH THE $$ to hire my own lawyer to review their agreement and recommend changes in my favor, instead of just accepting it blindly.

The less than $1,000 I have spent for these kinds of reviews have paid me back many-fold in the final agreement.

Particular things to watch for:

Requirements that you have extensive and expensive liability/E&O insurance. While I think everyone SHOULD have liability insurance, I have always been able to argue down the amount. And liability insurance ain't cheap.

Unfavorable payment terms. I have been able to get most clients to agree to net/10 payment, but almost all of them start by saying they'll pay in 60 or

Statements of Work

A statement of work (SOW) is a high-level definition of your project objec-tives that you should be able to put together in a two- to three-page document (not including cover). The SOW is typically written before you get into detailed requirements, although depending upon your client and your project needs, you may choose to create a hybrid document that best suits your needs.

In general, SOWs should be used to build consensus between your team and your client's stakeholders early on. The SOW will define the inputs and outputs of the project, as well as assumptions and limitations.

At this point, it is not uncommon for clients to ask you to provide a "ball-park figure" for the work you will be doing for them. It can be a little risky to

90 days. I've gotten everyone down some. We don't work with government, which is a likely exception to that point—they are NOT going to change their payment terms for you.

No-hire clauses. If you have employees, or if you anticipate having them, pay attention. The large client will always have a provision saying that you can't hire their staff within a certain amount of time of working with them. If you work with a really big company, this is crazy—because you might want to hire someone from a completely different part of the company, completely unrelated to the project, and that agreement will prevent you from doing so. Additionally, the big client rarely includes language that will prevent them from hiring YOUR employees. You have to add that.

Copyright and NDA terms. You usually can't change these, but you need to understand them completely and make sure that employees or subcontractors who work with you also understand them.

One final thought: The client is hiring you to do the work because you know it better than anyone at their company. However, don't be lulled into false security over that. It is vital that your client understands the scope of work as well as you do—otherwise, it will come back to haunt you.

answer that at this point. It is recommended that you do your best to avoid specifics or commitments without defining the details. It's just not possible to know how much a project is going to cost when you haven't yet written the proposal and/or requirements document.

That said, you have to make a judgment call at this point. If you are working on a project such as a basic website, and you have successfully completed several similar projects before and/or have worked with the same client before, then you have some wiggle room. Remember, erring on the side of caution is always better than an uncomfortable situation later on in the project.

A statement of work should be approximately two to three pages and, at minimum, contain the following:

- ▶ Title page
- ▶ Revision history
- ▶ Project reference number
- ▶ Project summary
- ▶ Start date
- ▶ End date
- ▶ Rate/price
- ▶ Project explanation
- ▶ Activities and deliverables
- ▶ Itemized costs and payment schedule
- ▶ Acknowledgement and sign-off

Do the elements look familiar? They should—you can put together an SOW utilizing a trimmed-down version of the proposal.

You have now learned how to put together two types of documentation that will allow you to identify the work you are performing for a client. These documents should be the foundation of any project work you do for any client and will give you and your clients a well-defined set of marching orders for your projects.

4 Project Objectives and Approach

Know Which Star to Navigate By

One of the keys to a good project is to start the team out with clear project objectives and a well-understood approach. Ideally, the project leadership will have this defined for you—but how do you know if they don't?

This chapter talks about forming project objectives and offers some questions that will help you solidify those goals. We'll also discuss some common project approaches (or *methodologies*) and how they may influence the way you work.

Carolyn Chandler

You're in the project kickoff, with the full team for the first time. The project manager hands out some materials and gives you an overview of the project. By the end of the meeting, ideally, you should have the following information:

- ► Why is the project important to the company?

- ► How will stakeholders determine if the project was a success?

- ► What approach or methodology will the project follow?

- ► What are the major dates or *milestones* for key points, such as getting approval from business stakeholders?

All of these questions concern the expectations that stakeholders have for the project: *what* the project will accomplish and *how* they will be involved in it. The first two questions pertain to the project's objectives and the last two to the project's approach.

A *project objective* is a statement of a measurable goal for the project. Let's talk about objectives in more detail.

Solidify Project Objectives

Objectives are an important focusing lens that you'll use throughout the project. They should spring from the client company's overall business strategy, so the project objectives should be in line with the strategic initiatives within the company. For example, if there is a strategic initiative to appeal to a new group of prospective customers (called a *market*), the site or application you're creating may be an effort to provide that market with online access to products and services relevant to them. The objective for that project would then be focused on reaching and engaging that market.

A clear objective resonates throughout a project. It helps you:

- ► Ask the right questions as you gather ideas from business stakeholders

- ► Plan research with users and focus your analysis of the results

- ► Detail the ideas gathered from stakeholders and users and convert them into a consolidated list of project requirements

- ► Prioritize those project requirements based on their value to the company

- ▶ Create effective interaction designs
- ▶ Manage requests for changes to the design once development begins
- ▶ Focus efforts during deployment activities (such as training and communications to users about the new site or application before and during its launch)
- ▶ Determine whether you've met the needs of the client company, once the project is launched

When you start a new project, you probably have project objectives from the project's sponsor (the business stakeholder who has direct responsibility for the success of the project), as well as a set of project-related requests coming from business stakeholders and from customers, but they all may be a bit fuzzy (**Figure 4.1**). Your goal is to clarify these into solid statements that you can use as a yardstick for the project's success.

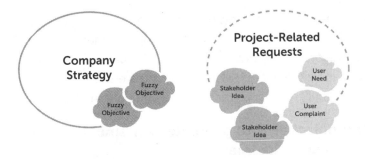

Figure 4.1 *Fuzzy objectives, ideas, and needs*

A solid objective has the following characteristics:

- ▶ **Easy to understand.** Avoid insider terminology
- ▶ **Distinct.** Avoid vague statements; instead, use wording that seems like it will be useful when you're prioritizing requirements
- ▶ **Measurable.** Make concrete statements that you can set an independent measurement against to determine your success

As you define a fuzzy objective, making it clear and measurable, it becomes a solid objective that you can base decisions on (**Figure 4.2** on the next page).

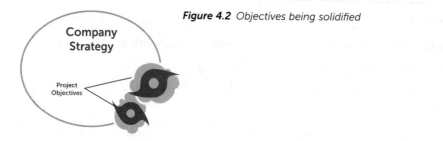

Figure 4.2 *Objectives being solidified*

You'll hear many statements that could be considered objectives. Analyzing fuzzy ones such as those below will help you solidify your objectives and communicate more effectively within the project team.

 Business Advocate **"Our objective is to become the market leader in industry x."**

This is an objective for the entire company, but is too broad for a specific project. Multiple initiatives at the company need to come together to make this happen; any one site or application may *help* with this but will be very unlikely to be able to handle the entire burden—unless the entire company is about this one site or application and it ends up being wildly successful.

 Business Advocate **"Our objective is to generate excitement among our customer base."**

This one is better, because a site or application could have an impact on this, but it's still too vague. Why is it important to generate excitement? How does that excitement translate into meeting a business need? And how can you tell if you've been successful?

 Business Advocate **"Our objective is to increase the amount of traffic on our website."**

Now we're getting there. This one is easy to measure, but it's too focused on an intermediate step. Suppose you do generate more traffic: It may not help you if people don't perform the actions you want once they get there.

Fuzzy objectives can give you a sense of a client's desires and larger goals. From these you can craft more solid project objectives, such as

▶ Increase the revenue from online sales by 10 percent

▶ Increase the revenue from online advertising by 20 percent

▶ Increase the number of current and potential customers in our customer database to at least 20,000

▶ Deliver highly rated and highly referenced content to our primary users (Note that this one requires some work to decide how to measure "highly rated" and "highly referenced," but the elements are there to build from)

Each of these can be measured and affected by your project. They can also map pretty closely to your designs and the features offered. For example, it's very common to offer an online newsletter as a way to meet an objective of growing the customer database: To deliver the newsletter you'll need to capture customer e-mail addresses, which will be added to the database. Objectives may also bring out new requirements. For example, if you're measuring success by the average rating given to articles on your site, you'll need a feature that allows users to give ratings. In these ways, objectives help you focus as you gather ideas for the site, and these may later become project requirements.

If there are multiple objectives, be sure to create a prioritized list with your business sponsor and project team. Objectives sometimes conflict with each other during design, and the team will need to know what takes precedence. The final prioritized list of objectives should come from your project sponsor, but you can be a key part of the discussion. Let's talk about how.

How Can a UX Designer Help?

If you find the project objectives are unclear at the beginning of a project, you can bring your facilitation skills to bear. Help the project team understand the business-related context of the project by holding a workshop with key stakeholders (see the next chapter for more on identifying the right stakeholders). Your goal in this session, which usually lasts two to four hours, is to bring out information on the company's strengths, weaknesses, opportunities, and threats. Called a *SWOT analysis*, this is a common business analysis technique and one way to discuss a company's position in the market. You can also use this time to discuss the company's competition.

Understand Strengths and Weaknesses

The *SW* in a SWOT analysis are the company's current strengths and weaknesses as they pertain to the project. Strengths and weaknesses could include internal processes as well as external perceptions—and often they influence each other. For example, a company with a large research and development (R&D) department could have access to a large source of original research that is published (a strength), but there may be no one to help make that content more accessible to the average user, leading to the perception that the company is "too academic" (a weakness).

Identify Opportunities and Threats

The *OT* is the future-facing half of the SWOT. Considering the things that differentiate the company from its competitors, what future initiatives could it pursue that will open up a new niche or strengthen a current one? What situations could threaten those plans?

For example, our R&D company may decide to hire writers to publish more accessible feature articles around its original research (an opportunity), but if the current site toolset doesn't have robust content-management features, the publishing process may be prohibitively slow. That could give competitors a chance to respond more quickly (a threat).

Compare Competitors

What is the company's main competition? Who are the competitors for the site being developed? They can be different, especially for large companies or brand new sites.

Are there sites that aren't necessarily direct competitors but that represent interesting models to consider? You can learn a lot from reviewing other e-commerce sites to see whether and how they sell what you're selling.

Pull It Together

SWOT and competitors are good topics to discuss at the same time because they interact with each other. It's hard to talk about future threats without knowing who your competitors are—and once you start talking about future opportunities, new competitors may come to mind.

Once you have a full picture here of the company's competitors and SWOT, your project objectives—as well as the overall fit of your project within the company strategy—should become easier to define, and the priorities among them should become clear.

Solidifying project objectives helps you understand expectations of what the project is going to accomplish. Next, let's talk about expectations concerning how the project will be run. Understanding the project approach will help you collaborate effectively and involve the right people at the right time.

Understand the Project Approach

Knowing the overall approach, or *methodology*, of a project is an important part of understanding when and how you'll be involved and how you should be involving others, such as your project team and business stakeholders.

Sometimes there seem to be as many project approaches as there are projects. How to choose the right approach for a project is a large topic in itself. The methodology you choose can depend on many things, including the structure and location of the project team, the technologies being used on the project, and the degree to which collaboration is a part of the company's culture. For the purposes of this book, we're assuming that you've joined a project where the approach has largely been determined by those responsible for the project's success, such as the project sponsor and project manager. In this situation, your main goal will be to understand the approach and help make it effective for the business stakeholders and your users.

Here we'll focus on two of the most common types of approach, as well as a third that shows a possible variation you might encounter on a project. The important thing to note is that most approaches involve the same steps:

▶ **Plan** the overall strategy, approach, and team structure

▶ **Define** the project requirements

- **Design** interaction and visual concepts and evolve them into detailed specifications
- **Develop**, test, and refine the solution
- **Deploy** the solution via messaging, training, and a planned launch
- **Extend** the project by making recommendations for improvements

The names for these steps may vary, as may the degree to which they overlap and the way information is documented. But the general activities in each step are common to most projects and to all three models presented here.

Waterfall Approach

A *waterfall approach* (**Figure 4.3**) involves treating the steps of a project as separate, distinct *phases*, where approval of one phase is needed before the next phase begins. For example, the Design phase does not begin in earnest until requirements have been approved by business stakeholders, who sign off on one or more requirements documents at the end of the Define phase.

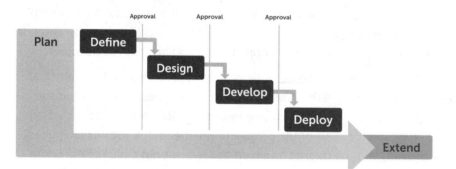

Figure 4.3 *Example of a waterfall approach, where each phase "falls" into the next*

The problem with a pure waterfall approach is that it assumes that each phase can be completed with minimal changes to the phase before it. So if you come up with new requirements in the Design phase, which is common, you must suggest changes to documents that were approved at the end of the Define phase, which can throw off the plan and the schedule.

Agile Approaches

Because change is constant, project teams are continually looking for more flexible approaches than the waterfall model. Many methodologies follow a more fluid approach, with some steps happening alongside each other; for example, versions of the website could be released on a rapid, iterative schedule using an *agile* or *rapid development* approach (**Figure 4.4**). An agile approach generally has a greater focus on rapid collaboration and a reduced focus on detailed documentation and formal sign-off.

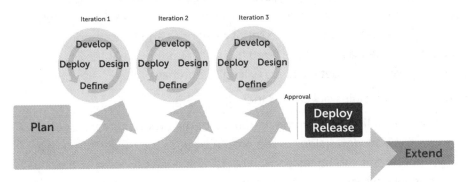

Figure 4.4 *Example of an agile approach*

A true agile approach (following the best practices developed by members of the Agile Alliance, for example) calls for small teams whose members are located next to each other physically, with little focus on defining formal roles between team members. Working this way allows a very high degree of collaboration, which reduces the need for heavy documentation between the stages of design, development, and testing. A team member can pose a question, come to the answer together with other team members during a quick whiteboarding session, and implement a solution without the delay of detailed documentation and approval. Stakeholder reviews occur with a fully functioning system when one of the many iterations is released, and the resulting input is taken into account as the next iteration is planned. (*Iterations* are draft versions of a particular site or application and may also be called *sprints*.)

Designers moving to an agile approach for the first time often face a conundrum. How do you go from a waterfall approach (which favors detailed documentation and sign off, taking weeks or months per phase), to an agile approach (which favors conversations and quick decision making over the course of days or weeks) and still make time for design thinking and user research? To see how some designers have made the transition, let's dive deeper into a particular kind of approach called Lean UX.

Lean UX

Lean UX is an agile project approach that's well-suited to products being developed in the face of great uncertainty (as most products for startups are). It reduces waste in the project's process by removing effort spent on features that don't really matter at the time of each iteration. For example, spending time designing an entire set of categories and subcategories of products may be wasteful if the team has not yet proven that they're offering products that their target users are willing to purchase.

Some of the principles of Lean UX include:

▶ **A focus on validated learning.** Iterations of the product are not seen as simply working versions of the product, but as the presentation of a hypothesis that can be tested with users. The goal is to *learn* as quickly as possible, by validating design decisions with customers and incorporating the subsequent changes that will help the team learn the next important lesson.

The Origins of Lean UX

Eric Ries developed an approach called the Lean Startup after studying Toyota's lean manufacturing processes, and Steve Blank's Customer Development model, which emphasizes the need for startups to have an early focus on customers. A Lean UX approach builds on this direction with its customer inclusion, its reduction of waste in the process, and its definition of product iterations as experiments.

Entrepreneurs can find out how experimentation and a focus on learning can help startup teams in the face of uncertainty, in *The Lean Startup* by Eric Ries (Crown Business, 2011).

▶ **A continuous loop of Build—Measure—Learn.** Lean processes prioritize the building of a testable iteration of the product as quickly as possible, in order to test assumptions that the team is making about how users will react to the product. Tests fail or succeed based on qualitative user feedback during research, and on quantitative measures that are put in place to track success. These measures should pull from actual user behavior—for example, the number of registrations for a site, the number of products purchased, and so on. Care should be taken that the measures put in place really test the assumptions of that iteration. For example, if people are registering for your site, but not taking any important actions in it afterwards, you've just learned that your post-registration experience needs to be more compelling! Incorporate that learning into your decisions on what goes into the next build, and complete the loop (**Figure 4.5**).

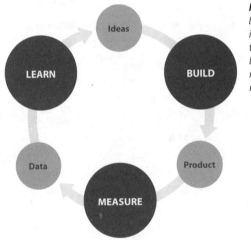

Figure 4.5 *Lean approaches focus on a loop of Build—Measure—Learn. The process is meant to increase the speed by which teams cycle through the loop, maximizing learning and allowing for quicker adjustments in strategy based on customer response.*

▶ **The importance of developing the Minimum Viable Product (MVP) at each iteration.** In a lean process, the focus is on testing a hypothesis about user behavior, rather than building a fully functioning product at each iteration. Teams don't need to create a fully functioning digital version of their product to test a hypothesis (although a more robust digital version will eventually exist after several cycles, if things are going well on the validation front). Especially in beginning stages teams can focus on developing a Minimum Viable Product, which Eric Ries defines as "that version of product that enables a full turn of the Build—Measure—Learn

Ask the Experts: Jeff Gothelf

Jeff Gothelf is the founder of Proof, a product innovation and design studio, and is the author of Lean UX: Getting Out of the Deliverables Business *(O'Reilly, 2012.)*

You've said that Lean UX is an approach that gets designers out of the deliverables business. But many UX designers use deliverables—documentation like detailed wireframes—in order to communicate design recommendations to their teams. Does Lean UX skip this step?

Deliverables aren't skipped in Lean UX. They're still used, to the extent necessary, to communicate to target audiences like stakeholders, developers, and customers. But they're not the focus of the project, and they don't create the bottleneck they would in waterfall where the team sits back and waits for the design to be "done" and then signed off before anyone else begins working. Also, there's still a large amount of work that you're doing as a designer outside of the actual documentation, because the goal is to validate your design hypotheses as soon as possible—so the more tests you're running with customers, the more right you'll be in the product you're building. The trick to getting to a level of efficiency with it is to build a shared understanding across your entire cross-functional team. The more you're out there with your team having conversations with them, discussing what you're seeing and why you think that is, the more they get a clear sense of why you're making the design decisions you're making and what direction the design is heading in. When they have a clear sense of that, they need less documentation in order

loop with a minimum amount of effort and the least amount of development time." For example, elements of the experience that should eventually become automated—like confirmation emails when a purchase has been made—may be completed more manually by a team member while the test is being run in an earlier iteration.

▶ **A move away from formal deliverables and detailed documentation.**
This is consistent with the overall agile approach. Deliverables like detailed wireframes and use cases, which may become replacements for direct communication and fast implementation of ideas, are removed from the process in favor of faster methods like sketching. Conceptual wireframes

to start building those experiences because they have the foundation and shared understanding from which to work.

How does a Lean UX approach affect the role of a UX designer on the project?

It assumes a leadership quality to the UX role on the team. The Lean UX process forces you to constantly communicate out to the team and solicit feedback from them. But it's not design by committee, either. Yes, you're out there soliciting feedback from your team early and often, but it isn't your job to take all their feedback and make sure it all makes it into the next iteration of the design. It's your job to prioritize the feedback based on what's needed to get to the next level of learning with your customers. Then you incorporate that and communicate the result out to the team so they're aware of what design decisions are being made, and why.

Is there anything the team should have from the beginning to ensure a Lean UX approach is successful?

There needs to be a freedom to fail in the organization. If people feel they have to get it right the first time, right out of the gate, than the whole process fails. This is a hypothesis validation process, and by the very nature of it you're going to come up with some wrong answers. The idea is to figure out what those wrong answers are as quickly as possible and minimize the wasted effort going down those paths. If you don't have the freedom to be wrong in your organization, then you will not be able to execute this process with any kind of success.

are often still used, but are meant to illustrate quickly as an aid to communication, and do not "live on" as records of design decisions.

When an agile approach is working as it's designed to, it's a beautiful thing. At most companies and within most consulting engagements, however, teams rarely follow a pure agile approach. In part, this is because companies often have distributed teams and remote workers, which makes it difficult to maintain the high degree of collaboration needed to take best advantage of the pure agile approach. However, a greater prevalence of virtual collaboration tools and digital sketching tools makes this distributed agile approach increasingly possible, as long as teams commit to clear communication, high availability, and effective decision-making.

> ### Surfing
>
> LUXr is a company founded on Lean UX practices. You can see an introduction to Lean UX and more detail on its principles on their site at http://luxr.co/lean-ux/9-principles-for-lean-ux/.
>
> All UX designers should be focused on reducing waste in the process, and prioritizing communication over documentation regardless of the specific approach of the team, as Whitney Hess points out here: http://whitneyhess.com/blog/2011/02/27/why-i-detest-the-term-lean-ux/

Modified Approaches

Many projects try to follow an approach that marries elements of waterfall and agile approaches, with enough structure and documentation to reduce the risks posed by distributed teams and turnover of team members, but enough collaboration and iteration to respond to changes in a relatively nimble way. For example, a project may follow a waterfall model but include an overlap in phases so that there are key collaboration points from team to team. This allows potential changes to surface earlier in each phase. This may also include an early release (such as a beta release to a particular user group) with a shorter iteration cycle. Feedback from that release can then be incorporated before the full deployment of the new site. (**Figure 4.6**)

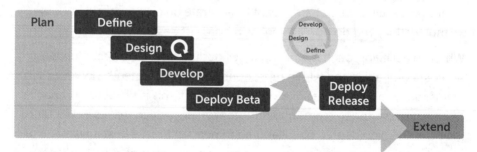

Figure 4.6 *Modified waterfall with beta release*

Notice the smaller iterations within the Design phase in Figure 4.5. That's one of the greatest values you bring to your team as a UX designer. Tools such as wireframes (Chapter 12) and prototypes (Chapter 13) can allow you to gather feedback on quick iterations of ideas, before a lot of development time has been put in.

This book loosely follows a modified waterfall approach like the one shown in Figure 4.6. However, many of the topics covered here will apply to your project regardless of the specifics of your approach, because the basic activities behind them—defining and designing, for example—are still necessary.

Deep Diving

If your project is using an agile approach, you'll have unique needs during requirements gathering, such as the writing of "user stories" as a way to capture requirements. We recommend *User Stories Applied: For Agile Software Development* by Mike Cohn (Addison-Wesley Professional, 2004).

How Does the Approach Affect Me?

Knowing your approach helps you understand a number of things:

► **What questions you should be asking, and when.** For example, if you're working with a pure waterfall approach, you'll need to put in extra effort to make sure the requirements captured in the Define phase contain all the information you need for the Design phase. (We'll be discussing requirements in the next chapter.)

► **Expectations on how project team members will collaborate and how close that collaboration will be.** For example, an agile approach requires very close collaboration. A waterfall approach may involve individual work most of the time, with touchpoints once or several times per week.

► **The level of detail needed in your documentation and the level of formality.** Documents submitted at sign-off points need to be formal, almost like legal contracts. Typically, you'll need more formal documents in a waterfall approach, where sign-off is required before you move on to the next phase. However, you may also have some formal sign-off documents when using an agile approach—for example, to capture information at major decision points, such as when a particular iteration is prepared for full release and deployment.

▶ **Important milestones that involve approval from stakeholders and deployment to different groups.** The approach will determine what different audiences need to provide at various points in the project, including approvals from stakeholders at sign-off points and feedback from potential users during a beta release.

Now that you've solidified your project objectives and gained an understanding of the project approach, in the next chapter we'll start with the primary work in the Define phase: gathering requirements.

5 Business Requirements

Know the Problem Before
You Create the Solution

By the time the project team gets together you'll probably have heard, or have come up with, a lot of ideas about what needs to be done. There may already be lists of features provided by some prominent members of the company (your business stakeholders), along with their opinions about which features are most important. These are *elements* of the business requirements for the project, and they're a good start. To make sure you have a complete solution at the end of the project, or a strong vision to help guide your iterations along the way, you'll need to generate and clarify requirements from multiple viewpoints. In this chapter we'll focus on gathering and detailing requirements from your business stakeholders.

Carolyn Chandler

Chapter 4 covered fuzzy objectives and discussed some ways you can help clarify them for yourself and the project team. In the early stages of a project, you're also likely to have a set of requests that are relatively fuzzy. These may be ideas from stakeholders, user complaints, or user requests. To make these useful and trackable components of your project, you'll need to coalesce these ideas into *requirements*.

Requirements are statements defining what the site or application needs to do. Ideally, a business requirement does several things:

▶ Provides insight into the overall need that must be addressed

▶ Represents and consolidates needs provided by different stakeholders

▶ Gives direction for design, without being too specific about how it will be accomplished

▶ Serves as a distinct unit of work for purposes of prioritization and tracking

Here's an example of an idea for a feature on an e-commerce website. You could receive this same idea from a couple of different business stakeholders early in the Define phase:

"Customers can track their orders online."

This is a good base for a requirement, but it's fuzzy. Start asking questions that get to the details of the requirement:

▶ Why is it important to the business that customers be able to track their orders online? For example, is it to cut down on the number of calls to customer support?

▶ Does the company currently have the capability to track packages online? If not, new requirements will need to be captured for the tracking features, or the company may need to partner with a third party.

▶ How accurate does the tracking have to be? What kind of information should be included in the tracking details? For example, does the site have to provide an updated estimate for delivery time?

Asking these sorts of questions will help you coalesce fuzzy ideas into solid requirements. It will also make it apparent that the same statement can mean different things to different people.

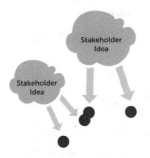

For example, one stakeholder may think tracking packages involves receiving a confirmation e-mail with a tracking number, which can be entered on UPS.com or another site so that the customer can see the latest stop the package has reached. Another stakeholder may think the company needs to push the envelope on package tracking and invest in developing the ability for customers to track packages via GPS, seeing the exact location in real time using an online map. As you can imagine, there's a significant difference here in user experience and scope!

It's important to outline these differences early in the project. Otherwise, you'll end up developing a solution that misses the intent of the business stakeholder—and potentially misses the project objectives. That leads to unhappy stakeholders and, if the feature needs to be redesigned, lost time and money.

So, clear and detailed requirements are a key part of your overall project. Getting to a consolidated list of project requirements involves the following steps:

1. Understand the current state of the site or its competitors.

2. Gather needs and ideas from business stakeholders as well as current and potential users. (See Chapter 6 for details on working with users.)

3. Coalesce ideas into requirements (**Figure 5.1**).

4. Prioritize requirements based on project objectives. (See Chapter 9 for suggestions on setting priorities.)

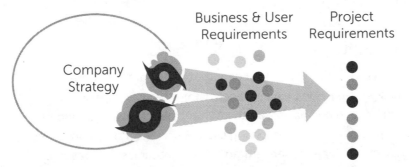

Figure 5.1 *Coalesce ideas from business stakeholders into business requirements, and ideas from research with users into user requirements. Then, use project objectives to focus prioritization efforts and create a consolidated list of project requirements.*

First, let's talk about gaining an understanding of the current state of your site so that you have a context for the ideas that will be coming your way during requirements gathering.

Understand the Current State

When diving into the specifics of the site or application you're designing, it's important to ground yourself by understanding the current state of the site (if you're redesigning one that already exists) or by understanding key competitors more thoroughly (if you're designing a new site or application).

You can learn a great deal about the current state through stakeholder interviews (more on this in a few pages). You can also gain a lot of understanding on your own, and this can serve as a strong base for stakeholder interviews and user research efforts. A great way to gain background information and generate ideas that could become requirements is to conduct a heuristic analysis.

By Any Other Name...

The word *heuristic* means a rule of thumb or best practice. A heuristic analysis has come to mean a review of a product against a set of rules (heuristics) for usable design, usually conducted by a UX designer. User-friendly sites will follow most or all of the heuristics you use in your analysis.

You may also hear this technique called a *heuristic evaluation*, *expert review*, or some combination of these terms.

Heuristic Analysis

A *heuristic analysis* is a technique you can use to evaluate the usability of an existing design, based on best practices within the user experience field. You can conduct such an analysis on the current site at the beginning of a redesign project or analyze competing sites to understand opportunities for offering a better user experience than other companies. The result is a document describing the strengths and weaknesses of the site, including recommendations for improvement. After it's complete, you'll have a deeper understanding of the site analyzed and a list of ideas to contribute to the requirements for the new site.

For example, a commonly used heuristic is this one, from Jakob Nielsen's list of ten usability heuristics (view the complete list on Jakob Nielsen's site, at www.useit.com/papers/heuristic/heuristic_list.html):

Visibility of system status. The system should always keep users informed about what is going on through appropriate feedback within reasonable time.

There are many situations on a site where this heuristic may not be followed. For example, let's say the user clicks on a Download button and gets no message that his file is being downloaded. The system has not informed the user that the file is in the process of being downloaded, even though the download has started. So the user may click the button again, thinking that he missed the button the first time ... and then click again....

This can lead to multiple downloads—potentially causing problems for both the performance of the site and the user, who now has multiple downloads in progress without realizing it.

During the heuristic analysis, you can note this as a problem area, describe it, and rate its impact. You may also share an idea that might address the problem, which could be added to the requirements list.

Why Conduct a Heuristic Analysis?

Conducting this kind of analysis is a relatively quick and inexpensive way of obtaining feedback on a design. A heuristic analysis can provide a general understanding of the design quality and help identify any potential design issues.

Keep in mind that this activity does not directly involve end users and shouldn't be a replacement for true user research. For example, it's possible that only 50 percent of your heuristic findings may actually be validated by later research. The analysis does, however, give the team a good handle on likely areas of concern. If you're working on redesigning an existing product or site, it can also be good for identifying obvious quick fixes that can lead to immediate improvements as the redesign efforts continue behind the scenes.

How Do I Do It?

The specific heuristics you use may vary from project to project, but the process for conducting the analysis will generally remain the same:

1. Gather product and project background knowledge.

   Make sure you have the objectives of the site, a list of the main user groups that need to be supported, information on the kind of environment users are likely to be working in, and a basic understanding of any specialized knowledge your users are likely to have. (Your analysis will be different for a site built for general consumers than a site built for pharmacists, for example.) If you need help with the last one, visiting a variety of competitive sites or applications can help you understand the most common terminology and areas of interest.

2. Choose the heuristics to use.

   There are many heuristics out there to reference. In addition to Jakob Nielsen's list, many UX designers refer to Bruce Tognazzini's list of design principles: www.asktog.com/basics/firstPrinciples.html. Once you're familiar with the subject matter of the site, you may want to add a few of your own—especially if you're analyzing more than one site. Be sure to keep your list to a manageable size (say, 8 to 12); too many heuristics can make the technique unwieldy for you and your readers.

3. Walk through prioritized areas of the site, identifying areas where the heuristics are followed well or missed.

   Each observation you make should have the following information:

   The general observation. A short statement summing up the finding. Ideally these will be numbered so that you can reference them quickly as you walk people through the report.

   A short description. A paragraph or two describing the context of the observation—for example, the point in a particular process where you noticed a problem.

   An impact ranking. This rating can be high, medium, or low for observations of issues, or it can be a note of a positive finding if you're sharing something that the site did well. In general, high-impact issues are those that you believe will cause many users to fail a particular task or permanently lose information (for example, an issue that causes a user to lose changes to a document she's been working on). Medium-impact issues are those that cause frustration and errors but don't cause irreversible issues. Low-impact issues are minor problems that may cause some confusion but don't typically lead to lost time or frustration.

Recommendations. These are next steps or ideas that you share, which may serve as a remedy to the problem you encountered.

Figure 5.2 shows an example of these elements together, as they might appear in your heuristic analysis.

| Observation #4 | HIGH |
| The search function does not appear to be bringing back all possible results. | Concern |

A sample test of the search function yielded mixed results. Searches using a name in a relatively new post, featuring a less commonly covered topic, occasionally returned no results. It also appears that primary search returns link to new stories only, not videos.

Recommendations
1. Ensure newly added content is indexed and searchable before, or very shortly after, being publicly available.
2. Consider surfacing related content when search results are brought back—for example, stories in similar categories or with similar tags—so users who are exploring have more threads to follow.
3. Consider universal search that presents results organized by category.
4. Use search term logs to understand commonly searched items. This may also provide insight into items that users are having trouble finding.

Figure 5.2 *A sample observation in a heuristic analysis report*

4. Present your findings to the project team and primary stakeholders.

   Walk them through your observations and recommendations. Discuss why you gave the ratings you did. (This is also a great time to have a prepared recommendation on how to validate your findings, using one of the techniques discussed in Chapter 6.)

How Does a Heuristic Analysis Help with Requirements Gathering?

Once you've completed your heuristic analysis, you'll have a deeper understanding of the current state of the site (or its competitors), and a list of ideas that can contribute to requirements gathering. You'll also have some ideas on how to structure the topics you'll need to cover during requirements-gathering sessions—which leads us to the next step of that process.

Gather Ideas from Stakeholders

As we saw in our example at the beginning of this chapter, if you don't get context for an idea, such as "Customers can track their orders online," you risk missing the differences in expectations between stakeholders, like those of our friend who wants packages to be tracked by GPS. One of the most common mistakes made on a project is to seize on a feature and call it a requirement without first understanding the problem and the expectations around a solution.

So why does the requirements-gathering process get shortened so often?

Gathering ideas—and coalescing them into requirements—can take quite a bit of time. It's easy to underestimate the number of questions you need to ask to outline requirements so that they can be prioritized. And if the process isn't well structured or participation is incomplete, there can be a lot of churn that can last throughout the project. (*Churn* is time wasted in extra meetings and work iterations caused by lack of communication and involvement. These are different from the more productive work iterations that are part of designing and testing valid solutions in an effort to find the best one.)

So how do you encourage a well-balanced requirements process that's focused on business needs but avoids being a churning time-suck? Here are some steps for an efficient process:

1. **Outline roles and responsibilities.** Make sure project team members understand the roles that they should be filling as requirements are gathered.

2. **Gather the right stakeholders**, in the right groups, to ensure time is used in the best way during requirements-focused interviews or meetings.

3. **Create a plan for the meetings**, including topics to be covered and questions to be asked during meetings.

4. **Run the meetings efficiently**, capturing ideas and getting clarification. Investigate ideas to dig down to the needs behind each one.

When your meetings are finished, don't forget to thank the stakeholders involved and keep them updated on progress once you move to a consolidated, prioritized list.

Let's examine each of these steps in more detail.

Outline Responsibilities

The act of gathering business requirements generally involves members of the project team interviewing key business stakeholders to gather ideas.

Business stakeholders are those within the company who have a business-oriented stake in the success of the project or have subject matter expertise to contribute, or both. These folks aren't on the project full time, but they need to be involved at key points in the process, and requirements gathering is one of those points. Keep in mind that they also have day jobs (so to speak), so their time is valuable and often hard to get, unless you plan ahead.

The *project sponsor* (or sponsors) is the business stakeholder who also has direct responsibility for the success of the project, often at a relatively high level in the company, such as director. He or she won't be on the project on a day-to-day basis for the whole project lifecycle but will likely be actively involved in requirements gathering and ensuring a high level of participation by business stakeholders. The sponsor may also sit in on some or all sessions.

The *project team* includes people officially assigned to the project as ongoing resources. They may be involved as the project manager, UX designer, business analyst, technical lead, visual designer, quality assurance lead, and so on. Depending on the size of the project, this may be their primary job.

Within the project team itself, responsibilities during requirements gathering are often unclear. Taking time to define responsibilities early on will help ensure an efficient gathering process.

Here are some questions to ask as you determine the specific responsibilities each team member will shoulder during requirements gathering:

▶ Who is primarily responsible for gathering and scheduling the right business stakeholders in the most productive groups? This could include both internal and external stakeholders (such as partners, vendors, and so on).

▶ Who creates the structure of topics and questions for the business stakeholder meetings? This is a great collaborative exercise for the team, if time permits. The main facilitator can then arrange them in a structure that flows well in a meeting.

▶ Who facilitates the meetings?

▶ Who takes notes, and how are they shared?

- ▶ Who follows up with whom afterwards?

- ▶ Will someone from the technology team be present at all the meetings? If so, how is that person involved (are they listening, providing input, or something else)?

As a UX designer, whether or not you're primarily responsible for one or more of these areas, you have important skills to bring to the process. Creating a structure for topics and questions requires a knack for clear categorization (which sounds like a good crossover with information architecture), and of course facilitation skills are important for keeping the meeting on topic, with participation from all attendees.

Gather the Right Stakeholders

The main purpose of interviewing stakeholders is to gain an understanding of relevant project-related ideas, needs, knowledge, and frustrations from various points of view, which can then feed into the project requirements.

There's also the sometimes-unstated benefit of involving many different groups so that each one feels like it's had its say in the project—and as a result will buy into the final solution. Although involving people to get their buy-in may seem more political than practical, it's often a key step that puts you in touch with a network that will support you throughout the project. It may also help you avoid eleventh-hour changes, which can occur when someone you didn't talk to raises an issue late in the process. So involving a large variety of people is frequently a good idea.

On the other hand, schedules and budgets must be kept in mind. Involving a large number of people takes time, from their standpoint and from yours, for the meetings alone—not to mention the time sorting through notes to identify trends and consolidate redundancies. For efficiency and your own sanity, it makes sense to prioritize the groups to talk to and to choose key people from those groups to serve as thought leaders for their team.

Who are possible stakeholders you could involve? These groups are often good sources for ideas:

- ▶ Groups with initiatives that depend on the site (for example, those with marketing campaigns that need to have information presented on the site)

- Groups that need to support the processes directly behind the site or application, such as providing content, entering and managing data, and responding immediately to information gathered

- The front line of customer service, such as phone or online support or anyone who deals with customers face-to-face (for example, at a retail location or via deliveries)

- Sales, product management, or consulting services, to represent the products and services being presented

- Human resources, for meeting recruiting objectives

- Public relations, for presenting information to investors and the media

- Any groups responsible for other relationships that need to be developed as part of the project and that will influence its design, such as relationships with partners or vendors

When choosing the individuals who should be included, get help from your project sponsor and any project team members who are familiar with the groups involved to help pick the right people.

Create groups that will get a good discussion going. There's no one right way to do this, but one common way is to group stakeholders by department, like this:

- Marketing (five people)

- Product management (four people)

- Customer support (two people)

- Sales (four people)

A smaller project might include one person from each of these groups, in a series of two or more collaborative work sessions where everyone meets together.

Once you have your stakeholders in mind, as well as a general structure for the meetings (discussed in the next section), you can start scheduling the meetings. Try to start scheduling at least a couple of weeks beforehand; it can be hard to get everyone in a room together.

Create a Plan for the Meetings

In parallel with your effort to choose the right stakeholders, pull together a list of topics to cover and questions that need to be asked (this will also help you refine your list of stakeholders). You should have a different plan for each group you meet with, although several of your questions may be the same from group to group.

You'll also need to decide on the level of detail you're aiming for in the meetings. If you're meeting with a large number of people only once (for example, members of various departments, as suggested above), you'll want to gather ideas, but you probably don't want to spend too much time diving into the gritty details during the meeting. In that case, if one of your stakeholders gives you the idea "Customers can track their orders online," you may want to simply ask why this function is important and if the stakeholder can think offhand of a site that does this well. These questions should help bring up the major differences among stakeholder expectations of the feature without spending the whole meeting on one statement. You can then work out the specific details of the idea with the project team, circling back with the stakeholder to make sure the requirements that you generated still represent his or her original idea.

Let's say you're redesigning an e-commerce site and you're meeting with a large variety of stakeholders, holding one meeting with each group. Here's an example of a plan for meeting with a group from a sales department.

Sales: Requirements-Gathering Meeting

Participants

Inside Sales: Jenny Bee, Tracy Kim, Joseph Arnold

Lead Management: Kevin Abernathy, Cat Parnell

Time frame: 2 hours

Objective: Understand the current sales process and identify issues and opportunities for how the web could better support that process.

Background: We have reviewed a PowerPoint presentation on the purchasing process, which provided a good background on how purchasing decisions are made. We also plan to talk to the Customer Service team.

Sales: Requirements-Gathering Meeting *continued*

Questions

Sales process:

▶ How is the sales process different for different product lines?

▶ Are there regional differences?

▶ Are some differences based on customer size (e.g., small companies versus large companies)?

▶ How has this process evolved over the last two years and how is it anticipated to evolve over the next three to five years?

▶ How does a potential customer understand all the things that need to be purchased and how they work together?

Overall impression:

▶ Who do you believe are the primary visitors to the current site? Why? What are they like? What are they trying to accomplish on the site?

▶ How does the web contribute to the sales process and/or the sales closure rate today?

▶ What information do customers need to make a purchasing decision? Is that information available on the site today? Is it easy to find? Is it accurate?

▶ How hard is it to maintain content on the site today?

▶ What metrics do you get from the site? What additional metrics would you find valuable? Why?

Envisioning the future:

▶ As you think about a future website, what could we do to better support the sales process?

▶ What current functions and features on the site are critical for sales?

▶ What is not necessary?

▶ What is missing?

Summary:

▶ Are there any other thoughts, suggestions, or concerns that we haven't addressed?

▶ What websites do you think do an excellent job of supporting sales?

▶ What is the number one thing the company could do to improve customer satisfaction?

Run the Meetings Effectively

Here are some practices that will help you with requirements-gathering meetings.

Ensure a Shared Vocabulary Is Used

A lot of confusion can be avoided if the team gathering requirements agrees on a common list of terms and definitions. For example, are the people using the system going to be called *users, customers,* or *clients*? Are people more familiar with the term *interaction designer* or *information architect*?

To avoid confusion, take some time at the beginning of each meeting to state which term is being used and what it means. You may also benefit from creating some visual elements that help explain relationships between different terms or roles (**Figure 5.3**).

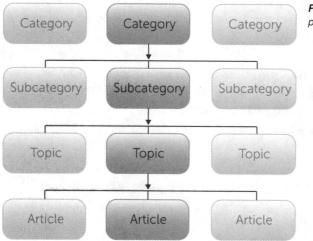

Figure 5.3 *Diagram showing project terms and relationships*

A common vocabulary for the deliverables that will be used in the project will also help stakeholders understand the process and the type of output they can expect to see. This can build trust that their time and effort isn't going to go into a black hole of ideas.

Generally, if you find yourself defining the same words more than once or twice (especially if you find the definitions are changing subtly each time), consider putting them into a project glossary and sharing it with the project team. Here are other examples of terminology that is good to clear up at the beginning of the project:

- Roles that will be interacting (for example, *job seeker* versus *client* or *content producer* versus *editor*)

- Primary deliverables that will be widely referenced (*functional specification, wireframes, site map*) and a brief description of how they differ

- Distinctions between different levels of information (such as our category information in Figure 5.3)

- Distinctions between *needs* and *ideas*

Listen to Ideas and Dig Down to Needs

Stakeholders may make statements that appear to be needs. Consider an example.

 Business Advocate   **"We need a blog on the site."**

This is really an idea, not a need. If blog functionality is then fully designed and implemented, it becomes a solution, but it is not necessarily the solution that best meets the core need of the stakeholders requesting it.

By asking why a blog is important, you may get a wide range of need statements:

"**We need to appear relevant and in touch**. Everyone is talking about blogs, and I feel like we'll be behind the times if we don't include them."

"**We need a way to get people to come to the site repeatedly** to generate more ad revenue, and blogs mean freshly posted content with a following."

"**We need to position ourselves as thought leaders**, and blogs are a more personal way to show our expertise."

"**We need to have a better way to communicate and innovate with our customers**, and blogs get us comments so we can hear their thoughts."

Each statement describes valid needs. By bringing them out, you'll learn about the drivers behind requests for a particular feature, which will help you build consensus as you consolidate and prioritize requirements.

Coalescing Requirements

When the meetings are over, take the ideas you've gathered and sort them into general areas of functionality. You'll start noticing a lot of overlaps; this is a good sign that a particular idea has a lot of buy-in from your stakeholders. Remove redundancies and try to consolidate a list of ideas that efficiently captures the intent of your stakeholders.

To turn the ideas you've gathered into useful and trackable components of your project, you'll need to coalesce these ideas into requirements. Think of raindrops forming from a cloud: You're moving from one large and undefined cloud to a larger number of well-defined raindrops.

So when you get an idea cloud such as "Customers can track their orders online," you'll need to convert it into distinct statements defining what the system needs to do. The resulting requirements should:

▶ Provide insight into the overall need that must be addressed

▶ Represent and consolidate needs provided by different stakeholders

▶ Give direction for design, without being too specific about how it will be accomplished

▶ Serve as a distinct unit of work for purposes of prioritization and tracking

As you start moving from ideas to requirements, make sure your technical lead (or another person who can represent the development team on your project) is involved to ask the questions that will help estimate the effort required when you're prioritizing later. If you have a dedicated quality assurance team member, that person can also provide some great detailed questions to help coalesce requirements.

To detail the tracking idea into requirements, ask questions such as

▶ How accurate does the tracking have to be?

▶ What kind of information should be included in the tracking details; for example, do we have to provide an updated estimate for delivery time?

These kinds of questions can be asked and detailed with the stakeholders who gave you the original idea, if they have a large amount of time dedicated to the project. If you don't have that much access to those stakeholders, you can work out the details yourself by having project team discussions and then reviewing the requirements with your project sponsor to ensure that your choices make sense for the business.

Table 5.1 lists the kinds of requirements that might coalesce from the tracking idea and how you could capture them.

TABLE 5.1 An Example of Business Requirements

ID	AREA	REQUIREMENT	BUSINESS NEED
1	Order Tracking	Orders can be tracked by entering a tracking code online	Encourage self-service during delivery (Support benefit)
2	Order Tracking	Users can track their package by GPS, following trucks or airplanes	Show innovation in efficient delivery (Competitive benefit)
3	Order Tracking	Users can view all past orders made in the last 365 days	Encourage reordering and self-service (Sales, Support benefit)

Notice that in some cases the requirements overlap with each other, as in the case of the first two requirements in the table—both are methods of tracking. They can live together in the same system because you can enter a code to find your package through the GPS view. They're separated, however, because the GPS-related requirement is probably a larger effort and should be prioritized independently of the other features.

As you consolidate the statements, note the business requirements that you think could come in *conflict* with user needs. For example, a business requirement could be to gather personal information from prospective customers, such as their e-mail addresses. But customers may have reservations about providing information. After all, it takes time to fill in forms, security and privacy is a concern, and this step may be interrupting the larger task they're trying to accomplish.

As you identify conflicts like these, they'll start to give you ideas that could help you meet both business and user needs. For the tracking example, you may suggest using a "Send to a Friend" feature to capture the e-mail address and provide a convenience to the user. This means Send to a Friend may become a requirement you put in the mix for prioritization. Ideas like this one can help meet both business and user requirements, so they're great to capture. They also live in that overlapping area between the Define and Design phases (see Chapter 4), because you're starting to think of design solutions to business problems (**Figure 5.4**).

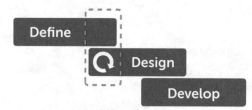

Figure 5.4 *The overlap between the Define phase and the Design phase*

Potential conflicts between business and user needs are excellent things to explore during user research, which we'll discuss in the next chapter. User research will also allow you to extend Table 5.1 into a full set of potential requirements, which will be prioritized into a list of project requirements (shown in Figure 5.1 and discussed further in Chapter 9). Remember, the gathering of business requirements usually occurs in parallel with the exploration of technical possibilities and the gathering of user requirements.

Next up: time to talk about users!

6 User Research

Get to Know the Guests You're Inviting to the Party

There are many user research techniques that can be used throughout the project lifecycle, either to better understand your users or to test out their behavior on versions of a site. This chapter will focus on some of the methods that are most commonly used in the beginning stages of the project.

These techniques will help you define the user groups that should be of highest priority during the project, put their needs and frustrations in context, and assess the performance of the current site (if one exists) using best practices in the field of user experience design.

Carolyn Chandler

Basic Steps of User Research

1. **Define your primary user groups.** This involves creating a framework that describes the main types of users you're designing for—allowing you to focus your efforts in recruiting users for research.

2. **Plan for user involvement.** This includes choosing one or more techniques for involving user groups in research, based on the needs of your project.

3. **Conduct the research.** We'll cover the basic techniques here, such as interviews and surveys, and provide tips on how to go about them.

4. **Validate your user group definitions.** Using what you learned from the research, you can solidify your user groups model. This model will then serve as a platform for the development of more detailed tools, such as personas (discussed in Chapter 7).

5. **Generate user requirements.** These are statements of the features and functions that the site may include. You'll add these statements to your business requirements (discussed in Chapter 5) and prioritize them to become project requirements (discussed in Chapter 9).

This chapter will cover the first three steps, starting with the first: defining your user groups.

Define Your User Groups

Planning for user research at the beginning of a project can feel like a chicken-or-egg dilemma (which comes first?). How do you make sure you're talking to the right people, if you don't know yet who those people need to be?

One way to get started is to create an initial or provisional definition of the users you'll be designing for. This describes your site's primary user groups, which can help you focus your research efforts for the right roles, demographics, or other variables that may have an impact on how users will experience your site. User group definitions can be high level (a list defining each of your target user groups) or detailed and visual (a diagram showing multiple types of users, as well as how they interact with each other).

A high-level definition for a company's primary .com site might include the following user groups: potential purchasers, current purchasers, partners, and job seekers.

As you begin defining groups for user research, you'll start prioritizing user groups in more detail.

Your initial definitions are based on the collective knowledge of business stakeholders and project team members regarding the potential types of users who may be interacting with the site. Those definitions can be built by collecting some of the goals and attributes that different user groups may have. Here are the basic steps for defining your user groups:

1. Create a list of attributes that will help you define the different users of your site (the next section will cover some of the most common)

2. Discuss the attributes with those at the company who have contact with relevant types of users (for example, customers)

3. Prioritize the attributes that seem to have the largest impact on why and how a potential user would use your site or application

4. Define the user groups that you will focus on in research and design

The next sections take a closer look at some brainstorming techniques to help you collect these attributes and how to prioritize and model them (creating representations of the different user types that will help you focus your research efforts).

Create a List of Attributes

A good start for your attribute list is to gather and absorb any research or other documentation the organization has that could provide direction with regard to users. Here are some potential sources:

▶ Documents explaining company strategies, such as company goals, competitive information, marketing strategies, and business plans

▶ Market segmentations of current customers and other demographic data gathered by the marketing department

▶ Previously conducted user research (see Table 6.1 later in this chapter for some examples)

▶ Surveys, such as user satisfaction surveys and feedback forms

▶ Customer service reports covering frequently occurring issues

Next, identify people within the organization who have some insight into current or prospective users. The number and variety of people you should include depends on the type of project and its scope and timeline. If you know the initial definition of your user groups may have a short lifespan (for example, it's in use for only a month or two while user research is being planned), you may include just two or three participants. If you think the initial definition may need to hold you through a good portion of the design process (for example, if you only have this one to work with until you conduct usability testing, after some design has been done), include more participants and ensure you have a cross section of perspectives.

Some possible participants include marketing staff who are responsible for brand representation, segmentation, and campaigns; sales staff; product managers; customer service or support representatives; and trainers.

It's also good to include project team leadership and other business stakeholders in this exercise.

Ask the group to think of the different types of potential users they tend to interact with. Then ask them to list some of the common attributes they've encountered. Here are some examples of what could vary:

▶ **Primary goals,** as they relate to the subject matter of your site. Why are users coming to it and what are they trying to accomplish? For example, purchasing an item, trading a stock, or getting a specific question answered are common goals.

▶ **Roles.** This can be defined in many ways, but one way is to tie roles to the user's primary goal: job seeker, support seeker, potential client, and so on. Once you have more user information, roles can be subdivided by different needs or styles; for example, on an e-commerce site shoppers could include bargain-hunters and connoisseurs.

▶ **Demographics,** including age, sex, family (single, married, children), income level, and region

▶ **Experience** including level of education, level of familiarity with relevant technologies (often referred to as *technical savvy*), level of subject matter expertise, and frequency of usage (one-off, occasional, frequent)

- **Organizational attributes,** including the size of the company users work for, their department, type of job (entry level, freelancer, middle management, executive), tenure (long-term or high turnover?), and work patterns (remote work, amount of travel)

Once you have a list of some of the attributes that come up most often when stakeholders are describing potential users, you can start to prioritize them by their level of importance and then use that hierarchy to begin defining and modeling user groups.

Prioritize and Define

Which of the attributes listed above do you think have the greatest influence on how and why different user groups might use the site? Focus on the ones that you think will have the greatest impact on a user's goals or behavior. Prioritize those attributes, and remember the objectives you created in Chapter 4—they will help drive your choices as well.

An example best illustrates how to prioritize attributes. Say you're working with a company that provides tools for online trading of stocks, options, and futures. This particular company has determined that part of its strategy will be to engage *nonprofessionals* who are trading stocks on their own, online, and to encourage them to try trading new types of products such as options and futures. The company plans to do this by providing trading tools that are easy to use and targeted to those who want hands-on learning in a safe environment.

In discussing attributes with business stakeholders, you may find that the following ones seem to have the biggest impact on how individuals might use these tools:

- **Current frequency of trading,** specifically, frequency of direct online trading (for example, once a quarter, once a day, several times a day). Those who just dabble in trading (say, once a month) may not be serious about trying something new, while those who are already trading full time may not find much value in tools targeted to newer traders. But those who are active part-time traders could have a strong interest in the company's tools.

- **Number of product types traded:** just stocks or stocks, options, and futures. Those who are already trading all types of products may already have a preference for their own tools, but those who only trade one type may be ready to branch out to others.

▶ **Level of subject-matter expertise** (for example, familiarity with trading terms). This will help determine how much help they'll need along the way, with tutorials and glossaries.

▶ **Level of technical savvy** (for example, familiarity with making purchases online and online banking and trading). This will influence how much reassurance they'll need about information privacy and how advanced or simple the online interface needs to be.

You can prioritize these attributes because they may affect the user types you'll be targeting for research. If where traders live doesn't seem to have a real impact on how or why they trade, the Region attribute can drop off the list as a consideration for research participants. On the other hand, if the importance of a particular attribute sparks a lot of discussion it may be a good subject for a survey question or interview question (we'll be discussing surveys later in this chapter).

Comparing two or more attributes can help you prioritize as well. For example, if you make a chart using two attributes for online traders, you can start to see how groups fall within some of the ranges. **Figure 6.1** is an example of a rough user model you could make using the two attributes of Frequency of Direct Trading and Number of Product Types Traded; it also shows the resulting user groups that might form out of the discussion.

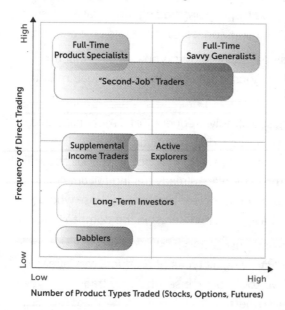

Figure 6.1 A chart of two attributes, representing a rough user model. Creating this model collaboratively can facilitate discussion about potential differences in user motivations and experience.

This user model provides a high-level way to discuss different user types. It's not meant to be the final model, and it doesn't label user groups exclusively (a user could be a long-term investor in stocks and also be actively exploring other possibilities in options or futures). But it does begin to express your understanding of different user groups and how they may be motivated to use your site.

This discussion concerning important attributes also helps you discover which ones you'll want to focus on when recruiting users for research. If you determine that Frequency of Trading is important, and that the priority will be to engage those who currently have a medium level of frequency, you'll want to define what *medium frequency* means (one to three times a week, for example) and recruit your research participants accordingly.

Speaking of research, let's talk about techniques you can use to involve users in your project.

Can You Design from User Models Alone?

There's debate within the user experience field about creating user models before research is conducted, because doing so can color your thinking before you have real user data, and because your project team or project sponsor may see the model as a replacement for user research. Using an unvalidated model does introduce more risk that your assumptions will be incorrect. In projects where you'll have no contact with users at all, however, a well-thought-out model (verified with sources outside the project team, such as a customer service group or training group) is better than having no model to use during design.

Choosing Research Techniques

Now that you have a rough idea of the user groups you want to include, it's time to plan the next step: your recommendations for the amount and type of user research activities to conduct during the project.

Table 6.1 presents some information on the most commonly used research techniques and when they are often most useful. Use this table as a reference to help you choose which ones best apply to your project. The next section describes each technique in more detail.

TABLE 6.1 Common User-Research Techniques

ACTIVITY	WHAT IT IS	WHEN IT'S USEFUL	CHALLENGES	TYPICAL TIME FRAME *
User Interviews	A one-on-one conversation with a participant who belongs to one of the site's primary user groups.	There is access to users, but type of access (in person, by phone, etc.) varies. You want to gain context but can't go to the user.	Getting straight-forward opinions. It can be hard to gather information about attitudes and context, especially if interviews are conducted remotely.	2–4 weeks for 12 interviews: Up to a week to plan, 1–2 weeks to interview, and up to a week to compile results.
Contextual Inquiry	An on-site visit with participants to observe and learn about how they work in their normal, everyday environment.	The project team has little information on target users. Users work in a unique environment (e.g., a hospital). Users are working with fairly complex tasks or workflows.	Gaining access to participants. Going to users' environment may raise concerns about security, intellectual property, and intrusiveness. For business applications, it can be easier to visit on a workday.	3–4 weeks for 12 inquiries: 1 week to plan, 1–2 weeks to observe, 1 week to analyze and report results.
Surveys	A series of questions consisting of mainly closed-end answers (multiple choice) used to identify patterns among a large number of people.	You want to state results in more quantitative terms (e.g., "80% of the target user group said they never purchase cars online"). You're more interested in gathering information about preference than actual performance.	Getting an appropriate sample. Making sure questions are well-written so that you get accurate answers without leading respondents to a particular answer.	3–4 weeks for a short-run survey: 1 week to plan and write the survey, 1–2 weeks to run the survey, 1 week to analyze and report results.

TABLE 6.1 Common User-Research Techniques (*continued*)

ACTIVITY	WHAT IT IS	WHEN IT'S USEFUL	CHALLENGES	TYPICAL TIME FRAME *
Focus Groups	A group discussion where a moderator leads participants through questions on a specific topic. Focuses on uncovering participants' feelings, attitudes, and ideas about the topic.	The team believes that users' attitudes will strongly influence their use of the solution (e.g., if there have been problems with it historically).	Understanding how to target your questions to get the right information out. Facilitating the group effectively.	3–4 weeks: 1 week to plan and write questions, 1–2 weeks to conduct focus groups, 1–2 weeks to analyze and report results.
Card Sorting	Participants are given items (such as topics) on cards and are asked to sort them into groups that are meaningful to them.	You're working on a content source site with many items and want an effective structure for your user groups.	Determining which topics would be best to include.	3–4 weeks: 1 week to plan and prepare, 1 week to conduct research, 1–2 weeks to analyze and report results.
Usability Testing	Users try to perform typical tasks on a site or application while a facilitator observes and, in some cases, asks questions to understand users' behavior.	An existing solution is being improved. Competitive solutions are available to test. You have a prototype that lets users complete (or simulate) tasks.	Choosing the appropriate tasks to focus on. Determining how formal to make the test.	3–4 weeks for 10 users and medium formality: 1 week to plan and write the tasks, 1 week to run the tests, 1–2 weeks to analyze and report results.

* Typical Time Frame represents the time often needed from the point users are scheduled. Two groups of six to eight users are assumed (except for surveys, where the number of users should be larger). This does not include time for recruiting, which can take one to two weeks after creation of the screening questionnaire.

How Many Research Activities Can I Include?

Before you choose among the activities, ask yourself how much money and time the team can dedicate to user research. Consider the following situations to understand how much appetite your client company has for user research.

If project leadership and the project sponsors are comfortable with user research and are interested in using it for known goals, such as ensuring the site meets specific project objectives, then you're likely to have more leeway in planning for two or more activities, or for one activity that you conduct multiple times (for example, testing a design, changing it based on your results, and retesting the new design).

Considerations When Planning Research

When planning for any research techniques, consider the following:

▶ Why you're conducting the research: what you want to learn from it

▶ Who you're including: the primary user groups you outlined above

▶ How you'll get participants: recruiting people to participate and screening them (that is, asking questions to make sure they fall into the user groups you're targeting)

▶ How you'll compensate participants

▶ What space, equipment, and software you'll need, based on whether you'll be in person or you will conduct research remotely (see Chapter 14 for more on remote research)

▶ What you're covering: the primary topics

▶ How you're capturing information: the number of people involved and the tools they're using

Chapter 14 will cover each of these considerations as part of a detailed look at one of the most common techniques used by UX designers: usability testing.

Surfing

Steve Baty wrote an article describing different methods and how to choose among them based on the phase of development, your information needs, and the flexibility you have to incorporate user research. It's titled "Bite-Sized UX Research," by Steve Baty, UXmatters: http://uxmatters.com/MT/archives/000287.php.

If no one at the organization is familiar with user research and there's some resistance to it altogether, you may be better off proposing one round of research and picking the technique that you think will bring the most value to you, the project team, and the business stakeholders. Once you have the results of the research, the project team will have a better idea of what's involved and how the project can benefit. You'll then have a strong case for including more research later, if needed.

If you have room for at least two rounds of research, a good approach is to include one round during the Define phase, or early in the Design phase, to better understand the users. Then include one more round before development starts, to validate the design. For example, for a task-based application you might conduct user interviews before designing and then perform usability testing on a prototype later in the process. Or for a content source you might start with contextual inquiry and then include a card sorting exercise.

Note *See Chapter 2 for more on task-based applications and content sources.*

Let's take a closer look at each of these techniques and the ways they're commonly used.

User Interviews

User interviews are structured conversations with current or potential users of your site. These can be conducted over the phone, via video webconferencing tools (such as GoToMeeting or Skype), in person in a neutral location (such as a conference room), or, ideally, in the environment in which the user is likely to use the site. (This last situation is also great for conducting a contextual inquiry, covered later in this chapter.)

Interviews help you understand participant preferences and attitudes, but they should not be used to make formal statements about actual performance. If you're looking for specific information on how people interact with a site, it's better to observe them using it (for example, in a contextual inquiry) or ask them to perform tasks on the site (during usability testing). Site analytics can also give you some insights into some performance information that can be particularly strong when paired with interviews or inquiries that provide context for the data.

The Basic Process

For user interviews, the UX designer creates a list of questions aimed at eliciting information such as the following:

▶ Relevant experience with the site or with the subject matter

▶ The company's brand, as experienced by the participant

▶ Attitudes, for example, toward the subject categories covered (for a content source), the process being designed (for a task-based application), or methods of marketing (for a marketing campaign)

▶ Common goals or needs that drive users to your site or that of a competitor

▶ Common next steps users take after visiting the company's site

▶ Other people who are involved in the experience. For example, does a user tend to collaborate with someone else as part of the larger goal they're trying to achieve? Are they likely to share information or ask opinions of others along the way?

▶ Any other information that will help you validate the assumptions you've made about user groups up to this point—for example, whether the variables you discussed when creating a provisional user model really seem to influence the way users are experiencing your site

If more than one person is conducting interviews, it's a good idea to have a set list of questions and a scripted introduction that can be used to maintain consistency across interviews.

Choose ahead of time how structured you want the interviews to be. If you're going for a formal report, you'll probably want a high degree of structure, where question order doesn't vary much and every question is asked, with few additions. If richness of data is more important than consistency, you may decide to opt for semistructured interviews, where you start with a list of questions but allow the conversation to follow a natural path, with the interviewer asking questions to further explore interesting comments (called *probing*).

The length of your interview can vary; 45 to 60 minutes is often the best range to shoot for. It gives you enough time to build a rapport and cover a wide range of questions without fatiguing your participant.

User interviews provide a rich set of data that you can use to write personas, which are covered in Chapter 7.

Interviewing Tips

The quality of the information you get out of an interview has a lot to do with the quality of the questions you ask.

Focus on participants' personal experiences. Don't ask them to speculate on what they may do in the future or on what others may do. This kind of information rarely predicts what they actually will do.

Don't ask *leading questions*—questions that imply a specific answer is the correct response or that influence participants to answer in a certain way. Ideally, questions are simple, neutral, and open ended. Some examples of leading questions are:

▶ What do you like about PseudoCorporation.com?

   This assumes the user likes using the site. Use this question only if you also ask what they dislike about it.

▶ Does PseudoCorporation.com meet your expectations?

   This can be answered with a simple yes or no, which doesn't give you much detail to help with your design efforts.

▶ Would you rather use PseudoCorporation.com or CompetitorVille.com and, if the latter, why do you think they are better than Pseudo?

   This has a couple of problems: It's asking two questions in one statement, and it forces an implied opinion on the participant.

Better questions to ask are these:

▶ Tell me about your last visit to PseudoCorporation.com. Why did you go there?

▶ What do you remember about your visit?

If you're doing a large-scale, more formal set of interviews, you may want to include some multiple-choice questions. For the most part though, these don't give you very rich information. They can be hard for participants to follow when asked verbally, and they don't allow users to elaborate. In general, save that type of question for screeners or for surveys.

Perform a test run with someone, perhaps someone within the organization who isn't a member of the core team. This will help you discover questions that may not be clear and will also help you refine the timing and flow.

If it's possible, and the participant consents to it, record the interview so that others can benefit from hearing answers straight from the participant's mouth.

Contextual Inquiry

Contextual inquiry combines user observation with interviewing techniques. The UX designer goes to participants, ideally to the environments in which they're likely to use the site. For example, for an office application contextual inquiry would involve sitting at the participant's desk.

This method gives you rich information about the context a participant works within, including these:

▶ The real-life problems users are facing

▶ The kind of equipment they're working with

▶ The space they're working within—in particular, the amount of space they have, how much (or little) privacy, how often they are interrupted, and how they use the phone and paper (pay special attention to printouts they've posted or notes they keep handy).

▶ Their preference in using a mouse versus keyboard. This can greatly affect your design choices, especially if you're designing a tool that requires a lot of data entry.

▶ How they're working with others, in terms of both collaboration and sharing resources. If more than one person is using the same computer, for example, it will affect how you design login and security features.

▶ Other tools they're using, both online and off. How people use paper is especially interesting—for some tasks, it can be hard to design an online solution that competes with paper!

Inquiries combine observation time and interviewing time. They can last anywhere from a few hours to several days.

If participants can't dedicate at least 2 hours, you should consider just performing an interview. During an observation, it takes some time for the participant to adjust to your presence and act somewhat naturally, and this doesn't happen after just 15 minutes.

The Basic Process

Prepare a 10- to 15-minute introduction you can use with each participant. It should include the purpose of the inquiry, a high-level description of what you'll be doing together (the observation and interview), and how the information will be used. This is also a good time to get signatures on consent forms and to assure participants that what they share will be kept confidential.

Begin with some high-level questions about the participant's typical processes, especially ones that are relevant to the design of the site.

Let the participant know when you're ready to stop talking and start observing. Observation can range from active to passive. With *active observation*, a common approach is to have the participant take the role of the master while you take on the role of the apprentice. The master explains what he is doing as if teaching you his process. Active observing often gives you more background on the reasons for the participant's behavior, but it may affect how the participant works.

In *passive observation*, you encourage the participant to act as if you're not even there. Your goal is to observe behavior that is as natural as possible. For example, if a participant is talking to you, she may be less likely to take a call or go ask someone a question on a problem she's trying to solve, but if you're observing passively, you're more likely to see this happen. You can then follow up during the interview portion to ask about the reasons behind some of the behaviors you observed.

Either approach can work well. Generally, if you don't have a lot of time with participants (let's say, only 2 to 4 hours each) you may decide to use active observation to ensure you get the depth of information you need. If you have a full day or more, passive observation offers a good balance of natural behavior and discussion.

Once you have information from your inquiries, you'll have a lot of rich data to sort through! So how do you identify patterns or trends in your results?

One way that's helpful is a technique called *affinity diagramming*. There are many great resources available on this topic, but here's a short description.

A Quick Guide to Affinity Diagramming

Affinity diagramming is the technique of taking a number of distinct and separate items (like statements made by users or observations made by a researcher) and grouping them together to form patterns and trends. Here are the steps involved in a simple affinity diagramming session:

1. Gather the team that performed the inquiries, with their notes

2. Give each person a pack of sticky notes and ask them to write a statement on each one, along with a short code that will allow you to track that statement back to a participant, such as their initials. Focus on statements that seem to have relevance to the site design, either specifically (a feature statement) or in a more general way (a statement that represents a participant's attitude to the company or subject matter).

3. Have everyone put their sticky notes up on the wall. You'll need a big blank wall if you're working on a large study; try to get one that you'll have access to for at least a few days.

4. Once all the notes are up, start grouping similar statements next to each other. This portion of the exercise can include the larger team. It's a great way to start sharing results.

5. Once groups start to form naturally, start labeling the groups to provide further structure. If some sticky notes belong to more than one group, you can write duplicates and place them in each appropriate group.

Note *This method works well for contextual inquiry but can be applied to many other situations. For example, it's a great way to collaboratively create categories for unsorted topics, so it can help you move card-sorting results into additional levels of structure.*

Patterns can emerge in many ways, so it's best to let them form on their own. However, here are examples of the kinds of categories that you might see, including the kind of statement you'd find in them:

▶ Goals: "I try to clear off all the open items here before I leave for the day."

▶ Mental models (includes statements that demonstrate how users are mapping external experiences to internal thinking): "I use this online tool as my briefcase, for things I reference a lot but don't want to carry around with me."

▶ Ideas and feature requests: "I wish this would allow me to undo. I keep moving the whole folder accidentally and it takes me forever to cancel out of it."

▶ Frustrations: "I'd ask the help desk about this, but half the time they don't know what the problem is either."

▶ Workarounds: "This takes so long to do here that I just end up printing out the list and working with it throughout the day. Then at the end of the day I enter in the results."

▶ Value statements: "This tool here saves me a lot of time, so if you're making changes don't take it away!"

 Deep Diving

The quintessential resource on contextual inquiry is *Contextual Design*, by Hugh Beyer and Karen Holtzblatt (Morgan Kaufmann, 1997). The book also includes detailed information on interpreting results through techniques such as affinity diagramming.

For more information on mental models and how to understand them, take a look at *Mental Models: Aligning Design Strategy with Human Behavior*, by Indi Young (Rosenfeld Media, 2008). This is especially helpful when you're working on the information architecture for a content source.

Surveys

Surveys involve a set collection of well-defined questions distributed to a large audience. They most often consist of closed-ended questions (such as multiple choice questions) that can be easily collected with a tool that can display patterns among responses.

Surveys are good tools when you want to be able to state results in more quantitative ways (for example, "Of those surveyed, 82 percent of those who work from home state they have some form of high-speed Internet connection") than you would get with the kinds of open-ended questions that are used in interviews. However, you can gather qualitative information from them as well, about user perceptions and attitudes.

In the user experience field, surveys are often used to measure user satisfaction (with existing sites or applications) or to build or validate user models like segmentations or personas.

The Basic Process

As with user interviews, you don't want to ask questions that require users to speculate. Don't ask "If you got Feature X, would you use it?"

Unlike with interviews, in surveys multiple choice or Yes/No, True/False questions are best and easiest to analyze afterwards. They're also quicker for participants to answer.

Use surveys when you have questions that are factual requests for demographic data, such as these:

> Of the devices listed below, which do you personally own? Choose all that apply.
>
> _____ Computer
>
> _____ Mobile phone
>
> _____ Game system, such as Xbox, Playstation, or Wii

Or use surveys when you need to ask questions that are attitudinal with a set range of distinct choices. For example:

Read the following statements and select the degree to which you agree or disagree with each of them.

The Customer Service at Pseudo Corporation is responsive to my needs.

_____ Strongly Agree

_____ Agree

_____ Neither Agree nor Disagree

_____ Disagree

_____ Strongly Disagree

In particular, questions like the one shown in the second example are often used to supplement usability testing tasks. You can use this type as a follow-up question to find out if participants were frustrated when completing a task. Participants don't always like to state a negative opinion out loud, but they are often willing to express one when faced with a ranking system.

This brings out another point: Surveys are an excellent supplement to other forms of research you may be doing. For example, you can gain quantitative data from surveys to supplement qualitative data gained from user interviews or contextual inquiry (see Chapter 14 for more on quantitative and qualitative data). Combining two research methods provides a richer picture of the user than one method can provide on its own.

Surfing

If you want a high degree of confidence in your results and have the budget for it, there are formal tools available for measuring user satisfaction with regard to ease of use. These tools include questions that have been tested to ensure they are not leading or confusing to a broad audience. Some of the most commonly used are

ACSI (American Customer Satisfaction Index): www.theacsi.org/

WAMMI (Website Analysis and MeasureMent Inventory): www.wammi.com

SUMI (Software Usability Measurement Inventory): http://sumi.ucc.ie

When planning a survey, consider the following:

▶ Who are you targeting?

Use your provisional model to determine this. It'll make a difference in how you answer the rest of the questions here.

▶ What method for distributing the survey will give you the best results?

If your primary user groups tend to congregate in a particular location, you may get more results if you go there and set up a table for people to fill out the survey on paper. If your user groups are active Internet users, having an online survey could be the best choice for a large number of participants. Or you may decide your user group will be best found with phone surveys using a list of current customers.

▶ How much time will participants probably be willing to spend filling out the survey?

If you're providing some kind of compensation or they get some other benefit from filling it out, you can usually create a longer questionnaire—one that takes maybe a half-hour to complete. If not, you'll need to keep it short to help ensure people complete it—think 5 to 10 minutes. Either way, make sure participants are given an estimate of how long it will take and update them on their progress as they go through it (use page numbers like "2 of 4," for example, or show the percentage completed).

▶ How will you know when to start analyzing the data?

You may choose to run the survey until you reach a certain number of participants or until you hit a certain deadline, whichever takes priority.

▶ What tool will you use to collect and analyze the data?

If you're running the survey online, the tool you use to collect the data may have options for viewing and analyzing the results. If not, you'll need a method to enter the data into your tool of choice. For paper-based surveys this means a lot of data entry, so be sure you're planning for that time.

Focus Groups

Focus groups involve bringing together a variety of people within a target audience and facilitating a discussion with them. Common goals are to elicit opinions on topics relevant to the organization or its brand, such as past experiences, related needs, feelings, attitudes, and ideas for improvement.

A focus group is a good technique for several purposes:

▶ **Hearing a variety of user stories.** Open discussion is a great way to bring out the storyteller in all of us. When a focus group is going well, individuals build off each other's stories and ideas and remember situations they might not in a more structured one-on-one interview. The group format and energy can give people the time they need to recall these stories and share them.

▶ **Understanding relevant differences in experiences.** Most people are natural information sharers and want to compare favorite tools with others in their interest group. Often you can learn of competitive sites or services, or you'll hear tips for workarounds, resources, and support.

▶ **Generating ideas.** Although you don't want to make the group itself the designer, you often get some excellent ideas for new features or designs either directly from the group or from hearing about their work processes or frustrations. As with stakeholder ideas, be sure to trace these back to the core need (see Chapter 4) so you can be sure it's being addressed.

▶ **Understanding multiple points of a collaborative process.** If you're designing a process that involves multiple related roles and collaboration, groups can be a great way for you to fill in the gaps in your understanding of how people are interacting. For example, if you're working with a content source like an intranet, it can be helpful to gather a mix of those generating the content, editing the content, and consuming the content to identify the points where the process could be improved.

There's a lot of debate about the use of focus groups in UX research. It's not a good technique for testing usability (since users most often work individually, rather than in groups), and sometimes the group setting can unduly influence participants' statements. If planned and facilitated well, however, focus groups can bring out many insights that will be valuable to you as you're designing. Chapter 14 discusses this further in the context of concept testing.

The Basic Process

When writing questions for focus groups, consider the same tips you would use for writing user interview questions (covered previously in this chapter).

Begin with some of the easier questions, such as "Tell me about your last visit to PseudoCorporation.com. Why did you go there?" Save any questions focused on idea generation to the middle part of the group, when participants are feeling comfortable with you, each other, and the topic.

Assign time blocks to each topic and keep to them; it's easy for discussions to really get going and for time to slip by! If you're worried about time, put your most important questions in the middle of the topics list, after people have warmed to the activity but before any potential time crunch that could occur near the end.

Many of the logistics for focus groups will be the same as those for usability testing. (Chapter 14 offers suggestions on screening, recruiting, and scheduling.) The primary difference with focus groups is that you'll need a larger room with a table allowing participants to interact with each other easily. Shoot for six to eight people per 1- to 2-hour group session.

Give each person a nametag or a place card at their seat, so everyone can address each other by name.

The format of the discussion itself should include an introduction, which often hits these key points:

▶ Your role as moderator, and what you're expecting to get out of the discussion (for example, some of the points above)

▶ Why attendees were chosen to participate (for example, "You are all current users of the Pseudo Corporation site, and we've brought you together to find out about your experiences")

▶ How this information will be used—both in the design and from the standpoint of confidentiality

▶ That as the moderator, you're there to hear about their opinions and experiences. You want them to feel they can share honestly, so ask individuals to be straightforward but also respectful of others in the group.

▶ That there are many topics to cover, so at some point you will end a discussion on one topic to be sure you can cover all of them

This can then go into a round of introductions for group members, often including some kind of icebreaker question.

Your goal is to get everyone to talk on the first question, even if they just tell a short story. You can either start with one person and work around the table or let people answer naturally and then call on the people who haven't answered yet by name. Often you'll end up going around the table for the first few questions and then, when you feel the group is ready, with body language you can open up the questions to everyone.

Snorkeling: Body Language

A good understanding of body language can be an amazing tool when moderating focus groups or any user research conducted in person. It can help you understand when someone is feeling frustrated, excited, angry, or threatened, so you can identify when you should try to make someone more comfortable or probe on a particular comment.

The following book on the subject may take more than a weekend to read completely, but it's designed to be easy to flip through: *The Definitive Book of Body Language*, by Allan Pease and Barbara Pease (Bantam, 2006).

When you call on someone who hasn't answered yet, be sure to repeat the question in case they didn't understand it or weren't listening to the last few statements in the discussion. Also, avoid making a difference in opinion seem like a disagreement between two individuals.

Don't say, "Bob, we haven't heard from you yet. What do you think about what Chris just said?" but rather (looking at Bob), "How about you, Bob? What kinds of experiences have you had with Pseudo Corporation's customer service?"

As moderator, you control the flow of the discussion and you pass the virtual microphone around. You keep control using eye contact, volume of speech, arm movements, and orientation of your body. Most people will be very aware of your body language, and these cues can be useful signals if someone is dominating the conversation. If an overly vocal participant doesn't get those hints, use a gentle but firm statement such as "OK, great, I'd like to open that thought up to others. Has anyone else encountered some of the same issues that Theresa has?"

When moving on to a new larger topic, give verbal notice that the previous discussion has finished and that a new one is beginning, so that people can clear their minds for the next topic.

Finally, when the activity is nearing its end, a simple look at your watch and shift in your body orientation can signal that the conversation should be wrapped up. As with any other activity, be sure to thank the group for their time.

Sharing results with your team typically takes one of two forms: findings are either shared according to the main topics being covered or are grouped into relevant categories much as they are for contextual inquiry. Affinity diagramming can be another effective way to bring together various trends and attitudes for illustration to the project team.

Card Sorting

In a *card sorting* activity, participants (working either individually or in small groups) are given items printed on cards and are asked to put them into groups that make sense to them. Either they group them into categories that are provided beforehand (called a *closed sort*) or they make their own groups and title each group themselves (called an *open sort*). At the end of the round of card sorting you should begin to see common patterns emerge in how people are sorting the items, as well as common areas of confusion or disagreement.

A common reason for doing this is to create a site map for a website or to create a hierarchy of content, categories, and subcategories containing items such as articles, documents, videos, or photos. This makes card sorting an excellent technique if you're working on a content source.

Note *See Chapter 2 for more on content sources.*

Say you're working on a common type of content source: the company intranet. Many intranets tend to categorize their information by the department that owns it, with navigation to human resources, operations, legal, marketing, and so on. For longtime employees this may not present an obvious problem, because they have probably learned the lines of responsibility of each department and built an understanding of where to find information.

But for new employees, or for those who need information that they don't usually reference, it can be difficult to locate information that could fall within more than one department (or doesn't seem to fall into any). For example, where would you go to find a policy on signing of contracts with newly hired employees? It could fall under legal, or it could fall under human resources.

With card sorting, you can find common patterns in how potential users would categorize information, regardless of departmental lines.

The Basic Process

Collect the items you'd like to include in the card sort; 40 to 60 is usually a good range. You need enough to allow for a potentially large number of card groups to be created, but not so many as to overwhelm the participants with options (or to overwhelm *you* when you need to analyze the results).

Choose items that you think will be easy to understand and free from unnecessary jargon. You can include some subject-matter terms that you believe your user groups are likely to know, but avoid including too many "insider" terms. If you include too many company-specific terms or acronyms (such as "the SUCCEED campaign" for growing sales), you'll be testing the effectiveness of the company's marketing and communications, rather than building a common information hierarchy.

For the intranet example, you might include the vacation policy, 401(k) plan information, new-hire contract, vendor contract, nondisclosure agreement, new-employee orientation, health insurance information, and computer security policy.

This list represents a mix of clearly worded items that could be categorized in multiple ways. You could have one participant who groups new employee orientation and vacation policy together under human resources, and you could have another who groups new employee orientation and new hire contract together and names it "employee onboarding."

Once you have your list of items, put them onto cards that can be easily grouped and ungrouped. You can print labels and stick them onto index cards or print directly onto sheets of card stock that are perforated to separate into individual cards.

Perform a test run by asking someone to sort the cards into groups and give the groups names—for example, by putting a sticky note on the stack and writing the name on it with a pen. Ideally, your test participant is someone unfamiliar with the items and the activity. This will help you get a rough idea of how long the activity might take. If the test run takes over an hour, you may need to cut out some cards!

Once you have a finalized deck, you can bring in a real participant and give these basic instructions:

1. Arrange these cards in whatever groups make sense to you

2. Try to have at least two cards in a group. If a card seems to belong to no group, you can place it to the side

3. At any time as you're sorting, you can name a group. By the end of the activity, please name as many groups as you can.

Some trends will become obvious simply by observing the sessions. Others may take a little more analysis to bring out. There are several tools for entering and analyzing the results of card sorts; many of them come with tools that allow you to run card sorts remotely (see the following "Variations on the Card Sort" section for more on this).

In particular, OptimalSort (www.optimalsort.com/pages/default.html) and WebSort (http://websort.net) provide both remote sorting capabilities and helpful analysis tools. Or, if you want to do your own sorting in a more manual fashion, take a look at Donna Spencer's excellent spreadsheet, complete with instructions, available at www.rosenfeldmedia.com/books/cardsorting/blog/card_sort_analysis_spreadsheet.

Variations on the Card Sort

The discussion so far has focused on a card sort carried out with an individual, in person, where the participant is asked to name the categories he created. This is an open sort, meaning that the main categories have not been given to the participant—instead they are *open* to being named. This is a good approach when you're determining a new navigational structure or making significant changes to an existing one. For other situations, you might consider these common card sorting variations:

- ▶ **Closed sorts.** In a closed sort, you provide the high-level categories and participants add to them. The results are relatively easy to analyze, because you have a small set of possible categories and can focus on understanding which items fell most often into which categories. If you're adding large amounts of content to an existing information architecture or you're validating an existing site map, a closed sort can provide quick and actionable information to help with your categorization decisions.

- ▶ **Group sorts.** Rather than having an individual sort items into groups, you can have card sorting be a part of a focus group activity, where participants work together to sort items. Although the results don't necessarily reflect how any one individual would group the items, you can get a lot of insight into how people think about the items and their organization by hearing them work through the activity together, debating the rationale for each placement.

- ▶ **Remote sorts.** Sorting with physical cards can be a fun activity, especially for group sorts. But there are many great tools for performing sorts online with individuals. This also allows you to reach a greater number of participants or particular participants that may be difficult to meet with physically. OptimalSort and WebSort, previously mentioned, are two of the tools that make this type of online sorting easy.

Usability Testing

Usability testing involves asking participants to perform specific tests on a site or application (or a prototype of it) to uncover potential usability issues and gather ideas to address them.

You can perform usability testing during the Define phase if you want to gather information on how the current site can be improved. Or you can perform it on similar sites (such as competitive sites) to understand some of the potential opportunities for a more user-friendly solution.

Most often, usability testing is conducted as part of the Design phase, ideally in iterative rounds (where a design is created, tested, refined, and tested again). We'll discuss usability testing again in full detail in Chapter 14, "Design Testing with Users." That chapter includes tips for recruiting and planning that can help you conduct the activities discussed earlier in this chapter as well.

After the Research

Once you've completed one or more of these user research activities, it's time to revisit the assumptions you originally made about your user groups. Put those assumptions away for a moment, and ask yourself what user groups you would create now that you have more information. If some of your earlier assumptions weren't valid, consider any gaps you may have in your user research because a key group wasn't included. If this gap is identified early enough in your research activity, you may have time to adjust and add another set of participants to research in progress, to ensure you're getting a full picture.

With your new knowledge, you can revise your user definitions to more accurately reflect the groups that should be the focus. This will help you create more detailed tools like personas (discussed in Chapter 7) and will help you create user requirements for the list we began in Chapter 5.

In that chapter, we discussed the process of taking statements from business stakeholders and refining them into requirements. You'll follow a similar process with users—your work doesn't stop when you capture the idea or request. Dig down to the roots of needs and goals to make sure you understand them. This will ultimately help you design a solution that best meets those needs for all relevant user groups.

In the next chapter, you'll learn how to use the insight you gain in conducting user research to create tools that can bring focus to your user groups throughout design and development: personas.

7 Personas

Find the Best Way to Put Your Team— or Your Client—in Your Users' Shoes

Personas are often a topic of debate among user experience practitioners. Opinions range from how much content is needed to how much research is needed to whether they provide any value to projects. Some people question whether or not they belong in the process at all. Regardless of where you position yourself, personas may be used to help your project team and your client empathize with their users. Personas can deliver a gut check to many parts of your project—business requirements, visual design, or quality assurance—by providing insight into who your audience is and what their expectations and behaviors are.

Russ Unger

What Are Personas?

Personas are documents that describe typical target users. They can be useful to your project team, stakeholders, and clients. With appropriate research and descriptions, personas can paint a very clear picture of who is using the site or application, and potentially even how they are using it.

User experience designers often see creating personas as a great exercise in empathy. Well-crafted personas are often used as a touch point whenever a question or concern arises about how aspects of the project should be designed. You can take out your personas and ask, How would *<this user>* perform *<this task>*? or What is *<this user>* going to look for in *<this situation>*? Although this process may not be as accurate as testing functionality and design with actual users, it can help move your project along until you are able perform more extensive tests.

Josh Seiden (www.joshuaseiden.com) points out that there are two distinct types of personas:

▶ Marketing-targeted personas that model purchase motivations

▶ Interactive personas that are modeled toward usage behaviors

This chapter focuses on interactive personas.

Why Create Personas?

In the user experience design process, personas help you focus on representative users. By providing insights into "real" behaviors of "real" users, personas can help resolve conflicts that arise when making design and development decisions, so you and your team can continue to make progress.

How real do personas need to be? The answer varies widely. A single persona document may be enough for one team, while another may create full "living spaces" for the user personas to deeply understand how they "live." You could even go to the extreme of creating individual online presences that can be interacted with to provide insights into online behaviors. However you choose to extend your personas is up to you.

Personas can be constant reminders of your users. A useful technique is for your team members to keep personas in their workspaces; this way they are continually reminded of who their users are. When you share a cube with "Nicolle," the 34-year-old certified hand therapist from West Chicago, Illinois, for a while, you begin to find yourself compelled to provide an experience that works well for her.

If it helps you, feel free to keep printed copies with you while you sleep and let the osmosis fairy impart empathy from the pages through the pillow and into your slumbering subconscious. The purpose of personas is to help you, your team, and/or your clients remove some of the confusion that can crop up when you reach a decision-making crossroads.

Finding Information for Personas

Effective personas must accurately depict a number of specific users of your product or website. To achieve that goal, personas must be supported by research. Chapter 6 presents techniques for researching and modeling your potential users to provide a firm foundation for your personas. Don't look for one method to be the answer, however; it's best to find as much data as you can *and* mix it with a blend of observational and interview data—this can also include utilizing online surveys and analyzing behaviors in social networks.

It's a common theme to creating personas: Get real data, but make the personas into real people on the pages. To learn how one company accomplishes this, see the sidebar "Case Study: Messagefirst Personas."

Creating Personas

Once you identify your audience and accumulate data to support your personas, your next step is to put pencil to paper and start to bring them to life. How many personas you need to create varies. In general, the minimum is three, but upwards of seven is not uncommon. Rather than aim for a specific count, consider the number of target segments you have and what you feel is the best way to get a fair representation of them.

This chapter's example persona is Nicolle, a 34-year-old Certified Hand Therapist from West Chicago, Illinois. She happens to be a nondriving commuter who spends 2 to 3 hours per day traveling to and from her job. The fictional client is a company called ACMEblue, a manufacturer of Bluetooth headsets for Apple's not-so-fictional iPhone.

Case Study: Messagefirst Personas

To create effective, data-driven personas, Messagefirst (www.messagefirst.com) uses no less than three different data input sources, drawing from the following:

▶ **Stakeholders.** We interview them to find out who they think the personas are and what they think their behaviors are. This is *always* included.

▶ **Customer advocate.** We interview people in the company who speak directly with customers, which typically means Sales/Marketing and Customer Service. Each of these has their bias, which we make sure we keep in mind as we document our findings. For example, the people who most commonly contact Customer Service are those with too much time on their hands (often retired or unemployed), or someone who's so upset about a product or service that they'll actually take time to contact you.

▶ **Customers.** We talk directly to the actual people who are going to use or currently use the product or service. This is included whenever possible.

▶ **Customer data sources.** We review any available blog traffic, surveys, and e-mails that are available to us.

▶ **Someone we know.** We pick someone we know who fits the initial profile of the persona. This helps keep us grounded, ensuring the persona is believable and realistic, and provides a real person to contact should we have additional questions. This is very important for validation, and *always* included.

Because each data input source we use has a particular bias, we use multiple sources to normalize the data. What's important for data-driven personas is not to go in with an expectation of how many personas you will have, but to let the data reveal how many personas there should be. When analyzing the data, I look for gaps in the behaviors and activities. These gaps reveal the individual personas.

—*Todd Zaki Warfel, President, Messagefirst*

That brief paragraph tells you a lot about Nicolle, but as you can see in **Figure 7.1**, the actual persona contains a much more thorough story about Nicolle. Note that the content is written *about* Nicolle, not "by" Nicolle. It's best to write your personas from the third-party perspective and not contend with writing in their distinct voices, especially when you're just getting started. As you expand your experience, you should naturally explore and find the style that fits you best and provides the most value.

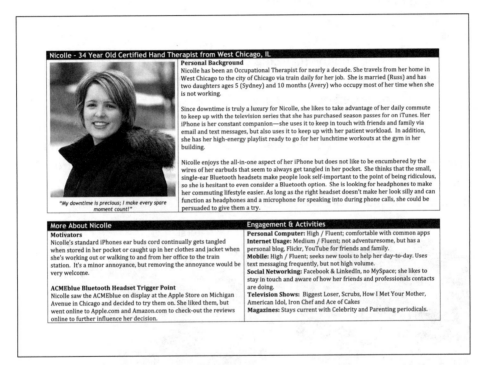

Figure 7.1 *Persona for a fictional client of ACMEblue*

What kind of information goes into personas? The kind of information that your audience will find relevant and believable, that's what kind.

Based on the research data you've gathered, you should be able to ascertain what is important to the client, brand, and project.

The majority of the personas you create will share a common set of required content mixed with any amount of data, statistics, and other relevant information that can be considered optional, because it will vary from client to client, if not project to project.

Minimum Content Requirements

When creating personas, you need to provide enough information to draw people in and make them relate to the person they are reading about on the page. To help your audience understand how your persona behaves and thinks, be sure to include six key pieces of information: photo, name, age, location, occupation, and biography. The next sections take a closer look at filling in the details for each item.

Photo

A photo is the first (and the real) step to putting a face to your persona. When choosing a photo for your persona, try to make sure that the picture doesn't look too posed or polished.

Photos that appear to be posed do not have the same effect as those that are in more natural settings. Personas seem to be more effective with photos taken in more natural settings, such as the photo on the right in **Figure 7.2**, where the subject is standing outside in her winter coat, conceivably during her commute. Make sure the photo fits the lifestyle of the persona!

Posed   **Natural**

Figure 7.2
Natural-looking photos are more effective

There are a variety of online photo resources. Some of the better options are iStockphoto (www.istockphoto.com), Getty Images (www.gettyimages.com), and Stock.XCHNG (www.sxc.hu).

Finding the right photo can be a complete time suck if you're not careful. If all else fails (or you have the time and budget), take your own!

Name

Simply put, you've got to put a name to the face. The photo you use will humanize the mix of research data and personality traits, and the name will be how everyone refers to your persona during discussions. Not only does Nicolle sound better than "Mid-30s Blonde Professional Mom," but it's a lot easier to remember and associate with a specific persona.

Try to keep the names you use for different personas on a project from sounding too similar. Nicolle and Noelle could be easily confused, for example, so look for distinct names. And, although it may be tempting to use the names of coworkers or clients, don't. When you use names that are like or the same as those of people involved in the project, it is easy for them to try to identify themselves in your personas. Choosing different names avoids any uncomfortable situations or hurt feelings. If you find yourself having difficulty choosing names, some online resources can help you with this: baby-naming websites!

- ▶ BabyNames.com: www.babynames.com

- ▶ Babyhold: www.babyhold.com

- ▶ Social Security Administration's Popular Baby Names: www.ssa.gov/OACT/babynames

- ▶ Random Name Generator: www.kleimo.com/random/name.cfm

One last thing about names: Make sure your name is believable for the persona. Nicolle works just fine for a Midwestern mother, but Nicoletta or Natalia may be a much better name for an Italian mother. Also, names that appear to be a little more fun or lively, such as Bob the Builder, aren't. They tend to make your personas look silly and can detract from their value.

Age

Although your research should identify the age range of your consumers, providing a specific age for your persona helps to add authenticity to the biography that you write. Behaviors of a 21-year-old college student and a 34-year-old professional mother are significantly different!

Location

At first, location may not appear to be vital information; however, it is important to remember that cultural and behavioral shifts can occur from location to location. In Italy, for example, different dialects are spoken in different regions of the country. In the United States, a person who lives in Chicago would most likely have a different cost of living than a person in Savannah, Georgia.

Occupation

Knowing what your persona does for a living helps you to identify with them by relating to the patterns of their day-to-day lives. A persona who works in therapy meets with many people on a daily basis, whereas a drawbridge operator may not interact much with others.

Biography

The biography is the compelling story that makes the persona real. This is where you provide details that you derive from your research data and infuse them with a bit of "real people." That is, the data is *very* important to the persona, but you do not want to simply quote that information in choppy sentences. Instead, you want to weave data, anecdote, and observation into a story that your audience can relate to.

It may seem a bit strange, but the biography needs to be believable, and it's certainly not cheating to bring aspects of a real person into your persona. Nicolle, for example, is based upon both statistical data and the very real behaviors of a person who shares similar activities, beliefs, and desires.

Depending upon your project, you may need to delve fairly deeply into the biography—sometimes the more details you have, the better. Don't feel as if you have to squeeze your persona onto a single sheet of paper. Go with what works best to make your persona true to life and as meaningful as possible to the project you are working on.

Optional Content

As you work with personas, you will find that different projects will require different sets of information to make the personas more applicable. The minimum content requirements might also be considered the least common denominators from most of the personas you will create. In most cases, you will blend some of these optional content elements with the core of your personas.

Optional content that may add value to your personas includes:

▶ **Education level.** Knowing how educated a person is can provide a bit more insight into some of their habits. A person with a high school diploma *may* have substantially different purchasing habits and brand perceptions than a person with a master's degree, and this information can influence how your persona is perceived.

▶ **Salary or salary range.** Money talks, and in many cases, the amount of income a person has substantially affects their standard of living and their disposable income. This information can provide significant insight when you are targeting certain levels of affluence.

▶ **Personal quote.** What would be the motto that your persona would claim as their own? Sometimes this can give a quick overview into the core of your persona's way of thinking.

what are your personal quotes?

▶ **Online activities.** This can get tricky; there are a lot of ways people spend their time online. Some people pay their bills, some people are heavily into blogging and social networking activities, and some people simply use their computer as an appliance that gets turned on when they need to perform a task. Given that so many projects have some online component, this element is a bit of a judgment call. You'll need to lean on your research to help paint the picture.

▶ **Offline activities.** Does your persona have a hobby? Is there additional information about what the life of your persona is like when they're not online? This element can be every bit as tricky as online activities, and can be every bit as important in influencing your persona.

▶ **Key entry or trigger point to client, brand, or project.** Often it is important to understand how a persona interacts with the client, brand, or project. Does the persona hear about it via word of mouth, online reviews, a billboard, television or radio, or from an online pop-up ad? Is your persona looking to solve a problem that can be addressed through the client, brand, or project? Using your statistical data to understand this point, and writing it into your persona, can help ground your approach to engaging users.

▶ **Technical comfort level.** Does your persona use a PC or a Mac? Does she own a computer at all? Does she use instant messaging, Flickr, or write a blog? Is she very comfortable with that activity, or is she confused by it? Would she be helped by a very simple solution directed toward a novice? Does she have an MP3 player or other portable device? Does she use a DVR or AppleTV or on-demand programming to watch television? The list can go on and on. And on. Depending upon your client, brand, or project, these notions—and a variety of others—may be important to identify.

▶ **Social comfort level.** Given the growth of social media and social networking, it may be important to identify very specifically how your persona engages in that particular space. Does she have a Twitter account? If so, how many followers does she have? How active is she? Is she a leader? Does she use Facebook, LinkedIn, or other aggregators or online communities?

▶ **Mobile comfort level.** As the usage of mobile devices becomes more prevalent, it is important to consider including how your personas find themselves in the mobile space—if at all.

▶ **Motivations to use client, brand, or project.** In some cases you may want to include the reasons the persona would want to use the client, brand, or project. If she is continually getting the wire for her headphones tangled in her coat and yanking them off her head, that may be a good reason for her to consider new headphones. Real scenarios based upon research data can help uncover key motivators to include in your personas.

▶ **User goals.** You may also want to identify what the persona is hoping to accomplish by using the client, brand, or project. This can help provide insights into the persona's drivers for using it.

These are just data points to get you started. You can structure your personas and present them in an infinite variety of ways. If you are interested in taking a deep dive into the world of personas, a great place to start is *The User Is Always Right: A Practical Guide to Creating and Using Personas for the Web*, by Steve Mulder with Ziv Yaar (New Riders, 2006).

Advanced Personas

Once you have an understanding of the basics of creating personas, there are infinitely many ways you can extend your documents. A simple persona often can meet most of your needs, especially when your project team is just trying to get an empathetic understanding of your users.

Things tend to get more interesting when you present personas to your clients. In those cases, you'll often find that you need to provide much more than the information that you put together for the basic persona. **Figures 7.3** through **7.6** illustrate some of the ways you can extend personas.

Feel free to borrow from these examples, remix and mash them up to create something even better for your project!

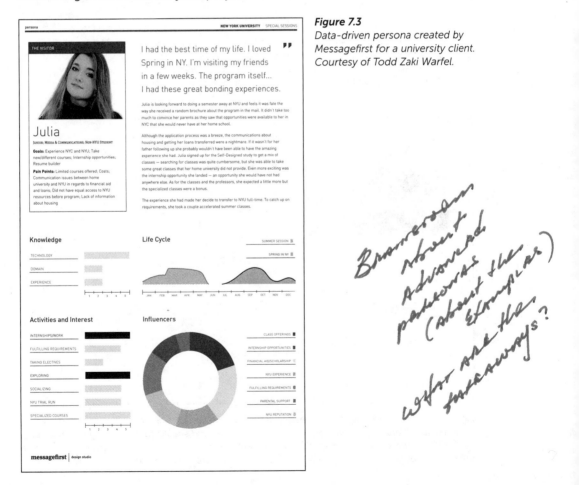

Figure 7.3
Data-driven persona created by Messagefirst for a university client. Courtesy of Todd Zaki Warfel.

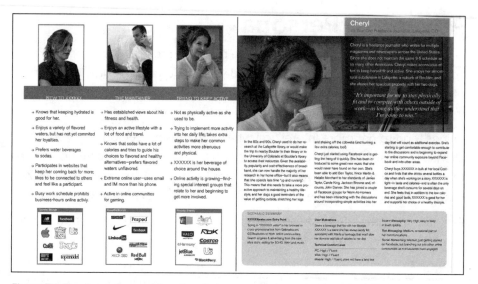

Figure 7.4 *Target overview and target audience persona (portrait orientation). The target overview at left provides high-level summary information and shows the brands the three personas interact with and relate to. The detailed description at right presents an overview and biography of a single persona, along with information about her behaviors and motivations.*

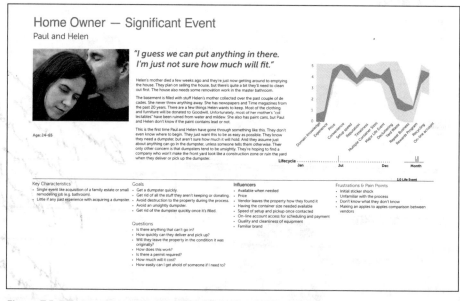

Figure 7.5 *Target audience group persona. This persona presents an age-range target, drawn from research data. The information it contains is broad and speaks to audience grouping, not specific individuals. This approach can be useful when you are making a business pitch or when the client's budget does permit detailed exploration of personas. Courtesy of Todd Zaki Warfel.*

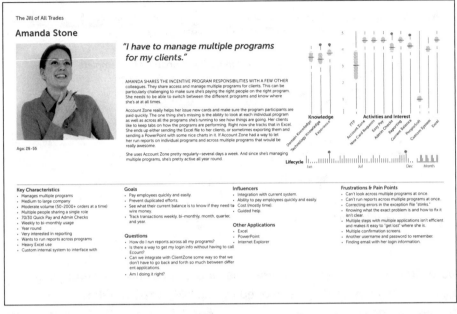

The Jill of All Trades

Amanda Stone

"I have to manage multiple programs for my clients."

AMANDA SHARES THE INCENTIVE PROGRAM RESPONSIBILITIES WITH A FEW OTHER colleagues. They share access and manage multiple programs for clients. This can be particularly challenging to make sure she's paying the right people on the right program. She needs to be able to switch between the different programs and know where she's at at all times.

Account Zone really helps her issue new cards and make sure the program participants are paid quickly. The one thing she's missing is the ability to look at each individual program as well as across all the programs she's running to see how things are going. Her clients like to keep tabs on how the programs are performing. Right now she tracks that in Excel. She ends up either sending the Excel file to her clients, or sometimes exporting them and sending a PowerPoint with some nice charts in it. If Account Zone had a way to let her run reports on individual programs and across multiple programs that would be really awesome.

She uses Account Zone pretty regularly—several days a week. And since she's managing multiple programs, she's pretty active all year round.

Age: 28-55

Key Characteristics
- Manages multiple programs
- Medium to large company
- Moderate volume (50-2000+ orders at a time)
- Multiple people sharing a single role
- 70/30 Quick Pay and Admin Checks
- Weekly to bi-monthly usage
- Year round
- Very interested in reporting
- Wants to run reports across programs
- Heavy Excel use
- Custom internal system to interface with

Goals
- Pay employees quickly and easily.
- Prevent duplicated efforts.
- See what their current balance is to know if they need to wire money.
- Track transactions weekly, bi-monthly, month, quarter, and year.

Questions
- How do I run reports across all my programs?
- Is there a way to get my login info without having to call Ecount?
- Can we integrate with ClientZone some way so that we don't have to go back and forth so much between different applications.
- Am I doing it right?

Influencers
- Integration with current system.
- Ability to pay employees quickly and easily.
- Cost (mostly time).
- Guided help.

Other Applications
- Excel
- PowerPoint
- Internet Explorer

Frustrations & Pain Points
- Can't look across multiple programs at once.
- Can't run reports across multiple programs at once.
- Correcting errors in the exception file "stinks."
- Knowing what the exact problem is and how to fix it isn't clear.
- Multiple steps with multiple applications isn't efficient and makes it easy to "get lost" where she is.
- Multiple confirmation screens.
- Another username and password to remember.
- Finding email with her login information.

Figure 7.6 Target audience individual persona. This persona is a heavily data-driven model. While the day-in-the-life story is a narrative, the rest is given in bullet points to serve as a design checklist. The diagram is used to communicate a significant amount of information in a small space. Courtesy of Todd Zaki Warfel.

As you can see, you can combine data in many different ways to present personas, tailoring them to a variety of situations. Start with the basic persona and expand it to suit your needs.

Guerrilla Personas: The Empathy Map

Every now and then it will be entirely probable that you may have neither the desired nor necessary time nor budget to create a research-driven persona. Yet, you may still feel that getting more detail on your target audience(s) is too important to overlook. This is when an Empathy Map (**Figure 7.7** on the next page) comes in handy. An *Empathy Map* is an activity that is geared toward identifying a specific persona and getting your audience (preferably stakeholders and others with user/consumer knowledge) to articulate what the persona is seeing, saying, doing, hearing, and thinking.

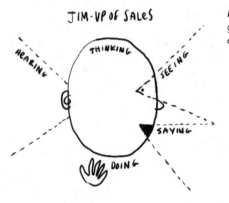

JIM·VP OF SALES

Figure 7.7 *Empathy Map template. Helps guide you in facilitating an Empathy Map exercise. Courtesy of Dave Gray.*

Dave Gray, Sunni Brown, and James Macanufo have pulled together a helpful "Empathy Map" activity, developed by Scott Matthews, in their book, *Gamestorming—A Playbook for Innovators, Rulebreakers, and Changemakers* (O'Reilly Media, 2010).

An Empathy Map activity (**Figure 7.8**) should take only about 15–20 minutes, and while it will not offer the same defensible data and rigor as more traditional personas, it may be an alternative when time and resources are not optimal and you need to provide your team with a focal point for design decision-making.

Note *For additional information on Empathy Maps, visit the Gamestorming Blog at http://www.gogamestorm.com/?p=42.*

Figure 7.8 *Empathy Map example. This Empathy Map was created to identify a male user segment for a t-shirt selling website. Courtesy of Brad Nunnally & Kim Nunnally.*

Final Thoughts on Personas

Many practitioners in the user experience design world do not believe that personas do a good job of articulating the needs, goals, and attitudes of users. They believe that personas can hinder creativity, innovation, or good design for any number of reasons. Other practitioners believe that personas meet a specific need that influences the design process in a very positive way—when they are based on solid research data and mixed with a dose of personalized reality. Which side of the coin you land on is entirely up to you.

This chapter is not meant to influence your decision one way or the other. Plenty of articles on the topic are available online, and plenty of professionals are ready to give you their view. All of these resources can help you figure out how personas will work best for your projects, so seek them out. Jared Spool, CEO and founding principal of User Interface Engineering (www.uie.com), also offers some insight on the topic:

> That value comes when the team visits and observes their target audience, absorbs and discusses their observations, and reduces the chaos into patterns, which then become the personas.
>
> What's in the team's head, as they are designing, is what will make a difference in the final design. The persona descriptions are just there to remind everyone what happened.

Jared's point is simple: By watching your target audience, infusing what you learn with research data, and synthesizing all of this into segments, you should be able to create personas that trigger the kind of empathy that keeps your team on track and building the best possible application, website, or product.

Ultimately, however, your personas are going to be a lot like Santa Claus: They'll only be valuable as long as people believe in them.

8 Content Strategy
More Than Words

Content strategy is your friend. It is one of those friends that you do not always recognize at first, because as a stranger it can be intimidating. There is always a little fear of the unknown and it is daunting when you set off to try something new, but once you start understanding the work that content strategy does and the outputs that come from that work—and how it can help guide you to better UX—it all starts to make sense. You need content strategy, and with a little bit of effort made to get to know it, you can find yourself with a new best friend that only makes you appear smarter to others, tells you that you smell really good, and says your butt looks great in those jeans.

Russ Unger
(Guided by the ever-brilliant Margot Bloomstein, Laura Creekmore, Tim Frick, Matthew Grocki, and Sarah Krznarich)

Content strategy, fortunately, is a lot easier to define than, say, user experience. That does not mean it is entirely simple to grasp. Fortunately, the leading experts in that field have pulled together some very palatable definitions that make it much easier to get everyone on—or really close to—the same page about what it is. The one definition that seems to get pointed to with frequency is from Kristina Halvorson, CEO of Braintraffic and author of *Content Strategy for the Web* (New Riders, 2010) and *The Discipline of Content Strategy* (A List Apart) at http://www.alistapart.com/articles/thedisciplineofcontentstrategy/):

> "Content strategy plans for the creation, publication, and governance of useful, usable content."

Let's get one thing straight up front: content does not mean copy alone. Content is all of those wonderful things that can end up in your project—from videos to PDF menus of your restaurant to that well-placed animated .gif of Orson Wells as Charles Kane performing a slow clap—and all of the things in between. These all count as content. This is kind of important, so consider putting it on a Post-it® note on your monitor until it is committed to memory.

This is a great place to start. You see, content strategy is about the planning for all that content that clients—internal and external—like to leave until the very last minute. What do you have currently, what can you cut out and what can you keep, how will the content be created, who will create the content, who will edit the content, who will approve the content, who will publish the content, how often will they publish the content, and what are the rules of the content road? These turn the wheels of content strategy.

It is rarely an easy wheel to turn.

Why Do You Need Content Strategy?

This subsection is probably better titled "Why *Don't* You Need Content Strategy?" as most UX work could be well-served by having a good content strategy in place. Matthew Grocki, Content Strategist at Grass Fed Content, and Laura Creekmore, President of Creek Content, both agree that while not all projects need a content strategist, all projects need a content strategy and that need most likely is determined by the scope of work that is going to be done and the time and materials available. Margot Bloomstein, Principal, Appropriate, Inc. and author of *Content Strategy at Work: Real-World Stories to Strengthen Every Interactive Project* (Morgan Kaufmann, 2012) supports this by adding:

> "If you're going to communicate, you need a goal and a plan—otherwise, it's just noise and prattle, and the world and the web have enough of that. Content strategy provides a structure for creating that goal and plan, from message architecture through audit, editorial calendar, style guidelines, and more."

Ask around and you will hear no shortage of tales where clients decided to worry about content later—after they addressed some pressing need to move forward with design and development for a deadline that is almost guaranteed to be more aggressive than the time and materials allowed. Planning, however, takes time and requires a lot of thought. As Tim Frick, President of Mightybytes, Inc., says:

> "Content shared across networks is likely to be the first experience a user or customer has with your brand, while the content within a website or application drives loyalty once brand interaction has been accomplished."

That is, if your content is going to stand a chance of being the first thing any of your users see, it should *not* be the last thing on your mind. Do not risk burying the lead because you didn't give the content proper attention and planning.

And that, friends, is a very good reason to have a content strategy in place.

When Do You Need Content Strategy?

Yesterday.

Because you have probably already started a project that needs content strategy and you want to know where you can and should start working on this aspect of the project.

The real answer is that content strategy needs to be right up front with everyone else in the project. Invoke your content strategy and/or content strategy needs as soon as there is discussion of a project. In the consulting world, this means trying to get a seat at the table during the RFP/Pitch phase to ensure a proper allotment of time and materials. In the internal project world, the bug needs to be planted in the ears of the stakeholders as soon as possible; content strategy needs a seat at the table.

Content strategy can help flesh out the business goals and get you thinking about how content is going to be created or curated, managed, and measured. In essence content strategy is not just part of your broader user experience, it can also tie nicely into your brand strategies, which should be getting the same resonating treatment across the organization.

To be frank, if you are reading this chapter—and you are already in the middle of a project—you needed content strategy before right now. That is not to say that all hope is lost; yours would not be the first project in the history of projects that got started prior to thinking through or understanding all of the needs of the project itself. Sometimes you have little choice but to build the airplane while flying it, regardless of how things should happen in a frictionless world.

So, let's keep moving!

Who Does Content Strategy?

Okay, this can be easy. Answer this question: Do you already have a content strategist on the project?

If the answer is yes—great! You have found your content strategist!

If the answer is no, look around you. Is there anyone else on the project who has claimed ownership of the content strategy?

If the answer is yes—great! You have found your content strategist!

If the answer is no, look into a mirror. Smile. Wave kindly, because the beautiful person you have found is your content strategist.

There is a chance that you could be the new content strategist on your project. The good news is that there are plenty of resources to help you and this chapter will provide a good start toward moving you in the right direction. You see, content strategy is kind of in the "sweet spot" of UX; it is a part of the UX, but it is also separate. Like how the delicious peanut butter is separate from the delicious chocolate, but together they are even more delicious!

How Long Does Content Strategy Last?

Your answer should be "forever." Since content is the front line between a brand/product/project and its users, there should be a component of measurement and adjustment whereever content strategy is involved. And from there—and in a perfect world—the process should start again.

Okay, maybe "forever" is a bit strong. There is a belief that "good UX never ends" and the same can be said for good content strategy. However, with a good governance plan put into place—and an adherence to it—the effort can certainly become less over time. Grocki adds:

> "I use the garden metaphor all the time. If you haven't touched it in 5 years (or ever), it's going to suck making it a functioning garden. Also, when the garden is finished, you'll still have to tend and weed, but it won't be nearly as impossible as the first time you worked on it."

This Sounds Familiar...

All of this content strategy stuff might seem like a lot of what you are already doing in the work that you do, as it pertains to UX. Information architects have been organizing, categorizing, and labeling information for as long as they have been information architects; and a lot of what a content strategist is doing might send their spider sense into action.

This is not a bad thing. If anything, it is the right thing.

Project culture seems to be trending toward "Lean" and "Agile" now more than ever. Do a keyword search on your local meetup groups or follow any mailing list thread (as long as they still continue to exist) and those words are sure to come up. The more time that a UX designer spends on deep dive of the content, the more time that UX designer is not spending on all of their other tasks (see also: several of the other chapters in this book). This is important, much like the differences between designing and developing are important: not everyone has the depth of skill necessary to perform the tasks that a content strategist performs, and further, not everybody wants to take on those tasks.

That is okay. What is *not* okay is ignoring the importance of the function and the importance that the role can play on your project team. It is also important to note that:

▶ **Content strategy is NOT information architecture.** While information architects deal with organizing, categorizing, labeling, and prioritizing information, the content structure, tone and voice, sources of content, governance of the content and all of the planning that goes into that is such a "political and hairy" area that one could get stuck in an infinite loop of herding cats in many cases. That means that sometimes it makes a lot of sense for these roles to be very separate—but working very closely together—on projects. As always, scope and time and materials will play a large role in making that determination.

▶ **Content strategy is NOT copywriting.** No. No, no, no, no, no. Copywriters, well, they are the ones who are writing the copy. In many cases, they are sure to work out how tone and voice and structure—and possibly even styles—are put together, but their primary focus is on generating the copy so that it is on-brand. Content strategy loves to take what the copywriters provide, which when articulated well is the story that is being told, and figure out how it works best for the project. To say that content strategy is copywriting is also to forget all those other wonderful content items (videos, documents, images, etc.) that need to have a home within your project. Then, in a frictionless environment where content strategy gets to analyze usage statistics, turn the data into insights and an updated plan for that part of the content.

Ask the Experts: Sarah Krznarich

Sarah Krznarich is Assistant Director of Content Strategy + Student Engagement at ASU Online (http://asuonline.asu.edu).

At ASU Online, content strategy sits smack in the middle of user experience and editorial direction, and works daringly close with website analytics and information architecture. It's a Content Strategist's sweet spot, if she knows what's good for her.

We strive to plan for, create and maintain content that serves both our business *and* user objectives, and to do that successfully means keeping these various disciplines at hand.

The most oft-changed content on our site is the hero story. I begin by discussing ideas with marketing—What are they interested in "selling?" Can this content support that? We use an editorial calendar to plan, freelance writers and photographers to produce, and finally data to analyze and improve through an iterative process.

The primary business goal of our website is to drive visitors to request information and apply to the University; the primary user objective is to easily find useful information. John Devoy, our User Experience Director, regularly navigates the myriad data in Google Analytics, and together we explore and ask questions: What pages see the most visitors? How much time is spent on those pages? Does the content lead the visitor to convert? What content contributes to our goals, and what pieces need some attention? We then conduct user and A/B testing to further determine whether design, content and navigation structure can be improved to support our primary objectives.

We're essentially obsessed with providing our prospects with an amazing user experience. Using quantitative and qualitative data lets us pay really close attention to our content. And that's my sweet spot.

Okay, so those are *not* as absolute as they sound. That is, the roles can intertwine to some degree. Content strategists can—and often *do*—practice information architecture, and vice versa. Likewise, content strategists can—and often *do*—practice copywriting, and vice versa. Heck, some information architects do copywriting, and vice versa, as well. In some cases, you may have a single person performing all three roles based upon the structure of the project or organization.

Tools of the Trade

Our brave panel of experts (and a couple of smart authors) have helped curate a listing of the types of artifacts that a content strategist, or someone who is performing content strategy on a project, may find useful in terms of communicating information to your client and team members.

The Artifacts

Some call these "deliverables" or "client/project documentation," but whatever they are called, they are the tools of the content strategy trade that help herd the content cats. This list is certain to *not* be exhaustive, but it should provide a really great start for you as you begin to explore content strategy. In addition, once you have an understanding of what these documents are, you will be well on your way toward crafting your very own content strategy.

Quantitative Audit

This is also called a *content audit* or *page inventory*. A *quantitative audit* (**Figure 8.1**) is a fairly basic audit that is easy enough to complete using any spreadsheet tool. The most core parts of a quantitative audit are the URL (if it's a web-based project) and/or page location (such as the page number in a site map), the page title, and the page contents.

Quantitative Audit Example		
Quantitative Audit for <Client Name>		
Version 0.1		
Date: 02/22/2012		
Notes: Excluded all syndicated and message board content.		
URL	Page Title	Description
http://instantbwong.com/	INSTANT BWONG!	Home page and only page of the website. Contains a large flash button that plays a sound when pressed.

Figure 8.1 A quantitative audit example

Depending upon your needs, this can be expanded to include additional information such as keywords, descriptions of various elements, etc.

Qualitative Audit

This is also called a *content audit*, a *page inventory*, or a *content assessment*. A *qualitative audit* (**Figure 8.2**) is a much more thorough examination of the content. In addition to all that is in the quantitative audit, additional information is added, such as a headline, a body description, a main message, image details and sizes, video details and sizes, other content types placed on the page, notes, traffic information (content usage), SEO information, content accuracy, content usefulness, how user-/target-audience friendly the content is, grammar, spelling, structure, etc. In some cases, you may also want to provide a grade or a level of measurement as to the quality or effectiveness of the content. To quote Kristina Halvorson, "A qualitative audit analyzes the quality and effectiveness of the content" (www.peachpit.com/articles/article.aspx?p=1388961&seqNum=5).

Creek
CONTENT
Site Audit

Number	Browser Title	Headline	Char Lim?	Body Description	Char Lim?	Main Message	Image
1.0	UserGlue - User Experience Design Strategy and Research, Information Architecture, and Usability	Sticky, Simple and Specific to Your Needs		2 paragraphs of branding copy		UserGlue provides user experience design and usability services. Specialize in integrating into your process.	Large full-wi Variety of im on reload
2.0	Russ Unger's Bio	Russ Unger's Bio		Multi-graph bio. Sample presentation. List of speaking engagements.		Russ Unger is a UX design expert consultant, author and experienced speaker.	Images of U books
3.0	The Work of UserGlue	The Work of UserGlue		Two sections: Where We've Been [Client listings by company], What We Do [Services provided]		List of clients and services	Wireframe i column
4.0	About UserGlue	About UserGlue		Multi-graph agency description		UserGlue's work process and expertise	Subway tun column
5.0	Contact UserGlue	Contact UserGlue		Contact form		Contact us	-
6.0	UserGlue UserBlog	-		Blog posts in main column. Right column: Search box, Recent post links, UX Blogroll, Categories, Archive, Meta, Social links, Syndication, Advertising		-	Small landsc images at to
6.1	UserGlue UserBlog > Blog Archive > Facebook Is NOT Making You Miserable. YOU Are.	Facebook Is NOT Making You Miserable. YOU Are.		Blog post page			
7.0	UserGlue Terms & Conditions	UserGlue Terms & Conditions		Multi-graph terms and conditions		User agreement	Small form i top

user glue
USER EXPERIENCES THAT STICK

Figure 8.2 A qualitative audit example courtesy of Laura Creekmore

Message Architecture

This is one of the first activities you should engage in. Margot Bloomstein calls message architecture, "A hierarchy of communication goals that reflect a common vocabulary. The qualities you want to convey, not the points you need to make." A message architecture helps you define these qualities in terms of language that everyone on the team can understand. Margot suggests using card-sorting exercises in a kick-off meeting to define "Who we are, who we are not, and who we'd like to be" over the course of three separate steps:

1. Categorizing adjectives to describe their brand or product

2. Filtering the adjectives while focusing on how the brand or product should be perceived through the work of the project

3. Prioritizing the goals by focusing only on the "we'd like to be" column

Margot's the expert here, and she has a full chapter dedicated to message architecture in her upcoming book *Content Strategy at Work* (Morgan Kauffman, 2012). This book is worth your read and features a great online presentation that provides even more insight at www.slideshare.net/mbloomstein/message-matters-confab-2011.

Content Matrix

A *content matrix* is pretty similar to—if not an extension of—the quantitative audit. The biggest difference is that the content matrix also tracks production status, related links, metadata, alternative text for images and other page assets, content source, content owner, whether or not content is approved or what the status is of the content, and the delivery deadlines for the content.

Content Templates

These are also called *page templates* or *page tables*. Content templates are not wireframes, but they play very nice with them by providing information on the page and/or template level. A basic *content template* provides a page title, descriptions of the content that will exist on the page, and samples of the content. You may also want to provide headlines, character limits on copy, captions, and other copy. These can get quite extensive when you get into catalogs and product pages, but they are useful when trying to wrangle content from a herd of cats. Erin Kissane has written a useful article entitled

"Content Templates to the Rescue" (A List Apart) at http://www.alistapart.com/articles/content-templates-to-the-rescue/ that takes a deeper dive and provides a sample that you can work from.

Editorial Calendar

This can also be called a *governance plan*. The *editorial calendar* is your project plan for future content. Editorial calendars hearken from the newspaper and magazine industries but apply nicely to content strategy, because we are all publishers now, and any content that can be planned, should be planned. According to Tim Slavin's *"How to Create an Editorial Calendar to Publish Blogs, Facebook Fan Pages, Twitter, and Email Newsletters"* (Reach Customers Online) at www.reachcustomersonline.com/2010/08/20/09.16.39/?doing_wp_cron=1328403570, an editorial calendar needs to have these core elements:

1. What to publish based on audience needs and your brainstormed ideas

2. Prioritized list of what to publish

3. Work effort required to publish each piece of content

4. Micro-content needed (e.g., page titles, headlines, navigation link labels, ALT tags, footers, blurbs)

5. Dates assigned for writing, editing, publishing for each piece of content

6. Publishing location (e.g. print, blog, email newsletter, Twitter, Facebook)

An editorial calendar helps you plan for future content needs and provides anyone who has responsibility or impact on the future content with advance notice. When considering your editorial calendar and/or governance plan, you will need to consider the following questions:

▶ Who owns what content?

▶ How much content will be largely static?

▶ How much will need to be revisited with some regularity and/or scheduled?

▶ When will content be retired?

These questions help you with thoroughly planning the future of your content.

Note *DivvyHQ has an online editorial calendar tool (for a fee) that can help you with managing this process at www.divvyhq.com/.*

Content Flow

This is also called *editorial workflow*. *Content flow* is a diagram that shows how content is created and moves through editorial and approval channels, then goes live. Richard Ingram provides an example online at http://richardingram.co.uk/downloads/110318_pr_workflow_example.pdf. This may look familiar to you if you know swimlane documents (see Chapter 11, "Site Maps and Task Flows").

What is the One Artifact You Need?

You may get varying answers depending upon whom you ask. Three of our five experts chimed in quickly with the content audit documents, and the others agreed on performing a customized, up-front workshop or defining message architecture during the kickoff. If you are new to content strategy, your safest bet is to start with one of the content audit documents so you can get your feet wet while learning a lot about the content that you are, or will be, working with. As you begin to learn more and get more comfortable with the materials, do not be afraid to dive right in and start planning your own message architecture with your clients and teams.

Additional Resources

The great thing about a growing field is that there are so many resources to help you along your way to learning. There are great books by smart authors:

► *Content Strategy for the Web* by Kristina Halvorson (New Riders, 2010) — Second Edition due in 2012 with Melissa Rach

► *The Elements of Content Strategy* by Erin Kissane (A Book Apart, 2011)

► *Content Strategy at Work: Real-world Stories to Strengthen Every Interactive Project* by Margot Bloomstein (Morgan Kaufmann, 2012)

► *Return on Engagement: Content, Strategy and Design Techniques for Digital Marketing* by Tim Frick (Focal Press, 2010)

► *Clout: The Art and Science of Influential Web Content* by Colleen Jones (New Riders, 2010)

► *Letting Go of the Words* by Janice (Ginny) Redish (Morgan Kaufmann, 2007)—Second Edition due in June, 2012

And there is a near endless bevy of online resources to keep you up-to-date with current trends:

▶ A List Apart has several articles in their content strategy section at www.alistapart.com/topics/content/content-strategy

▶ Richard Ingram has a great blog worth diving into for more content strategy learning at www.richardingram.co.uk

▶ Contents Magazine has recently launched and already has smart content at http://contentsmagazine.com

▶ Sara Wachter-Boettcher has a blog on content strategy at http://sarawb.com/blog

▶ Brain Traffic has a blog that you should just hook into your content feeds now at http://blog.braintraffic.com. In addition, they have one of the best curated blog listings in their "Check These Out" section.

▶ Shelly Bowen's Pybop has a great listing for additional resources for content strategists at www.pybop.com/2010/03/content-strategy-books

▶ Intentional Design, Inc. has a listing of content strategy deliverables at http://intentionaldesign.ca/category/content-strategies/deliverables

▶ Donna Spencer provides a content inventory spreadsheet that can help you start your audits at http://maadmob.com.au/resources/content_inventory

In addition, there are conferences that can help you deep dive into content strategy:

▶ Confab (www.confab2012.com)

▶ Content Strategy Forum (http://csforum2012.com)

▶ Intelligent Content (http://rockley.com/IC2012)

▶ Content Marketing World (http://www.contentmarketingworld.com)

▶ Langley Center for New Media Content Marketing Retreat (www.langleynewmedia.com/programs/marketing-pr/bootcamp/content-marketing-retreat)

▶ ...nearly any web design and development conference or UX conference

▶ ...and don't forget your local meetup groups (go to http://meetup.com and search "content strategy")

Ask the Experts: Tim Frick

 *Tim Frick is President of Mightybytes, Inc. (http://mightybytes.com), a creative firm in Chicago that works primarily with cause-driven clients and socially responsible businesses.*

Most of our projects involve some level of content strategy. Naturally, this can vary based upon contractual agreements and obligations, but when we are responsible for the full circle of content strategy, we start with the most granular element—the keyword—and move out from there to include:

▶ **Business rules and marketing goals** to define primary objectives for all teams.

▶ **Keyword analysis** to define the terms that define the business from search phrases to brand statements, from directory structures to file names.

▶ **Content audit** to assess the baseline from which we will create content structures.

▶ **Content assessment** document that includes:

  ▶ Keyword/phrase recommendations based on search volumes, trends, and brand standards.

  ▶ SEO recommendations for optimizing page data, keyword density, anchor text, etc.

  ▶ Writing standards for voice, clarity, and other content elements necessary to maintain brand equity.

  ▶ Topic recommendations for maximizing engagement (the 'value filter').

▶ **Project content** delivered in two drafts.

▶ **Content edits** and tweaks as site or app progresses through design, prototyping, and development.

Most of this is delivered at various points in the early part of a project, which we consider the Discovery phase. During Discovery, we also provide interface wireframes, information architecture documents that include navigation structure recommendations, and so on. Our approach will also vary depending on whether or not the project is subscribing to an agile or waterfall methodology.

After launch, if Mightybytes is contracted for ongoing maintenance that includes content development, we also provide:

▶ **Strategy documentation** outlining a content development approach for three months, six months, or one year.

▶ **Community building strategies** for ongoing engagement, social campaigns, promotions, etc.

▶ **Editorial calendar** and guidelines for creating and curating content over time.

▶ **Content development** that includes blog posts, new page content, email campaigns, tweets, status updates, etc. as outlined above.

▶ **Performance measurement reports** based on pre-defined objectives and delivered monthly or quarterly.

▶ **Actionable insights** for performance improvement based on analytics data from website, email, and social sources.

As a project progresses toward launch and moves into the inevitable maintenance and growth phase, we typically provide recommendations for some of the key points above in the form of documentation, hands-on training workshops, or a combination of both.

Since Mightybytes is equally focused on client marketing objectives and user experience, our approach may vary slightly from a more traditional marketing agency or a standard web firm. Our hybrid approach allows us to bring out the best in each discipline, which means we will often provide more artifacts than what you might see in a project more driven by UX.

There are even some smart content strategy people that you should be paying attention to, so track them down on your social networks, at conferences, or at local events:

▶ Margot Bloomstein, Tim Frick, Laura Creekmore, Sarah Krznarich, Matthew Grocki, Karen McGrane, Kristina Halvorson, Erin Kissane, Melissa Rach, Erin Scime, Ann Rockley, CC Chapman, Scott Abel, Ann Handley, Mandy Brown, Rahel Bailey, Daniel Eizans, and the list goes on and on. These folks are great people to start learning from.

Things to Look Out For

Content strategy is a lot more than what you will find in the pages of this chapter; this is really just scratching the surface of what it means to perform content strategy or to be a content strategist. With so much more to learn, there are some things you can look out for to help you avoid mistakes that others before you have made.

▶ Deleting content is good. Deleting content without a plan or a reason is bad.

Ask the Experts: Laura Creekmore

Laura Creekmore is President of Creek Content (http://creekcontent.com).

I worked on a project several years ago where the site had already been live for 7 or 8 years, and it had thousands of pages of content (around 40,000 real pages). The client wanted to delete the majority of it, but what we struggled with was, because those URLs were so old, they had incredible "Google Juice" (SEO value). They had amazing search engine optimization, and they didn't seem to care. The topics were really relevant to their audience and most of those thousands of pages had incoming links and continued to collect traffic for the website. They ended up removing a lot of pages, changing their CMS and the URL of every single page with no regard to their SEO; not even simple redirects to new and/or relevant content. They will never have the search position that they had previously.

▶ Content can be incredibly political and messy. It is not just about what goes where on a website or pages, but it is also about who owns it. You can work on a website that has a single page with multiple owners of content just for that page, and each of them could have completely different priorities or goals to meet.

Ask the Experts: Sarah Krznarich

Sarah Krznarich is Assistant Director of Content Strategy + Student Engagement at ASU Online (http://asuonline.asu.edu).

I once worked in an organization where if I thought something was not very good, I could choose not to print it. But when you have multiple stakeholders with different objectives and sensitivities, you find yourself in a political quagmire. There can sometimes be fragile egos involved when you ask someone "Why?" Why do we need this content you have developed? Why do you want this mission statement on your home page? Why does your marketing department want this tagline on every page? Why do you need a Facebook page?

▶ Who is paying for the content strategy? It is not uncommon for content to be the afterthought of a project. If you do not think this is true, ask anyone in the industry if they have ever used "Lorem ipsum dolor sit" in a wireframe or any other design-related document. That means that content strategy can be a line item in an already thinly stretched budget, and that can be difficult to contend with. If all else fails, bring out the old standard: "Failing to plan is planning to fail."

▶ Time and resources management for ongoing content strategy can be a challenge. Everyone is busy, and asking people to take on new content responsibilities can be a challenge, but if this does not happen, the strategy can fall apart. There needs to be a commitment to sticking to the plan.

▶ Content strategy as an afterthought. It has been mentioned several times in the pages of this chapter, but content strategy can lead projects. It deserves a seat at the table. When your project starts, your content strategy should be starting, too.

Ask the Experts: Tim Frick

Tim Frick is President of Mightybytes, Inc. (http://mightybytes.com).

Topics were easy to come up with. Finding time and allocating resources (dollars, personnel, etc.) within the confines of a small web firm has been an ongoing challenge.

We overcame this challenge by implementing the following:

▶ Scheduling short weekly meetings to discuss what's next, industry news, etc.

▶ Creating an editorial calendar that serves as a guideline for topics.

▶ Sharing content duties across staff (Joy covers design, Tai covers front-end web, Tim covers marketing, strategy, and business, etc.).

▶ Designating a content editor who oversees creation and publishing.

▶ Utilizing external resources to fill in gaps when internal resources are otherwise occupied.

It took a while to get our entire team on board with this process because it required writers, designers, project managers, and programmers to constantly think like marketers throughout an entire project's life cycle. Likewise, measurement for ongoing performance improvement requires a specific skill set not typical of a content writer or visual designer. We don't expect team members to veer too far outside their comfort zone but working within agile methodologies often means constantly being in sales mode, which requires all team members to be aware of every step in our process and other members' capabilities. Since content strategy stretches across all these steps in one form or another, standardizing our approach across the team can be a challenge.

There is a lot more for you to learn about content strategy. Do not be shy about reaching out to the content strategy community, plying them with adult beverages and kindness (translation: beer and scotch and cool shoes). They will be more than happy to provide a little guidance. Attend a content strategy meetup or conference and go exploring with the many links you have been provided with. Treat this chapter as the springboard it is meant to be and take a dive into the ever-growing content strategy ocean.

9 Transition: From Defining to Designing

Time to Visualize, Prioritize, and Plan

You now have a nice fat list of business requirements and user requirements. And you have information from your users to focus your discussions. So now what?

Unless you're on the Shangri-la of projects, you'll have a budget (tight), a timeline (crunched), or both that are telling you you'll need to focus and manage that list somehow. This chapter discusses some of the ways you can transition from definition to design, including tactics to help your team visualize the solution that needs to be designed, prioritize features to create a unified set of requirements, and plan the design activities that will follow in the next phase of the project.

Carolyn Chandler

C hapter 4 touched on different project approaches, or methodologies, and how they affect the way you collaborate with the project team and business stakeholders. It compared a waterfall approach, which has Define and Design phases separated by an approval step, with a modified waterfall approach that has some overlap in phases.

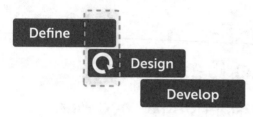

This chapter discusses the activities that can occur in the overlap between the Define and Design phases.

This point in the process is the right time to

▶ **Ideate** *and* **visualize** **features that did not emerge during stakeholder interviews or user research.** Doing this with the project team before prioritizing enables you to consider and plan for innovative features that meet both business and user needs.

▶ **Prioritize project requirements.** This involves taking the integrated list of business requirements, user requirements, and project team ideas and determining their relative importance in meeting the project objectives. At this point, you'll be working with the development team to understand the general level of effort required to meet each requirement.

▶ **Plan the activities and documentation you'll be using during design.** This planning determines how you'll work with other team members and what types of tools or documents they'll receive from you, such as site maps and wireframes (discussed in Chapters 11 and 12).

This chapter covers each of these three areas, beginning with a method for ideation and visualization that is easy for a UX designer to use in collaboration with project team members.

A Common Scenario

The requirements are defined and approved, and you're in the midst of design-ing the site features in the plan. In the middle of the design process you realize that providing a particular tool will be really helpful to your users. It's an exciting idea, but there are no requirements describing that new tool, so including it now requires a change to the prioritized requirements.

You'll need to make a strong case for changing the requirements list, especially if doing so means something else needs to fall off the list (it'll take time to decide what that is)—or that the project schedule may slip. There's a possibility the idea won't be included simply because it came too late in the game.

Although new ideas may come at any point in the project, setting aside some time to ideate features after requirements gathering is complete, but before prioritization, helps you generate those ideas earlier and increase the likelihood that they'll be included. It also ensures you take some time to consider innovative features that may not have occurred to your business stakeholders or users.

Ideate and Visualize Features

UX designers have a unique set of skills that help bridge the mental gap between words (such as requirements) and images (such as site maps and wireframes). As much as people may talk about requirements and argue over language, often they won't really get onto the same page until they can see the concept represented visually.

On the other hand, if you go into specific visual details too quickly, you risk focusing the conversation on smaller details (say, whether a choice in a form should be a radio button or a drop-down option) before you resolve the big questions (such as whether your users should have to fill out that particular form in the first place).

There are many conceptual design techniques you can use throughout the process that help visualize context, flow, and story in a way that engages others before detailed design begins in earnest. These techniques will also bring out the need for features that can be added to your requirements document before prioritization occurs.

One such technique is the collaborative creation of *storyboards:* visualizations of particular user scenarios sketched on paper or a whiteboard during a brainstorming meeting. The UX designer then works from these sketches to add details.

The Basic Process of Storyboarding

Prepare for the storyboarding session by creating a list of scenarios that you'd like to explore. To build the scenario, consider the following questions and bring the answers to the session:

▶ **Who is the main user in this scenario? What role is he playing?** This is where your user model or your personas will come in handy. If you have them, bring them to the meeting—they will both focus the conversation and ensure your project team has a better understanding of how they can use user-modeling tools throughout the design phase.

▶ **Is the chosen user a first-time user of the site? If not, is he a sporadic user, or does he use it frequently?** This will affect the level of the features you'll discuss; a first-time user might be overwhelmed by the number of choices that a frequent user might like. You may want to talk through the scenario twice to reveal different features that could be needed for each group, such as in-context help for new users or customization features for frequent users.

▶ **What immediate need has led this user to the site? What is he trying to accomplish, and why?** You can generate thoughts on this by looking at the high-level tasks covered in your business or user requirements, such as "find product recommendations." Perhaps the user wants to find product recommendations because he needs a pair of snow boots and wants to make sure they won't leak and get his feet wet.

Gather your brainstorming team for the session. This team can be just you and one other person, or it can be a small group of three or four other people. (More is possible, but it can be difficult to gather everyone effectively around a whiteboard and keep them focused on the task at hand.)

Ideally, at least one person in the group will be responsible for representing the user viewpoint. Another should represent the business viewpoint (for example, a business stakeholder or a business analyst if that role is represented on the project). This doesn't mean you can't switch perspectives; you can, and should, consider both user and business needs as much as possible during the discussion. See the section "Maintain a Good Tension" for more on balancing user and business needs.

Once you have your team together, tell them the purposes of the activity: to understand some of the features that may be needed to meet business and user needs and to focus future design efforts. Present the answers to the questions listed above and the list of scenarios to be discussed. Then step up to the whiteboard (or put your pencil to the paper) and ask the group questions about the scenario, such as

▶ How is this user likely to get to the site? Consider online searches, banner ads, word of mouth, and other avenues.

▶ If online searches come to mind, do the requirements accurately reflect the types of features or activities (such as tagging for SEO needs) to support this search?

▶ Once on the site, what does the user see that will be relevant to their need?

▶ What path will the user take to complete the task? Sketch this out with high-level details.

▶ Are other people involved in the task? If so, how might they be involved (phone, e-mail, collaborative site features), and how might they influence the decisions or behaviors of the main user?

▶ Where is a user likely to need help along the way? How will he get it?

▶ What happens when the user finishes his task? A common design mistake is to think you're finished when the user's task is complete, but that's a great time to encourage the user to explore other areas of the site or consider purchasing related products.

Consider an example from a common business scenario: the need to post a new job to the company's .com site. For the sake of this scenario, say that you've conducted stakeholder interviews and found that the hiring process is primarily managed by one person—call him Jeff—in the human resources department, who works with those who need to hire.

Jeff is pretty familiar with the job descriptions that currently exist. He usually finds out a new one is needed when the potential manager for the new position asks him to post a job. It's then a collaborative process between Jeff and the manager (let's call her Emily) to write up and post the job description.

Figure 9.1 illustrates how the storyboard for this scenario might look.

The figure shows just one part of the storyboard you could create here. You might want to start earlier in the scenario to show the approval process Emily had to go through, or you might want to continue the storyboard to show a job hunter finding and applying for the job.

The important thing to note here is that a storyboard like this allows you and your project team to see the workflow as more than a series of pages. It brings in the human element and the context. And without the human element of a persona (Jeff), your team may not have thought to include the feature of pulling in an existing job description to start from—even though all of us have done this as a way to save time and ensure we're including everything we need.

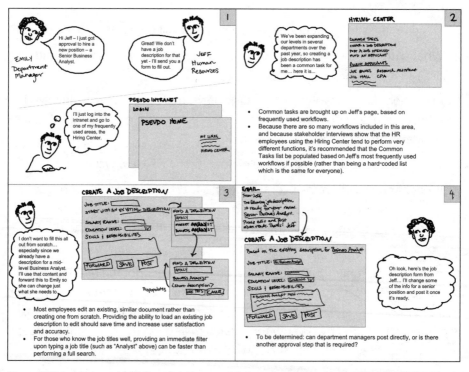

Figure 9.1 *A storyboard initially created on a whiteboard, then sketched out and detailed in Microsoft Visio using a Wacom tablet*

One thing to keep in mind when using storyboards and other types of sketches (such as user flows and conceptual wireframes) is that they are primarily meant to be brainstorming tools. Although some great ideas come out of the exercise, these sketches are not meant to be detailed designs. This fact may be apparent from their sketch form (as opposed to prototype form), but it is still an important point to make with business stakeholders, because seeing features visualized even in a sketch can sometimes lead to expectations that they'll exist in the final product.

Another risk here is that participants can get sidetracked in debates on user interface elements, such as whether something should be in the page or in a pop-up. It's very easy to get into those detailed discussions because those kinds of problems are often easier (or more familiar) to solve than the bigger problems that scenarios are meant to address. To keep things streamlined and use time efficiently, ask participants to save those kinds of discussions for the point where you're designing against your prioritized list of requirements.

And that takes us to the next step in the process: the often lively, sometimes painful process of prioritizing those beautiful requirements you've spent so much time collecting!

Facilitate the Prioritization Process

You've got your set of business requirements that have been fleshed out with features based on user requirements and your ideation work. Now comes one of the hardest parts: whittling it all down to a prioritized list of high-value requirements.

As you walk through the requirements that need to be prioritized, have the project objectives handy, as well as your user model, to help you focus the discussion on your target groups. In addition to you, in your role as *user advocate*, the prioritization process should also include:

▶ Someone who represents the viewpoint of the business (the *business advocate*).

▶ Someone who represents the viewpoint of the development team (the *development advocate*).

▶ Someone who represents the needs of the project (such as the *project manager*). This person may not need to be in the prioritization meetings but will set any constraints that affect prioritization (such as deadlines or budget) and ensure the final list fits within them.

The UX Designer's Role in Prioritization

It can be tempting to consider prioritization a shared responsibility between the project sponsor, the project manager, and the lead of the development team rather than an issue for a UX designer. There is nothing further from the truth.

Prioritization discussions are where successful solutions are made or broken. User experience designers have a *responsibility* to bring their skills to bear for these important conversations.

If you're already part of the prioritization process, this section will give you tips on participating. If you're not, do what you can to get yourself involved. This means you need to inform the project team of the skills you bring to the table—such as facilitation—and the balanced perspective you can bring. It's essential to demonstrate that you can understand different team members' perspectives and work together toward a unified understanding. See the section "Maintain a Good Tension" for more on how to achieve this balance.

The prioritization team walks through each of the requirements to answer the following questions:

▶ **What is its level of importance to the business?** How important is the requirement in achieving one or more project objectives? How great is the impact if this requirement is left out?

▶ **What is its level of importance to the user?** Does the requirement meet a common user need (or high-impact needs for priority user groups)? How does it affect the user experience if this is left out? Are there other requirements that are very similar and may compete?

For this last question, keep in mind that multiple solutions to the same problem can compete with each other and cause user confusion (as well as require more effort to support). For example, the *New York Times* may have a large enough development staff to support all the sharing features on nytimes.com (called out in blue in **Figure 9.2**), but some of its users may be confused about whether they should click Recommend, E-Mail, or Share to send the article to a friend. If your users may not be familiar with all the sharing options that have exploded over the past few years, you should probably start with a smaller set of features.

▶ **What is the technical feasibility of developing the requirement?** What kind of time is needed to develop it? If you're working with a relatively new technology, the time estimate will be higher here.

▶ **What is the resource feasibility of developing it?** Does the project team have the people, skills, and money required to develop the feature? (Consider the costs of purchasing and learning new technology tools.)

Figure 9.2 *A shot of www.nytimes.com, highlighting the many sharing features the online newspaper provides*

Create a worksheet that captures your decisions for each requirement. This could include a low, medium, or high rating based on the questions above, or you could use a numerical scale so that you can add up the numbers for sorting purposes. As you work down the list, you may find you'll need to consolidate similar requirements or break a large requirement into a number of smaller requirements that represent potentially independent units of work.

Keep in mind that this system is simply meant to help sort and prioritize; it isn't based on a scientific analysis of the requirement's feasibility. It is, however, very useful in managing a large list, inspiring discussion, and capturing relative importance.

Figure 9.3 shows an example of a prioritization worksheet that uses high-level categories of importance and feasibility (low, medium, and high) to assign relative values to each requirement.

Prioritization Worksheet

	Requirement	Description	Business Importance	User Importance	Technical Feasibility	Resource Feasibility
1	Contact Info Form	Users must provide contact information before seeing a list of distributors	High	Low	High	High
2	Email Confirmation	An email is sent to confirm an order has been made	High	High	High	High
3	Order History	Users can log in to see all past orders made in the last 365 days	High	High	High	Medium
4	Order Tracking	Orders can be tracked by entering a tracking code, given once an order has shipped	High	High	Medium	Medium
5	GPS Tracking	Users can track their package by GPS, following trucks or airplanes	Medium	Medium	Low	Low
6	Order Fulfillment Reviews	Users can read other customers' reviews of the company's fulfillment process	Low	Medium	High	Medium
7	Order Fulfillment Chat	Users can chat with other users about their order fulfillment experience	Low	Medium	Medium	Medium

Figure 9.3 *An example of a worksheet for requirements prioritization*

Assigning values to each of the categories will inspire a lot of conversations among the prioritization team. How can you help facilitate discussion and decision making?

Two of the most important things you can do are to understand (and sometimes represent) the different viewpoints that are key to defining a balanced solution, and to help resolve areas of conflict within the project team.

First, let's talk about representing the right set of viewpoints during prioritization. This involves creating and maintaining tension between user advocacy, business advocacy, and development advocacy—a good kind of tension, because it ensures a balanced solution that provides a good user experience, meets project constraints, and aligns with business objectives.

Maintain a Good Tension

As you gather requirements, and throughout the rest of the project as well, you may notice three roles pulling against each other during team discussions:

 Business advocate: The team member representing the business needs and requirements and ensuring they are captured and met as faithfully as possible. Primary concerns for the business advocate include meeting strategic objectives for company and department, ensuring the business vision doesn't get lost during the project, and setting and maintaining focus on project objectives.

User advocate: The team member representing the needs and perspectives of the primary users who will experience the site. Primary concerns for the user advocate include ensuring the site meets expectations for usability, providing a satisfying and engaging experience, and encouraging behavior that supports the project objectives.

 Development advocate: The team member representing the needs and constraints of technology and quality assurance teams. Primary concerns include ensuring the development team works efficiently and within scope and that it delivers a product that meets the quality standards expected by users and the business stakeholders.

Picture this as a three-way tug-of-war among the advocates. If tension is respectfully well-maintained among the three (meaning no one advocate dominates) then the three sides can work toward a well-balanced solution that meets project objectives.

Each team member should be aware that they have an interest in maintaining a balance throughout the project. If one side dominates, the other roles lose ground and the project risks missing its objectives—or achieving them at a much higher price than expected. **Figure 9.4** shows examples of what can happen when the tension is not balanced.

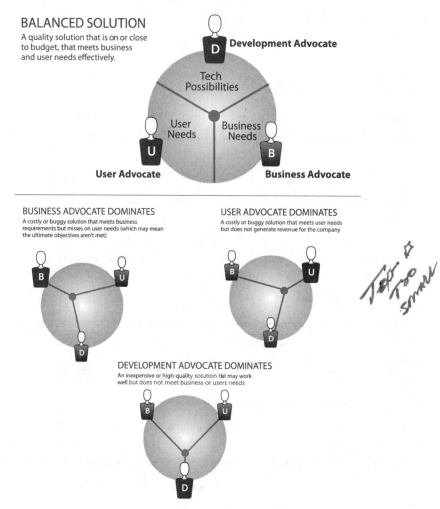

Figure 9.4 *Consequences when a good tension isn't maintained*

Can you play more than one of these roles on a project? Absolutely! Ideally different team members have primary responsibility for each role, but that doesn't mean you can't switch places once in a while. In fact, you may switch roles from discussion to discussion—or even from topic to topic. As the UX designer you'll be playing the user advocate most often, but you need to understand the viewpoints of all three roles and ensure they are consistently represented in order to create successful designs.

Although switching roles from time to time is healthy, be wary of designating yourself the primary person responsible for more than one of these roles. You may start making unchallenged compromises as the project progresses because you won't have a consistently present "devil's advocate" to ask you those uncomfortable but important questions. If you must take on more than one role, try to find a part-time resource who can play the other roles for you occasionally, to help ensure that good tension is maintained.

Up to this point, we've focused largely on the roles of business advocate (particularly in Chapters 4 and 5) and user advocate (particularly in Chapters 1 and 6). Let's take a moment to discuss the third primary role in our prioritization discussions: the development advocate.

The Development Advocate

If you're a UX designer at heart, you thrive when putting yourself in the shoes of others to understand their needs and goals. This skill is invaluable both for performing your role as user advocate and for ensuring effective communication and collaboration with those within your organization. Let's take a moment to use that skill to outline the goals of the development advocate.

One of the great design debates concerns the extent to which the development advocate should participate in, and influence, the requirements-gathering process—and what his or her role is during it. If the development advocate presents technical possibilities and limitations too early, it may curtail some of the brainstorming that could lead to some very innovative solutions. After all, today's blue-sky idea could be possible with some additional technical explorations. Even if the idea isn't feasible, discussing it may bring out an underlying need that you can address. (Mapping feature requests to needs is addressed later in this chapter.)

These are the goals and related responsibilities of the development advocate:

- ▶ Meet the requirements on time and within budget
  - ▶ Ensure team efficiency (avoiding redundant work, ensuring good communication)
  - ▶ Make the best use of the tools and platforms available
  - ▶ Select cost-effective additional tools
- ▶ Ensure future changes do not require a lot of extra work
  - ▶ Make the solution scalable, to accommodate growth
  - ▶ Make the solution modular, so that individual parts can be modified easily
  - ▶ Make the solution as standardized as possible: The fewer modifications made to a purchased system, the less redevelopment work will be needed down the road
- ▶ Ensure that the development team functions well
  - ▶ Limit turnover by providing relatively interesting and rewarding work
  - ▶ Limit the burnout that can happen with last-minute pushes

If the development advocate isn't involved early enough, however, the team may move far down the path of a certain option only to find that it's too expensive to include—or the development advocate ends up missing one or more of her own goals. And last but not least, the development advocate is a great source for bringing out some of the capabilities in the technology that could really make your solution sing, such as new technologies or under-utilized functionality.

An effective approach is to plan key reviews with the development advocate once brainstorming is complete, high-level requirements have been captured, and the prioritization process is about to begin. This allows the development advocate to spend the initial part of the process exploring the selected tools to get more detail on what may or may not be possible, and then participate more heavily in the requirements process itself once certain themes and ideas have more weight.

If you feel some requirements-gathering sessions are key for the development advocate to attend, make sure you're both on the same page beforehand regarding his or her role in the meeting and how you'll be capturing any potential concerns the advocate may have after listening in. You could also record these kinds of sessions to review with the development advocate later. You may need them yourself when you're in the thick of designing!

This kind of clear communication and follow-up during information gathering is vital to building strong relationships between team members, which can make a big difference in how smoothly the prioritization step goes later in the process. But sometimes, despite your best efforts, conflicts arise as you try to prioritize requirements. Let's talk about how you can help the project team manage this conflict.

Managing Conflict During Prioritization

If there are large areas of disagreement, prioritization can be a long process. And if those disagreements aren't resolved, they will continue to surface during design and development.

These conflicts can have many different root causes; here are some of the most common:

▶ The team is not on the same page about the project objectives or underlying business strategies (either misunderstanding, forgetting, or disagreeing on them).

▶ Opposing team members are closely tied to a certain set of features. (Perhaps the features excite them, or they've promised them to a set of influential customers or stakeholders).

▶ There are conflicts between business needs and user needs that are not easily resolved.

▶ The technologies being used are relatively new to the development team, so they're uncomfortable making estimates.

Let's take a couple of the situations above and discuss how you, as a user experience designer, can be involved in resolving them.

Choosing Your Battles

During the prioritization process, some of your favorite features may be on the chopping block. It's easy to start feeling unhappy about this, especially if it seems that user requirements are the ones most often being dropped from the list.

If you passionately defend every requirement equally, you risk having prioritizing decisions made for you. Here are some questions to ask yourself as you decide when to push for a particular requirement and when to compromise:

▶ How does the requirement support project objectives?

▶ Does it significantly reduce a particular risk? For example, does it reduce users' exposure to spam, reducing negative opinions about the site?

▶ Do other proposed site requirements rely on this one to function properly?

▶ What is the impact if the feature is not included?

▶ Is the value of the feature worth the effort needed to develop it (even at the cost of other features you hold dear)?

If you have a strong answer for all of these, bring them to the prioritization table to make your case. If not, consider letting it go, but be sure to share your reasons so others see that you're compromising for the overall good of the project. That will demonstrate your ability to consider the larger business context and solidify your involvement in future prioritizing discussions and change requests.

Lack of Alignment on Project Direction

The team is not on the same page about the project objectives or underlying business strategies.

Let's separate this source of conflict into two areas: communication and consensus.

If communication of project objectives or business strategies is the issue, ask yourself how you personally can help improve communication. Is it a matter of posting the objectives or strategies where all team members will see them (such as in a war room or online collaboration area, or the top of every meeting agenda)? Or maybe what's needed is a visual representation of the objectives or strategies that will help bring them into focus for the team and get team members excited about the vision they're working toward. Remember the visualization skills discussed at the beginning of this chapter? Use them to create an image that can be easily printed and posted or quickly sketched out on a whiteboard to help focus conversations.

If consensus is the issue, ask yourself how you could help bring everyone together. Is the conflict caused by anxiety about the risk involved in releasing a very different feature set to users? Perhaps there's research you can conduct to help resolve some of the disagreements, such as surveys, interviews, or contextual inquiries (see Chapter 6). Or perhaps you can bring your facilitation skills to bear by holding a structured discussion about disagreements, working through issues point by point until they're resolved.

Conflict Over Favorite Features

Opposing team members are attached to their own sets of features.

Suppose the director of the training department wants integrated, topic-based tutorials and the head of sales wants one exciting demo to send out to generate interest. Meanwhile, you have ten other business stakeholders in various roles—and *they* all have urgent needs. How do you help build consensus?

One method is to apply a variation of a method you read about in Chapter 6: affinity diagramming. In this method, you can work from an existing set of requirements or have the stakeholders brainstorm their own requirements (especially useful if it's still early in the requirements-gathering process). If you're working from existing requirements, you can print them out on individual pages and tape them all to the wall. Otherwise, ask stakeholders to write their top-of-mind requirements on a set of sticky notes.

What you'll need:

▶ A room large enough for your stakeholder group to move around in and that has one or more large blank walls you can apply sticky notes to

▶ A pad of large sticky notes, at least one for each stakeholder

▶ Sticker dots (you can find these in office supply stores; they come in various colors), one set of ten dots per stakeholder

Gather your primary stakeholders together in a room and ask each to take some time to write key requirements down, one to a note. Give them 15 to 20 minutes to do this. (No peeking!)

Ask everyone to put their requirements up on the wall. Then ask them to walk up and describe what they posted. As you go around the room, start grouping similar requirements together (if the stakeholders agree they're similar).

Once the requirements are explained and grouped, hand out the sticker dots. Tell the stakeholders that they can indicate which requirements are of highest priority to them by allocating their dots among the notes. They can choose to place all ten of their dots on one requirement, for example, if they feel it's that important, or they could choose to place a dot on ten different requirements. You'll start to see some clear favorites form as people place their dots.

When they're done placing the dots, walk through the results together. When they are forced to choose this way, stakeholders will bring forth their own internal priorities, and the conversation will probably become a lot easier.

 Surfing

For more on a variation of this technique to be used in prioritization, see this article "The KJ-Technique: A Group Process for Establishing Priorities," by Jared M. Spool: www.uie.com/articles/kj_technique.

This kind of technique can help you jump-start the prioritization process or reset a process that has stalled due to disagreement. Once you've achieved momentum and a common understanding, completing the prioritization document (such as the one we saw in Figure 9.3) will become much easier.

In parallel with your prioritization activities, you should be preparing for the full design effort that will soon follow. Having a plan for your work will help you estimate the effort that will be involved in creating detailed designs, integrate your work with that of others on your project team, and coordinate efforts to align with project milestones. The next section covers some of the considerations that will help you plan.

Plan Your Activities and Documentation

Once you have completed a prioritized list of requirements and, ideally, some early conceptual work (such as the storyboards illustrated earlier in the chapter), your project manager will probably start asking you for details on what you're going to do as you design.

There are several types of design activities, and each will have a different impact on how you design, the amount of time it will take, and the type of document you'll end up with. This is a "document" in a general sense; it could vary from a whiteboard sketch, to a wireframe, to a prototype.

We'll be covering some interaction design activities in the next three chapters. As you plan the activities to use, keep these questions in mind:

▶ **How iterative will the overall process be?** Ideally you can begin by exploring several different concepts quickly (for example through sketches), then agreeing on one to develop in further detail. This approach could also involve taking one or more design concepts to users (see Chapter 14 for more on design testing).

▶ **How will collaboration happen during design?** If you're working closely with a team at the same location, you can include more collaborative whiteboarding sessions. If the team is dispersed, consider web conferencing sessions with tools that allow a high degree of collaboration despite the distance.

▶ **How will your design documents be shared with the larger team?** Are you e-mailing them out to a small team or posting them to an online collaboration site? What does that mean in terms of size limitations and your process of tracking versions?

▶ **How much detail will your designs need to carry, later in the development process?** If your documents are part of a formal quality assurance (QA) process, you should make sure you involve someone from the QA team early on so they understand what kinds of detail they'll be receiving from you.

▶ **How long do your documents need to "live"?** With complex projects, the minute you stop updating a document such as a set of wireframes, it starts to "die"—the details become more inaccurate as time goes on. (This isn't always a bad thing, as long as you're involved in the discussion of those changes.) Documents that are focused on providing general guidelines, such as a brand guideline document or a library of interaction design patterns, tend to live longer.

▶ **Who are the primary users of each type of documentation?** This answer may be different at different points in the project. The primary users of your conceptual design documents are usually business stakeholders and the design team, who use them for communicating and socializing ideas. Detailed design documents are primarily for the developers who need to implement the designs; those docs provide specific direction.

▶ **What other types of documentation will yours need to align with?** You'll need to provide some kind of tie between the prioritized list of features you created above and the designs you create. You may need to keep an eye on several other kinds of documents, as well, to ensure everyone is on the same page. These docs may include brand guidelines, content development plans, functional specifications, or use cases (see Chapter 2 for an overview of different roles and the types of documentation they may be producing).

▶ **How can you estimate the effort needed for each type of document?** This one is tricky since there are a lot of variables on a project that can affect the time. But, by setting a baseline for a rough estimate, you'll have a place to start, and you can validate the numbers as you get more information. For example, you could set a baseline estimate that each detailed wireframe will take you about 6 hours to create. If you estimate a particular feature will require about five pages (for example, based on the results of the storyboarding sessions described earlier in this chapter), you'll have an initial estimate of 30 hours for that feature. If it ends up taking you eight pages per wireframe, try to figure out why. If it's something that you think will continue, you'll need to revise your estimate and possibly reprioritize.

▶ **What additional factors will affect the timing of the document?** Total time includes review time with the team and with stakeholders, as well as the time for the number of revisions you think you'll need to make. For detailed sites, it could also include time needed to reconcile your design documents with other documents, like detailed functional requirements (such as use cases). Write those assumptions down for yourself so you can check against them later.

▶ **Will you be working with multiple designers and, if so, how are you going to split up the work?** If you're working on parallel but distinct areas of the site, you can be working fairly independently on the documents you create. If you're breaking up work in a way that's very interdependent, you'll need to plan for time to reconcile your designs, and you may also need a way to track and merge different versions on documents. Save yourself a big headache later by working out a process at the beginning, and set some design guidelines early on so you're on the same page about such key elements as navigation.

Now that we've talked about some of the things you should consider when choosing your design activities, let's explore those activities. In the next three chapters we'll discuss a variety of documents, including site maps, task flows, sketches, wireframes, and prototypes.

10 Design Principles

Bring Focus to Your Design Decisions

The stage is set and it's time to move into the meaty part of the design process. Maybe you're starting with a blank screen. Or maybe, with a screen that's so full to bursting that you don't know where to begin to cut down on all the elements screaming for attention.

The good news is that there are many accepted principles in the field of design that can serve as a starting point for you. The challenging (but fun) news is that every design problem has something unique about it and should have a unique solution. Understanding common design principles, *and* creating your own, will help you create and maintain a design vision that can be used to keep your designs simple, targeted, and engaging as you move from conceptual design to implementation.

Carolyn Chandler

Whether you're working within a current design or creating one from scratch, it's extremely helpful to have a framework to work within. You can define a framework using *design principles*—commonly understood rules, assumptions, or guiding statements that define the relationships between the elements of your design. In this chapter you'll learn how to create your own design principles, in the form of guiding statements that help you make design decisions for the unique demands of your products. But first, you'll get an introduction to commonly understood principles that apply to most digital designs within these areas:

▶ **Visual design principles regarding the relationship between elements in a view (such as a web page).** This includes concepts such as unity, hierarchy, and balance. They provide focus on how users may *see* your product.

▶ **Interaction principles regarding the way users move through the site's spaces.** This includes flows within a page (such as through an online form), and navigation. They provide focus on how users may *act* within your product.

▶ **Psychology principles affecting the way users may perceive and engage with your design.** This includes common perceptions that may influence if they trust your information, their engagement with other users, and their motivation to learn. They provide focus on how users may *feel* when using your product.

There are many great resources covering these topics in more detail; here you'll find some of the most commonly discussed, and tips on where to find more.

Let's start with the first thing a user is likely to notice about a site; its visual design.

Visual Design

The visual design of your product affects a user's understanding of its brand and often affects the trust placed in the product. (After all, if someone put money into a great visual design, there's a good chance something good is going on behind the scenes as well, right?) An effective visual design also affects viewers at a subconscious level, enabling them to glean value, relevance, and importance without making conscious judgments about the product.

A Note on Accessibility

Many of the design principles covered in this chapter are true for those users who are able to see and directly interact with the elements of your design. However, it's important to also consider the accessibility of your product for users with disabilities. Those who are visually impaired, for example, may have screen readers that read elements of your page aloud and provide a method for navigating via words rather than images. If not well planned for in your design, this can be a painful or impossible task. If accessibility is a priority for your product (and for most government sites, for example, it's mandatory), visit the W3C's Web Accessibility Initiative (WAI) at http://www.w3.org/WAI/gettingstarted/Overview.html to learn more about related design standards and techniques.

Your visual design doesn't have to be beautiful to be effective—Craigslist. com exploded despite its unadorned look, and "no-frills" can be a draw in itself. However, there are basic visual design principles that are good to focus on when designing to ensure a pleasing and usable product regardless of how sophisticated it appears. Here are some of the most common.

Unity and Variety

Unity is the degree to which elements in your design have an obvious association with each other. You can demonstrate unity in many ways—for example, with color, with shape, with style, or with the way elements are positioned in relationship to each other (also called *proximity*).

Of course, if everything was the same, that wouldn't make for a very visually interesting design! By introducing some *variety* in the elements of a design, you can make it clear when there are differences between elements, and can add to a sense of freshness or exploration (**Figure 10.1** on the next page). Part of the challenge of design is figuring out how to achieve unity in visual experience (which will help users understand) while still representing some of the different users or needs a particular product is targeting.

Figure 10.1 *Feeding America launched a site for Hunger Action Month (which is September). The Manifest Digital designers had the challenge of balancing unity and variety—clarifying that Hunger Action Month is associated with Feeding America, while still giving the initiative its own unique identity. The Hunger Action Month logo in the middle right of the page demonstrates unity with the photos around it through shape (the semi-rounded rectangle) and proximity. The logo also demonstrates unity with the Feeding America logo in the upper left through color (the word Feeding is the same orange as the base of the Hunger Action Month logo), symbol (the wheat stalk), and font style and size. Variety is demonstrated through the distance between the two logos, the difference in shape, and additional colors used in the Feeding America logo.*

Another challenge may be in representing elements in your design that vary from each other in character, but that work together for a particular purpose. For example, you may want to associate text-based information with button-based actions that you'd like users to take once they've read that information. In this case, you may take visually different elements and associate them with proximity, grouping or chunking information together so they appear related. If elements are disassociated by too much space, those relationships won't be as easily understood.

See the section later in this chapter on proportion for more on situations that could affect your ability to control the proximity of elements in your design.

Hierarchy and Dominance

Hierarchy is the established order of the elements being viewed. Things higher in the hierarchy are more prominent and more likely to stand out to the viewer, while things lower in the hierarchy tend to be supportive and may seem less important. Hierarchy influences the path that a user's eye will take when scanning a page. This is useful to keep in mind if you're trying to encourage a particular action, like choosing to buy a product.

Some of the factors that determine a user's understanding of hierarchy are location, color, and size of the action object (like a button) and the tone and length of any text. Generally, objects that are larger, brighter, and have higher contrast against other objects on the page have more *dominance*, and text that is short and commanding will attract attention as well. "Click here to add this item to your shopping cart" is less dominant than "Buy Now!" both because of visual reasons (Buy Now can be scanned by the user's eye more quickly) and because of more active tone and urgent punctuation.

Note *Limit the number of dominant items on the page in order to have a clearer hierarchy of elements, and to make your primary actions stand out.*

Images also tend to attract attention. Faces can be visually arresting, and dramatic photos will dominate the page (**Figure 10.2** on the next page). Marketers are well aware of this, and many banner ads will include photos like this regardless of how relevant they are to the products being sold. Subtle— or not so subtle—animation can draw the eye.

The location of elements also influences the user's understanding of hierarchy. This is one of the areas where cultural differences come into play; for most Western languages, the order of reading is from top to bottom and from left to right, so eyes will naturally tend towards that direction when scanning a page. An element in the lower right hand side of the screen will likely be prominent when the eye rests there at the end of a scan. Arab and Semitic writing, and Chinese calligraphy, are examples of writings that are read from right to left and the natural path for eye scanning will vary for users with that familiarity. Yet another reason why it's good to know your target audience!

Figure 10.2 *healthychildren.org creates a visual hierarchy on the page by using size of text and prominence of image, as well as animation. The most dominant element is the photo of the baby, with an association drawn to the heading of Car Safety Seats and a clear and simple button for the action of navigating to that topic (the GO button). This area rotates through topics and associated photos, using animation to draw the eye. The Ages & Stages section and the Hot Topics section are next in prominence due to their locations and the relatively large size of their headings.*

Before starting to design a specific page or view, it's helpful to list and designate the weight of all of the elements on the page, giving each a status of *primary*, *secondary*, or *tertiary*. This practice will help you make choices about location, size, and color to reinforce the hierarchy on the page. As your view takes shape, take a moment to step back and consider its overall hierarchy. Are the right elements dominant? If you're not sure, give it a *squint test*—squint your eyes so you can't look at all the elements individually, and pay attention to the things that really jump out at you. Or, run your designs through a usability test to see the elements users are drawn to (or missing). See Chapter 14 for more on usability testing.

As you consider your design more holistically, take a moment to understand the types of graphic elements that will span multiple pages or views. For example, you may anticipate two types of actions for the forms you design—those that help the user fill out the form (like a lookup of airport codes in a flight booking application) and those that submit the form, moving the user to the next step in the process. The latter should have more prominence because the action of submitting the form has more weight—it's the main purpose of the form, it saves information, and it navigates the user to the next step. In defining these relationships, you'll be creating a *visual language* for the site or application—a consistent treatment of elements and their place in the hierarchy, which will subtly help users understand their meaning and behavior. You can communicate visual language even in simple wireframes when the visual design is not yet set, by varying your treatment of elements (for example, using buttons for prominent elements and links for others).

Note *See Chapter 12 for more on wireframing.*

Economy of Elements

Picture yourself walking into a cocktail party with a small gathering of 10 people. You strike up a conversation with one and cover some interesting topics. All of a sudden, another friend in a completely different conversation calls you over to answer a question. Immediately you hear him, your attention is drawn, and you walk over to him.

Now picture you're at a party in the same room, with 100 people all involved in conversation. There's a general buzz that makes it harder to hear everyone as individual voices. Your friend is going to have to shout even louder, or perhaps even come over and touch your shoulder in order to get your attention.

The same applies to design elements. A very busy design with many elements may seem like a lot of voices shouting to the user—she may not know which one to listen to, and when! In fact, a common comment heard in usability testing is that a page is too busy, or that it's unclear where to go next. When a design has a good *economy of elements*—when elements on the page are purposeful, relevant, and information-rich, and when those that aren't are removed—you are able to ensure the information can be easily digested and acted upon.

Edward Tufte is a proponent of economy in design. He introduced the concept of *chartjunk* as a way to describe all of the design elements that are added to chart but that have no valuable use in communicating the data (**Figure 10.3**). It's often amazing just how many elements can be removed from a chart, cleaning it up and focusing on the real information that needs to be shown. 3D effects are a frequent culprit here!

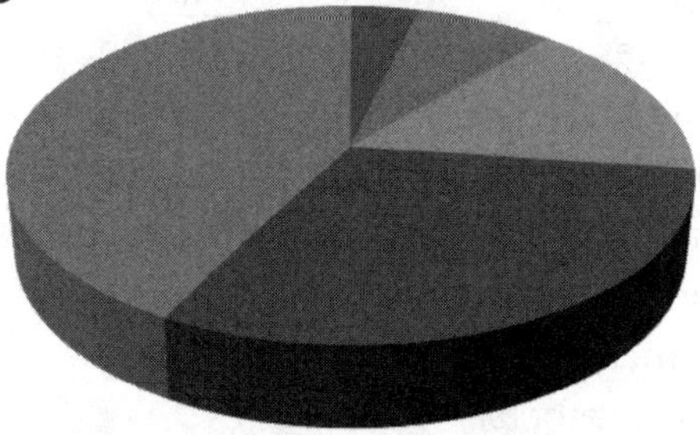

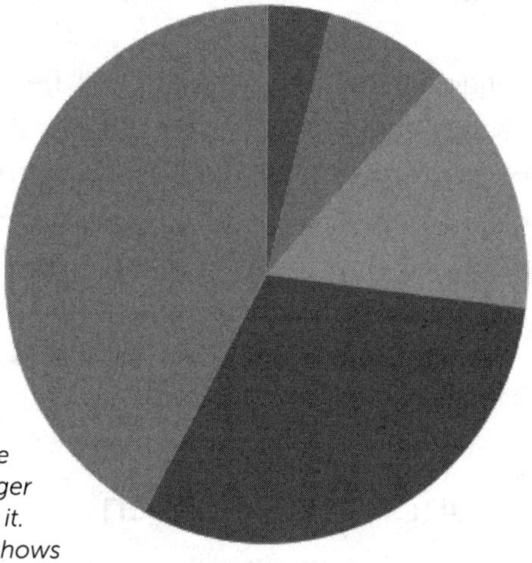

This is inaccurate — NOT just junk

Figure 10.3 *3D effects on pie charts are a great example of chartjunk. The tilt in perspective, and the way it skews the lines of the chart, make comparisons inaccurate. On the left, slice #4 (the one that appears closest to you) looks much bigger than slice #3, which is just counter-clockwise to it. Seeing the same pie without the special effects shows a smaller discrepancy between the two.*

A simple element can also be information-rich if you use more than one method to communicate its purpose. For example, these status icons use color, shape, and symbol to communicate their purpose, all in a relatively small and clean design). This is particularly good in the case of status, where relying simply on color would affect usability for color-blind users (**Figure 10.4**).

Figure 10.4 *These status icons each contain three levels of information, which help reinforce their meaning. One level is shape (a circle vs. a triangle), another is symbol (a checkmark vs. an exclamation point) and the third is color. Typically the checkmark symbol would be green for a status of "good" and the exclamation would be red to serve as a warning. However, those color indicators will be lost for a color blind user, or in cases where information is printed in gray-scale, so having all three levels makes a strong combination to cover those situations. Test your designs in grayscale to make sure your message is still clearly conveyed.*

Proportion and Balance

A design's *proportion* refers to the size relationships of its elements to each other, and to the outer dimensions of the overall design. When dealing with a fixed design, like a poster, the proportions never change, even if you change its orientation (**Figure 10.5**).

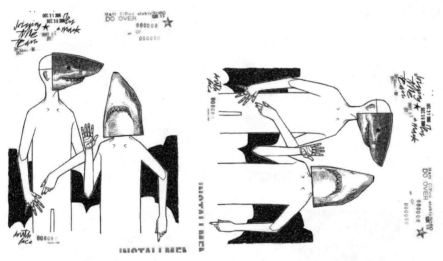

Figure 10.5 *This print by Matt M. Cipov is completely fixed in proportion (as is everything in print form). Whether you hold it in a portrait orientation or rotate it to landscape, the image has exactly the same relationship to the text and to the sides of the page—the size and relative position of elements do not change ("Joining the Team," www.mattcipov.com, 2011).*

When dealing with a more fluid design, like an application for an iPad that must be able to shift between portrait and landscape mode, discussions around proportion become more involved!

In most digital design, where you may not have control over the dimensions of the user's screen, you'll need to be explicit about how fluid your design will need to be. If you want elements to change proportion between different devices or dimensions, set rules about the way elements change to adjust. **Figure 10.6** shows an example and Chapter 12 explains how this affects design for mobile interface design.

Figure 10.6 The Boston Globe *has done an excellent job of creating a fluid design. The proportion and layout of elements change dynamically to adjust to the dimensions of the user's browser window. In the first example, the window has a relatively low width, so the photo is smaller and paragraphs of text adjust to fit. In the second example, the browser window has been significantly widened, and the proportions are adjusted dynamically. The photo becomes larger, associated paragraphs widen, and a new column of content appears on the right. The proportions have changed in that the photo is now relatively larger than fixed-size elements, like the logo for* The Boston Globe. *Even the main navigation has changed, with* Sections *grouped in the more narrow view, and expanded in the wider view.*

Generally, larger areas of text will be fluid, and primary navigational elements will remain grouped together but may "stick" to the top or side of the screen to ensure the user doesn't have to keep searching for the relative location of a menu item.

Proportion is often controlled by using a grid. Grids are very apparent in most content-heavy websites, for example, where you may have grid sections for left navigation, content in a larger middle section, and related content called out on the right. Another pattern is to have all navigation at the top and dedicate more columns to content (**Figure 10.7**).

Figure 10.7 *A basic grid as demonstrated using* The Boston Globe *screen. Note that the* Globe *uses two different grids—this one has three columns, while the narrow version uses a grid with only two columns.*

Grids help users understand the structure of the page. Strict adherence to a grid may be very functional, but could lead to a design that appears dull or overly utilitarian. Visual designers will often intentionally break the grid in order to make some elements stand out, or to make the design more visually appealing. A balance between the two techniques can help create a design that's both appealing and usable.

Deep Diving

For excellent examples of other visual design principles, such as scale, rhythm, and movement, see *Exploring the Elements of Design,* by Poppy Evans and Mark A. Thomas (Thomson Delmar Learning, 2008).

For more on using grids in web designs, check out *Ordering Disorder: Grid Principles for Web Design,* by Khoi Vinh (New Riders, 2010).

Be sure to test your grid with a variety of content, especially if you're designing a product that has dynamic content (like news stories and articles that get posted on a regular basis). In this case it's very important to make sure the design and content guidelines work together to create a good visual balance. Large and unintentional areas with no content can make your screen look awkward, and can also affect the usability of the page through excessive scrolling or separation of elements that should have proximity to each other.

Prevent this by talking with your content team to understand the types of content that need to appear on different views of your product, and setting guidelines such as amount of text for articles or news items so that everyone knows how to handle long and short content.

Now you've seen some of the most common principles to keep in mind when working with visual design elements. It's time to move on to how the user interacts with them by looking at common interaction principles.

Interaction

An interaction doesn't start with a click or touch. It starts with a desire to act, and the understanding that something can be acted *on*. This is where visual design and interaction design overlap—before a user knows which button to click, he or she has to realize that it actually is something that *can* be clicked. It sounds simple, but it's a rule that's often broken.

There are many rich sources of information on interaction design that go into depth. This section will break down the simplest steps of a user's interaction—understanding the ability to act, acting, and then getting a response—and cover some commonly accepted principles that help guide designing for interaction.

First, more on ways you can communicate something can be acted on.

Associations and Affordance

Go to your favorite eCommerce website. Take your hands off the keyboard and mouse, and really look at the page. Can you clearly tell what you can click on and what you can't?

If you're on a typical site, you probably see some of the most commonly used metaphors for interaction—tabs and buttons. You can't rifle through the tabs like a real set of folders, and you can't press your screen and get the tactile movement and click of a button, but your *associations* with these objects in the physical world gives you a clear understanding of how they should work in the digital space.

Using associations like this can be very strong, but be careful—it's also very easy to start breaking the rules and stretching your visual metaphor to the point of breaking. Around 2000, Amazon.com ran into this problem when trying to add categories to the site, making them all visible and breaking the tab metaphor (**Figure 10.8** and **Figure 10.9**).

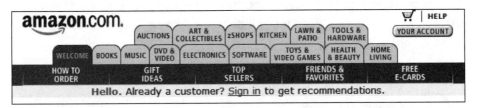

Figure 10.8 *Amazon.com broke the rules of the tab association several years ago when trying to show all categories and still maintain tabs (they weren't the only ones). Look at this closely all you'll see the issue. If the user clicks "zShops" in the top row, does the tab stay in the back but still change the main page to go to zShops? (This breaks the way tabs work in the real world). Or does the zShops tab move to the front, rearranging all the other tabs to fit? (This breaks the user's ability to remember tab placement when browsing, or on return visits). Thankfully this was a short-lived design and was replaced the next year with the design in Figure 10.9.*

Figure 10.9 *In 2001, Amazon.com replaced their confusing, metaphor-breaking tab design with this one, which is more consistent with the associations that users have with tabs. This still wasn't an ideal representation of all of the content on the site. Amazon has since moved away from tabs as their primary navigational metaphor as you can see in Figure 10.11, opting for a longer list of categories along the left hand side, and prominent search at the top. (Historical designs can be seen using the Internet Archive Wayback Machine at http://www.archive.org/web/web.php.)*

When designing objects that need to be acted on, most of the time you should make sure it follows one of these rules:

▶ Use an association with something of common use in the physical world that provides clues on how it is used digitally (such as tabs or buttons)

▶ Follow the common standards of interactive elements online, such as showing links in an obviously different color from regular text

▶ Consider the likely *perceived affordance* of the design element

An object's affordance is the degree to which the properties of the object make it clear how it can be used. In the classic example, a baseball is round and fits well in one hand, whereas a bat is long and takes two hands to hold at the base. Someone would be more likely to throw the baseball than throw the bat. Their shapes provide affordance to how they should be used. Digital objects don't have the physical properties, but their look, feel, and behavior can build perceived affordances that help communicate their ability to be acted on.

Deep Diving

It's a classic in the field of user experience design, where among other things, Don Norman applies the concept of affordance to the world of digital design. If you haven't read it, pick up *The Design of Everyday Things,* by Donald A. Norman (Basic Books, 2002). It will forever change how you look at phones and teapots.

Elements that can be interacted with ideally are distinguished visually with color, or with effects like beveling on buttons (seen for the featured stores in Figure 10.9), which help users understand they're clickable.

A subtle animation, like the increasing or decreasing of a glow on an object, or the movement of a page curl, can also enourage users to click.

> **Note** Limit the number of dominant items on the page in order to have a clearer hierarchy of elements, and to make your primary actions stand out. If your users are missing a clickable element on your screen, consider the dominance of that element (see the previous section on hierarchy) and the kind of affordance it provides, to make sure it's clearly perceived as something that can be acted on.

A common design error is to assume that a hover-effect on a design element is enough to indicate that it's clickable. For example, if a link isn't clearly distinguished as a link, but the user moves the mouse over the text and an underline appears, it's clearly a link, right?

The hover-effect approach (as the only indication of interactivity) assumes that the user is randomly moving the mouse over elements in the design in the hopes that something is clickable (**Figure 10.10**). Although this might be appropriate for exploratory products where you want to build some mystery—like a game where users are looking for clues—it should be used very intentionally as a design for exploration and not as a common navigational technique.

Users rarely want to spend a lot of time moving around your site to find clickable elements. For products where users are trying to do work or find information quickly, it's best to pay attention to the next topic—designing for economy of motion.

Figure 10.10 *This site gives the wrong visual clues about what is clickable. You might think you could click Lunch or click Dinner at the top to see a menu, but those aren't links. You might think you could click NAVIGATE in the lower-left, but that's not clickable either—it's a sign pointing to the eggs in the middle. Those eggs only become obviously clickable when the user hovers a cursor over the eggs—then some of them enlarge. As you can imagine, it's unlikely a user is going to consider eggs an affordance for links.*

Economy of Motion

The user has gone from understanding that an action can be taken, to taking it. How quickly and effectively she can do that depends on the distance she has to travel to get to the object, and the ease with which she can act on it. On a web page, for example, a small button far from her cursor is going to take longer to use than a large one right next to it. This is the basis of Fitts' Law.

> **Note** *Fitts' Law predicts that the time required to rapidly move to a target area is a function of the distance to the target and the size of the target. It's based on a mathematical model created by psychologist Paul M. Fitts in 1954.*

So why is it that most navigation is far away from where the user is likely to be—at the top and bottom edges of the screen? Partly this is to make sure it's out of the way of changing content in the middle—but also, because the navigation is "pinned" to the edge, users are less likely to overshoot when moving to it with a cursor or pointing with a finger—so the position actually makes it a larger target.

Thinking of distance and target size may seem obvious, but it demonstrates an understanding of an *economy of motion* that you should be considering when designing navigational elements, and that can be easy to forget when you're in the middle of design. When placing elements consider this:

▶ **How far is it from the where the user probably is?** Good form design, for example, takes this into account—if a user is moving through a series of fields on the far left side of the screen, buttons on the far right will take longer to click than buttons directly below the last field. If this is a highly used form, this could be annoying and inefficient.

▶ **Are you requiring users to switch methods of input—for example, from keyboard to mouse?** Switches like this are inefficient, so consider the way users may interact with a page or a task using both input methods. Keyboard-centric users will appreciate the ability to hit the Enter key, for example, rather than having to go from entering form info with they keyboard and then moving to the mouse to find and click the Submit button.

▶ **How easy is it to act on the object?** A larger target is easier to hover over and to click on—a simple large button is an example of that. Nested menus, where users have to hover to open other options and keep the menu open while they select one, can be difficult to use for some users, especially if the menu is unforgiving and disappears if the user accidentally moves the cursor off when trying to select an option (**Figure 10.11**).

In addition to the economy of motion within a page, consider the number of clicks required for a user to complete a particular task. Here as well, for something used every day for critical work, a large number of clicks will become inefficient and frustrating for users.

Figure 10.11 *Amazon uses nested menus, which expand when the user hovers over them with a cursor (as shown here). This design only uses two levels; it's only two because none of the options in the Books menu have additional hover states. Sites with three levels become increasingly hard to act on because the path is lost if the user moves outside of the active hover area and the menu disappears. Nested menus like these are effective when dealing with a large number of categories, but they are more difficult to act on than a simple button or link—especially for users that have difficulties with vision or fine motor control.*

Is it possible to take economy of motion too far? Yes, like most things, it is. Having all options closely gathered and present can be overwhelming. It's not rare to hear a business stakeholder say, "I don't want anything to be more than three clicks away," as if clicks are the only economy that matters. In design you need to balance discoverability and access (which is provided if all options are up and close together) with simplicity and economy of elements, discussed in the Visual Design section above.

The user has acted, and now it's time for the system to respond.

Response

When users act, they often have expectations for what will happen next. In products with great user experiences, their expectations are either met, or users are delightfully surprised to get something more powerful or interesting than they had expected (**Figure 10.12**).

Figure 10.12 YooHoo & Friends is an online game experience for kids. Hovering over different elements causes a variety of different (and delightful) responses. For example, the YooHoo & Friends title spins, the navigation at the top sways gently back and forth, and characters themselves display different skills. (http://yoohooworldwide.com/games/fling-the-furry-5/)

In most cases, however, a difference between expectations and reality leads to frustration or annoyance instead. Some of the common culprits are:

▶ **Poor performance, such as search results taking a long time to return.** The development team you work with will often communicate potential issues with performance when in the design process. It's a limitation that can be a design challenge, but an important one to acknowledge.

▶ **Poor error handling.** This can come in the form of a design that doesn't do enough to prevent errors in the first place. Once an error does happen, however, the tone and clarity of the error message (and the suggestion on how to fix it, when it's in the user's control) are essential. **Figure 10.13** shows an example of a common problem.

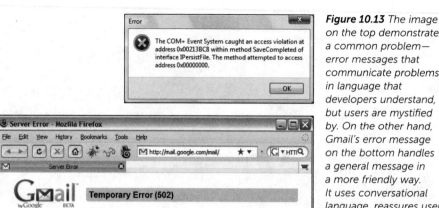

Figure 10.13 *The image on the top demonstrates a common problem—error messages that communicate problems in language that developers understand, but users are mystified by. On the other hand, Gmail's error message on the bottom handles a general message in a more friendly way. It uses conversational language, reassures users that they have not lost information, and gives users a clear next step to move beyond the error with a link to perform that step whenever they are ready. Of course, it would be better if the error message wasn't necessary at all.*

▶ **Lack of feedback on results.** If the user is successful in their action, ideally they know it through clear changes in the design. For example, many applications don't give a response when the user clicks Save, but for something so important, a subtle clue that saving is happening (an animation on the Save button or a "last saved" timestamp) can be very reassuring.

Good responses reward the user with a positive result of one kind or another. It turns out that a lot of the more addictive products online—like social sites and games—are well designed to reward users with a splash of good old dopamine, a hormone that lights up the pleasure center of the brain.

Research in psychology focuses on responses like these, and on motivations for returning to products with good experiences. The next section covers some of the principles that have come out of this research.

Psychology

Up to this point the principles covered have focused mainly on aesthetics and movement—more cognitive and mechanical aspects of design (dealing with psychology at a more visceral level). However, the truly fascinating aspect of design is the pursuit of understanding the psychology behind a user's attraction to, and engagement with, a product or experience.

The role of psychology in design is a rich area in itself, and it's worth a deep dive into several of the resources here that cover the topic. This section will give you just a taste of some of the insights psychology research has brought to the design field, including:

▶ The emotional effect of an attractive design

▶ The personal, or *intrinsic*, motivation people have to take on new challenges within your product (in particular, the principles of flow and gamification)

▶ Social proof—or the effect that second, third, and 164th opinions and behavior can have on a user's decisions regarding your product

First, here's more on the importance—and unintended consequences—of an attractive design.

The Effect of Attractive Design

If you're already working in the design field you may have heard one of the phrases that make a visual designer cringe:

Business Advocate **"Then we'll hand it to the designers so they can make it pretty."**

For consumer products from chandeliers to mobile phones, where similar models are being compared side by side, the attractiveness of the product is clearly one way to differentiate. But is it as important for more utilitarian products like ATMs or banking websites? Aren't features and usability more important than look-and-feel in those cases?

In his book, *Emotional Design,* Don Norman brought together some surprising findings in his argument for considering the emotional side of design regardless of the type of product:

▶ **People generally perceive that an attractive product is easier to use.** It turns out usability isn't just about usability. Cross-cultural studies on ATM design showed that simple aesthetic improvements in an ATM interface, which did not affect the usability of the ATM, led to a significantly higher *perception* that the product was easier to use. A visually pleasing design contributes to more pleasing interaction whether or not the user's task is completed more quickly or effectively. (This can be an issue when you're testing a design for usability—see the sidebar below for more detail).

▶ **An attractive design builds trust.** Ever hear the story about how Van Halen trashed a concert venue after finding brown M&Ms backstage, despite the fact that their rider explicitly stated "M&Ms (WARNING: ABSOLUTELY NO BROWN ONES)?" In David Lee Roth's biography, he claims this rider was intentionally placed there to test the venue staff's attention to detail. The band brought large amounts of heavy, and potentially dangerous equipment into venues that hadn't handled that type of show before, and a staff that didn't fully read the contract could lead to major issues with the production. The presence of brown M&Ms signaled a lack of attention to detail that could be trouble. Similarly, a regard for aesthetic details (for example, alignment of elements, clear visual hierarchy, and other considerations covered in the section on visual design above) communicates an attention to detail that users often feel will carry over to other, less visible areas of the product. This has a positive impact on a user's trust of the product.

▶ **Pleasurable products create positive feelings and, as a result, increased creativity.** When people feel stressed they tend to see problems in very narrow, black-and-white terms. This emotional response makes it more difficult for them to be creative in their approach. Customer support staffs encounter this all the time, as users frustrated with a computer issue may not consider solutions that seem obvious (hence the common support question for digital products, "is it plugged in?"). On the other hand, pleasurable products relax people and encourage a more exploratory approach to problems. Any product that requires creative thinking on the part of its users will benefit from attention to the attractiveness of the design.

Do these findings mean that aesthetic design is more important than usability? Far from it—the two work hand-in-hand to create a positive and engaging user experience. A beautiful product that doesn't work well may get purchased, but quickly ends up in the junk drawer (physically or digitally speaking). A utilitarian product that meets a real need will get used, until a more attractive and equally useful product becomes available. Both aesthetics and usability work hand-in-hand to create something that users return to and enjoy.

Because people perceive an attractive design as easier to use, make sure you account for this when conducting usability testing. People are less likely to criticize an attractive, fully-formed design than criticize a sketch, which feels still "in draft" and easier to change. They'll also be more likely to rate an attractive design highly even after encountering some usability issues. If you must test a complete visual design, consider testing two or more variations so users will compare the designs against each other, which helps reduce a bias towards positive feedback.

Just as attractiveness is often underrated in the design of functional things, so is the element of fun. The next section will cover some of the factors that make the interactions within a product engaging and meaningful.

Flow & Game Design

After decades of research into the positive aspects of human activity—moments of happiness and joy, for example—Mihaly Csikszentmihalyi (pronounced me-high chick-sent-me-high-ee) proposed the concept of flow in his book, *Flow: The Psychology of Optimal Experience. Flow* is the state of deep immersion that people feel when engaged in an activity that provides a challenge appropriate to their perceived level of skill. Along with spending time with friends, flow states brought the greatest degree of happiness among the many people who participated in Csikszentmihalyi's research.

When people enter flow states, time passes differently. For athletes, time can slow down and seconds pass like minutes as each movement of an arm or leg has their focused attention. For artists, hours can pass as they paint the detail on a face, and to them it feels like time has been suspended.

You can never really control when the people you design for will find the level of immersion required for flow experiences, but by supporting them in your design, you're more likely to create engaging products that help users learn the features or topics that you're providing. Some of the conditions that contribute to flow states are:

▶ **Presentation of an activity that has a clear set of goals.** A knowledge of what needs to be accomplished, and the basic rules that apply in the activity, provides structure so the participant can focus on the activity itself.

▶ **A particular balance between the challenges presented and the skillset that the participants perceive they have (Figure 10.14).** This is where it's extremely valuable to have an understanding of the target users of your product, and their likely skill sets; see Chapter 6 on User Research, and Chapter 7 on Personas for more on developing this understanding.

▶ **Clear feedback regarding the participant's performance as they perform the activity.** This allows the participant to try something, see a result, and try again, learning something new at each step and building their skills.

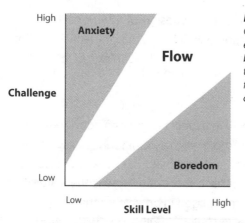

Figure 10.14 This is a version of Csikszentmihalyi's graph demonstrating the emotional conditions that exist at different balances of challenge vs. skill. Flow states tend to happen when a user feels they are facing a great challenge that they have, or can develop, the skills to face successfully.

Game design takes flow into account, as any gamer who has lost two days to World of Warcraft or Halo can attest. Successful games provide:

▶ Well-structured, clearly explained, and consistent rules of interaction

▶ A series of well-defined and sequenced goals (for example, quests or levels within the larger scope of game play)

▶ Immersive game play, engaging multiple senses (for example, using visual, audible, and tactile elements)

- ▶ Feedback on performance, with the ability to try challenges multiple times to increase skill

- ▶ Social interaction, either with fellow game-players or via a community that shares tips and results

Jesse Schell, author of *The Art of Game Design*, defines a game as *"a problem-solving activity, approached with a playful attitude."* And increasingly, the concepts of game design are being applied to new situations to build on a participant's intrinsic motivation to complete an activity (*intrinsic motivations* are those that individuals feel based on internal drive rather than external rewards or penalties). For example, Quest schools use a game-like curriculum to create a fun and immersive learning environment, where students are highly motivated to explore and solve challenges (**Figure 10.15**).

Figure 10.15 *Quest schools are designed by the Institute of Play, with locations in New York City and Chicago. Students learn cross-disciplinary skills within a challenge-based, game-like curriculum that integrates disciplines (such as math, biology, and ethics) into core classes, and also learn by designing and playing games. A digital media focus also allows them to express their creativity and develop skills in the digital space. (http://q2l.org)*

An increasing number of digital products are tapping into play as a motivator for user engagement. *Gamification* is the process of using game design concepts to engage users in ways that aren't traditionally considered game environments. For example, in Spigit's FaceOff (**Figure 10.16**), members suggest product or service ideas, and other users vote on their favorite. Popular ideas show up on a leaderboard, enhancing the feeling of competition.

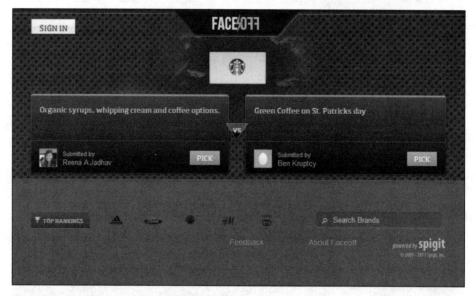

Figure 10.16 *Spigit focuses on generating value for companies via products using gamification. In FaceOff, popular ideas are worth more points for the person who suggests it, and the company sponsoring that competition gets the benefit of ideas generated and validated by users (as well as the overall engagement of users with their brand, which may be even more valuable).*

Gamification can also be used to encourage behavior changes that add to personal or social good. Health Month combines social gaming mechanics with information on healthy lifestyle habits, encouraging players to set and meet goals around nutrition as well as financial and mental health (**Figure 10.17**).

"Fun is the act of mastering a problem mentally."

—Raph Koster, *A Theory of Fun*

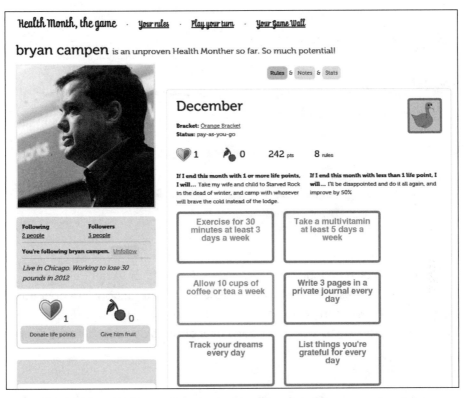

Figure 10.17 *To play Health Month, users set goals and track their progress online. Points are awarded for tracking consistently and for meeting goals (more points are awarded for goals which the play anticipates will be more difficult to meet). A variety of technologies can be integrated, such as scales, pedometers, and blood pressure monitors that automatically send information to Health Month for easier tracking.*

Simply adding competitive elements, like points and badges, are not enough to make a product a truly immersive game-like experience. When trying to motivate and engage users in a playful way, be sure to focus on what their needs are, and what style of play is most appropriate. If designing a game-like experience for a non-profit, for example, competitive game play (pitting player against player) may not be as effective as collaborative game play (where players work together to achieve a goal).

When designing an experience that requires learning and problem-solving skills, consider these motivational aspects of play. Could your product provide clear goals, pleasurable activities, and constructive feedback to make the experience fun and effective?

Deep Diving

For more on the concept of flow and the studies behind it, read *Flow: The Psychology of Optimal Experience,* by Mihaly Csikszentmihalyi (Harper Perennial Modern Classics, 2008).

Jesse Schell describes game design and its influence on the creation of engaging experience in *The Art of Game Design* (Pearson, 2010).

For an overview of gamification more directly tied to the solving of business challenges, pick up *Gamification by Design* by Gabe Zichermann and Christopher Cunningham (O'Reilly Media, 2011)

Whether it's to take on a dragon in World of Warcraft, or to get help finding the best web design book to buy, online social interactions are powerful things. The next section covers a principle that conveys the way users look to others to make decisions, and how digital designs can support that desire.

Social Proof

It's been said many times; the human being is a social creature. Not only do we look to others for companionship; we rely on each other, even complete strangers, to help make decisions in the face of uncertainty.

You may have been here before: something unexpected happens in a crowd of people, like a loud argument or potential fight, and a long pause stretches out as people look to each other to figure out if someone should intervene. When situations are overwhelming or uncertain, an individual often looks to the people around him in order to understand whether an action should be taken (and if so, which one).

Online it's no different. Faced with an overwhelming number of choices and limited time or money, the power of *social proof*—of popular support of a particular choice or action—may help people choose a better investment. This can help users decide anything from which product to purchase (**Figure 10.18**), to which document to spend time downloading and reading from a corporate intranet.

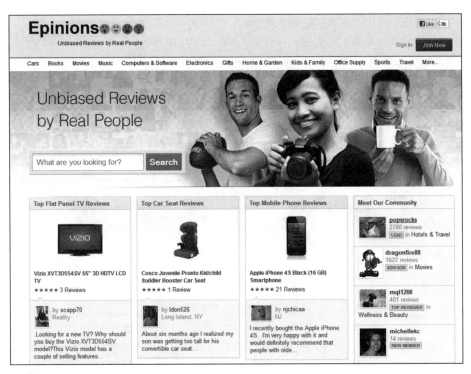

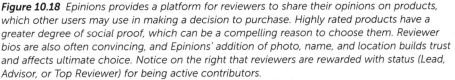

Figure 10.18 Epinions provides a platform for reviewers to share their opinions on products, which other users may use in making a decision to purchase. Highly rated products have a greater degree of social proof, which can be a compelling reason to choose them. Reviewer bios are also often convincing, and Epinions' addition of photo, name, and location builds trust and affects ultimate choice. Notice on the right that reviewers are rewarded with status (Lead, Advisor, or Top Reviewer) for being active contributors.

Even if users can't post content like reviews within your product, you can still bring user activity to the surface in your design to show that there are people using it, and to help support decisions in what to pay attention to (**Figure 10.19**).

Products that don't reflect any patterns of how they are being used are likely to appear disconnected. And in addition to appearances, they are probably missing a powerful method for both engaging users and adding valuable information that helps in decision-making.

So what happens if, early in the project, you realize that better support of decision-making is a key way to meet the needs of your users? How do you create a focus on this need and maintain it through the design process, as features are added and removed based on timelines and budget? The next section covers a method for creating your own design principles, collaboratively, to provide a consistent focus through product iterations.

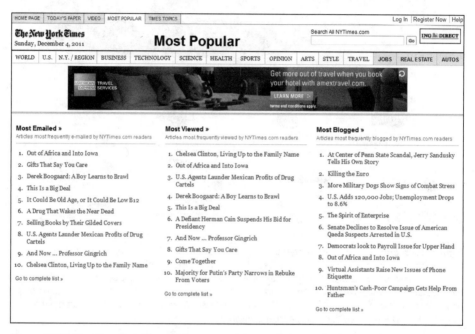

Figure 10.19 The New York Times *brings up activity around stories, whether they are viewed, emailed, or blogged about. For some readers, this provides a cross-section of the articles generating the most interest—a smaller list than they would encounter if trying to visit each major section individually.*

Snorkeling

These books are fast and enjoyable reads, and cover the concept of social proof (also called social validation).

The classic is *Influence: The Psychology of Persuasion,* by Robert B. Cialdini (Collins Business Essentials, 2006).

Susan Weinschenk covers many principles in psychology that affect design decisions in *100 Things Every Designer Needs to Know About People,* (New Riders, 2011).

It's a great and fun read on aesthetics, and the principles that motivate users to engage with products: *Seductive Interaction Design* by Stephan P. Anderson (New Riders, 2011).

Creating Your Own Guiding Principles

Up until this point, you've learned about design principles that are generally widely accepted by the design community, based on research that applies to most types of users. But it's easy to get lost in a sea of recommendations and possibilities if you don't focus your efforts on a set of guiding principles fitting your own user needs and design direction.

This section will cover the process of creating design principles in the form of research-based, memorable guiding statements that your team can use to set a vision through the unique challenges your product team encounters.

Chapter 5 introduced heuristics, which are good examples of guiding statements. The example used was:

Visibility of system status. The system should always keep users informed about what's happening, through appropriate feedback within reasonable time

This guiding statement applies broadly, which is why it's one of the more widely-referenced. It's relatively short, with a bit of qualifying description afterwards to make it more easily understandable.

Here are some tips on creating your own design principles:

▶ **Base your design principles on research conducted with your target users.** This ensures the principles are relevant, concrete, and defensible when you're in the throes of a debate on a design decision.

▶ **Make the main statement snappy and memorable.** Ideally team members won't need to consult a list to remember the main purpose of the principle. A small number (8–10, for example) of short, catchy statements will help the team reference them ad hoc when standing at the whiteboard.

▶ **Only add a principle if it helps to focus the team and differentiate the product.** Vague or widely-applicable principles don't help you say "no" to features or to create a unique design—both of which are goals of good design principles. A statement like "make it easy to use" is a waste of your time, for example. A design principle should take a particular stand, like saying "choose simple relevance over precision" to help the team focus on providing a small number of relevant choices to the user rather than every possible combination. (If user-need changes over time, you can adjust your principles if you need to.) It should also help the team brainstorm ways to delight the user by exceeding expectations set with past experiences with your company or your competitors.

▶ **Refine your principles collaboratively across the project team.** Everyone on the team should be familiar with these principles and take ownership in using them as a focus during feature definition and prioritization.

Here's an example of the creation of a design principle:

Pseudo Corporation was behind the curve in gathering useful information about its customers. In the rush to gather as much rich data as possible, the web design team has inadvertently created a site that requires users to enter an intimidating number of fields with their personal information, with no obvious statement on why that data was needed.

User research found that customers were frustrated with the amount of data entry required, especially when they were in the process of solving an issue (a situation that didn't lend itself to a lot of patience with requests like this). To them, it felt like Pseudo was taking their time and their data without clear returns. Research uncovered the need for a principle to help the project team understand when and how to gather user information in a way that was beneficial to users as well.

To provide focus, the following principle was created:

When gathering customer info, "give and take and give."

This was a short principle that was memorable due to its play on the phrase "give and take." In refining the statement collaboratively, the team added these test questions to help them determine when features or design decisions were being true to the principle:

When gathering customer info, "give and take and give."

Can we give users a good reason for needing this particular data at this particular time?

Do we only take data that we can't get some other way? Are we taking it in a way that is easy for users to reference and enter quickly?

Do we give the user an immediate benefit after they've shared their valuable information? Can we give them more than they're expecting?

Surfing

Jared Spool is a proponent of setting design principles for each project, as a way of establishing and maintaining a design vision across the years of a product's life. For more information, see "Creating Design Principles: 6 Counter-intuitive Tests" at http://www.uie.com/articles/creating-design-principles/

Some designers, like Whitney Hess, advocate setting design principles at a higher level (across a product suite or at the level of company strategy). This can be especially powerful when presented in conjunction with a company's brand vision and values.

Dan Saffer discusses the process of moving from the stage of ideation into the creation of design principles in "Design for Interaction: Ideation and Design Principles," http://johnnyholland.org/2009/09/10/ideation-and-design-principles/

The Pseudo team then used this principle whenever a requirement for another form, or another field, was added. It helped them both determine if the data should be required, and where to ask for it in the overall task flow. It also provided a prompt to discuss where additional value could be provided to the user.

Once you've developed a framework to help you brainstorm ideas and focus design decisions, you're ready to open up your sketchbook or your favorite diagramming tool. The next chapters will cover some of the techniques like flows, sketches, and wireframes. It's time to visualize!

11 Site Maps and Task Flows
Structuring Your Project from Here to There and Back Again

Site maps help to identify the structure of websites and applications. They can show hierarchies and connections that allow your audience to gain an understanding of where users may locate content. Task flows take site maps a step further by identifying the various courses of action that a user may traverse within a section of the site. Task flows also draw the connections to error states, content, or page views based on decision points throughout the process. When used together, site maps and task flows can provide your audience with a clear picture of content structures and how users may navigate through them.

Russ Unger

Starting with the most basic of definitions, a *site map* is simply a visual way to display representative pages of a website (**Figure 11.1**). A simple site map generally fits on a single sheet of paper and resembles an employer's organizational chart. Site maps are not just for websites, however; you can use them for any type of application that would benefit from identifying pages, views, states, and instances of whatever is being displayed.

In most cases, you will use a site map to show teammates and clients how content will be organized for a website. It will provide an overview of the website navigation and, in some cases, will display all the connections each page can have.

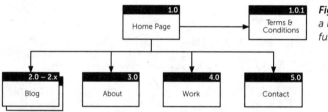

Figure 11.1 *A site map for a basic website with blog functionality*

Task flows identify paths or processes that users (and sometimes a system) will take as they progress through your website or application (**Figure 11.2**). Although site maps and task flows may look similar at first, the two types of diagrams serve different purposes: A site map tells you the visual hierarchy of a site's or application's layout, while a task flow gives you details of users' options and the paths they will be able to take.

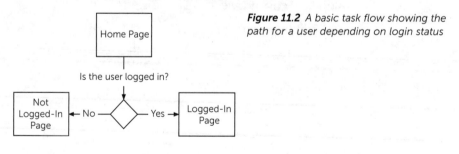

Figure 11.2 *A basic task flow showing the path for a user depending on login status*

Tools of the Trade

If you are just getting your start in the user experience design field and need a tool to start creating work product, you have many options:

▶ Microsoft Visio (http://office.microsoft.com/visio)

▶ Axure RP Pro (www.axure.com)

▶ OmniGraffle (www.omnigroup.com/products/OmniGraffle)

▶ Adobe InDesign (www.adobe.com/products/indesign)

▶ Adobe Illustrator (www.adobe.com/products/illustrator)

▶ Microsoft PowerPoint (http://office.microsoft.com/powerpoint)

▶ OpenOffice Draw (www.openoffice.org)

▶ HTML

▶ Blueprint CSS (www.blueprintcss.org)

So how do you choose? You can ask other designers; everyone has a favorite and they're usually happy to name it. Just don't be surprised if they, like your authors, answer "pencil and paper." You can also test out free trials online or opt for a no-cost solution, such as OpenOffice Draw, which is part of the OpenOffice.org suite of tools and outputs the same formats as popular office suites.

Beyond pencil and paper, what do we use? Michael Angeles, Director of User Experience at Balsamiq (www.balsamiq.com) and owner of the popular website konigi.com, has a number of templates he has created for use with Omnigraffle available online at http://konigi.com/tools/overview. In addition to Michael's templates, check out the offerings of the Information Architecture Institute, which houses many of these tools on its Learning IA page at http://iainstitute.org/en/learn/tools.php.

Whatever tools you decide to use, there are countless examples online from other professionals who are happy to share them and help you along in your career. These are largely free and can provide you with the framework you need to create—at the barest minimum—very professional-looking documentation.

Basic Elements of Site Maps and Task Flows

The most basic of elements within your drawing program will be more than enough to get you started creating site maps and task flows. To ensure that your creations can be easily interpreted by a wide audience, however, it's best to use a standard set of shapes.

The Visual Vocabulary for Information Architecture is one such standard, and the one used in this book. Created by Jesse James Garrett, one of the founders of Adaptive Path (www.adaptivepath.com), it is available online at www.jjg.net/ia/visvocab. The site provides many elements to help you articulate your site maps and task flows, all of which are available with detailed descriptions and as downloadable stencils for many of the popular drawing and sketching programs (more on these in a bit).

To help you get started and become familiar with the basics, the next sections take a look at the Visual Vocabulary's core set of elements and what they represent.

Page

According to Jesse James Garrett, a *page* is "the basic unit of user experience on the Web." "Instances" or "views" of content may be more realistic today, but a page is still very meaningful. There are a number of ways to draw these pages, but the simplest, most commonly used format is a plain rectangle (**Figure 11.3**). As you progress through creating site maps and task flows, you will want to find the style that best suits you for labeling and numbering your pages.

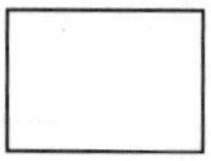

Figure 11.3 *Page element from Jesse James Garrett's Visual Vocabulary*

Pagestack

A *pagestack* represents multiple pages of similar content (**Figure 11.4**). An easy way to comprehend pagestacks is to think of dynamic content, such as a common blog page created using a publishing system. These pages are designed once and are in a design template, but you have the ability to click through many different pages of content—without actually leaving the original template design.

Figure 11.4 *Pagestack element from Jesse James Garrett's Visual Vocabulary*

Decision Point

A *decision point* is used to show the path that a user can take depending on the answer to a question (**Figure 11.5**). The decision point 10a might be "Are the user's login credentials correct?" The answer to that question would determine which page (or content view) would be displayed. A failed login results in an error message, while a successful one takes the user to the site member's home page. Take the time to appropriately label decision points; you'll be glad you did, particularly when sharing your work product with teammates or clients.

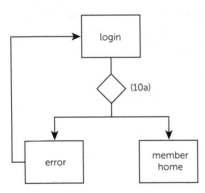

Figure 11.5 *Decision point element from Jesse James Garrett's Visual Vocabulary*

Connectors and Arrows

Connectors and arrows are used to show movement or progress between pages, pagestacks, decision points, and so on. Connectors generally appear where there is a call to action from one page to another. For example, a link to the About Us page from the Home page could be the connector between the two pages. Arrows (top of **Figure 11.6**) indicate "downstream" movement toward task completion.

Connectors with the crossbar (bottom of **Figure 11.6**) can be used to iden-tify when movement back to the page you originated from ("upstream" movement) is no longer available. For example, once a user is logged into a website, what was the home page content may now be personalized for the user, and the generic page, or the login page, will no longer be available to the user from the path they just followed.

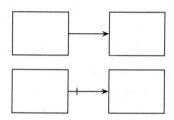

Figure 11.6 *Connector and arrow elements from Jesse James Garrett's Visual Vocabulary*

Conditions

A dashed line is a fairly common way to display a condition. It can appear in site maps, task flows, and other work product you may create or invent.

You can use a dashed line as a connector (**Figure 11.7**) or as a box around an area to highlight that a connection to a page—or an entire section of pages—is conditional based on some other action or event.

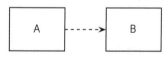

Figure 11.7 *Condition element from Jesse James Garrett's Visual Vocabulary*

Common Mistakes

You wouldn't go into a presentation with a lump of peanut butter on your chin or a coffee-stained shirt. Not only would such a blunder undermine all your hard work, it could also prevent you from landing a good project. A sloppy site map or a task flow that looks unprofessional can do just as much damage.

To help you recognize those little lapses with big consequences, the next sections take a close look at some bad designs. Learn to spot these common mistakes—then avoid them.

Sloppy Connections

Sloppy connections (**Figure 11.8**) are just that: sloppy. They're badly drawn. They look very amateurish, and they give you—the author—the appearance of not paying a lot of attention to detail in your work, to say the least. Most tools have some method of assisting you with connecting your lines to your boxes. Please take advantage of it.

Do *not* get lazy, regardless of the time constraints and pressure that you might be under. In most applications, using a combination of Shift and other keys allows you to drag elements from a starting point in 45-degree angle increments. Take advantage of this built-in functionality and ensure that your connections are, well, connected. If you are showing pencil sketches, you should have an eraser on hand just in case.

Make it a rule: Always make sure any lines that touch any other object are connected with accuracy.

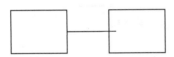

Figure 11.8 *A missed connection between two pages*

Misaligned and Unevenly Spaced Objects

Depending on the tool you are using, it can be difficult to ensure that your objects are accurately aligned or evenly spaced apart on your site map or task flow (**Figure 11.9**). There are some fairly simple ways to ensure that you get this basic rule down.

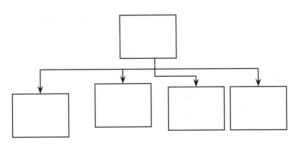

Figure 11.9 *Pages that are not aligned and are unevenly spaced*

For starters, turn on the grid in whatever application you're using. That way, regardless of whether the tool offers options that ensure evenly spaced, appropriately aligned objects, you can always *count* the number of grid units between your objects. Fortunately, when you are using pencil and paper, you can use graph paper and apply the same basic principle.

It is that easy to make your documents look professional. Unfortunately, it is also that easy to make your documents look like you really don't care about the quality of your work.

Poorly Placed Text

Careless text placement (**Figure 11.10**) seems simple to avoid, yet it is another common mistake. Find a way to make your text fit nicely in the shape you have created, and make sure any labels that are placed outside of their elements have appropriate connections (**Figure 11.11**).

Figure 11.10 *Inconsistently placed text*   **Figure 11.11** *Well-placed text*

It may seem basic, but proper placement of your text—along with appropriate font size and usage—will make your documents easier to read and use.

Lack of Page Numbering

It's time to establish another rule: Number every page of every site map that you create. Don't create a vague, numberless map like the map shown in **Figure 11.12**.

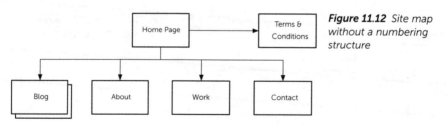

Figure 11.12 *Site map without a numbering structure*

Any page that you identify on your site map needs to be given a number, and your numbering system must allow for downstream changes to occur as new iterations and versions of your project are created.

You can use a variety of approaches for numbering pages; the most common is to identify your home page as either 1.0 or 0.0.0.0 (**Figure 11.13**). Over time, you will be able to determine which of these works best for you, but until you get comfortable and understand the advantages and disadvantages of both approaches, start by identifying your home page as 1.0. This method allows you to account for any decisions and pages that may occur prior to your home page—such as a Flash preloader, a login or register screen, or a number of other page types—as 0.X.

A numbering system on your site maps allows other documentation to sync up with it. The numbering system can proliferate to other documents, such as:

▶ **Content matrix.** Content creators can map their copy and other content to specific pages (and to a specific element in a wireframe; more on that later).

▶ **Task flows.** Task flows can use the same numbering system to show how a user will proceed through the pages of a specific task.

▶ **Wireframes** (see Chapter 12). The pages of your wireframes should share the same numbering system as the pages on your site map to provide a clear connection between the two documents.

▶ **Visual design.** Visual designers can sync design pages and elements to specific pages on your site map. This allows them to segment their inventory when it is time to hand off their designs to developers.

▶ **Quality assurance documents.** Quality assurance teams may author testing scripts that are dedicated to a specific page or pages on the site map.

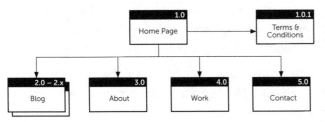

Figure 11.13 Site map that correctly connects pages, with elements that are aligned, evenly spaced, and appropriately numbered

Your attention to detail and structure at this point helps keep everyone else who touches the project on track and provides them with structure for their tasks.

In short, numbering the pages on your site map will make everyone else's life easier—and that means your life will be easier, too.

The Simple Site Map

In addition to containing page numbers, Figure 11.13 is a good model for creating the map of a basic website that has limited dynamic functionality and a mostly static nature. The pages identified for this website were:

- Home
- Blog
- About
- Samples of work
- Contact

As you can see, this simple site map incorporates the core elements from the visual vocabulary and maintains a professional style and appearance. Most importantly, it provides a very clear picture of the navigation, pages, and conditions available to users of the website.

Advanced Site Maps

A simple site map can generally fit on a single sheet of paper and most likely it looks something like an employer's organization chart. More advanced site maps, however, can expand to multiple pages.

When creating site maps that are more advanced or for larger scale websites and applications, one approach is to use your first page to identify any of the steps required to reach the site's home page. (That's correct, we're suggesting you use a task flow as part of your advanced site map.) In addition, you should identify all your top-level pages, global navigation elements, and footer elements. This allows you to show a very high-level overview of the site up front and provides your team and clients with a clear picture of the project.

The first page is also an appropriate place to include a legend or key to help in reading your site map (see **Figure 11.14**). Your team and your clients will need one. Don't skip this step!

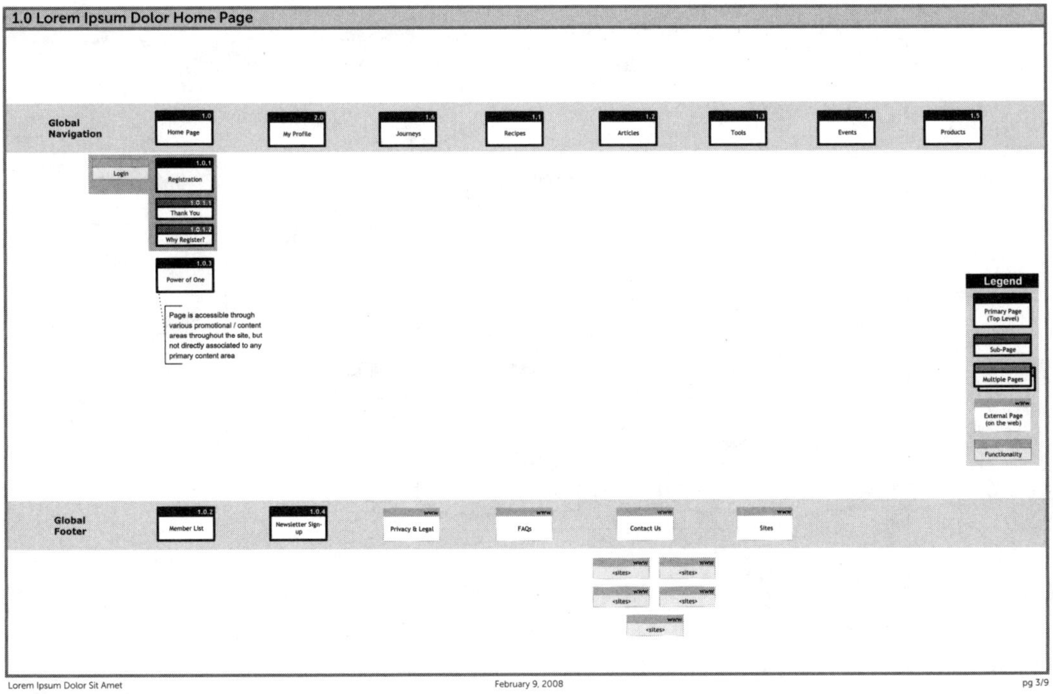

1.0 Lorem Ipsum Dolor Home Page

Global Navigation

| 1.0 Home Page | 2.0 My Profile | 1.6 Journeys | 1.1 Recipes | 1.2 Articles | 1.3 Tools | 1.4 Events | 1.5 Products |

Login | 1.0.1 Registration
1.0.1.1 Thank You
1.0.1.2 Why Register?

1.0.3 Power of One

Page is accessible through various promotional / content areas throughout the site, but not directly associated to any primary content area

Legend

Primary Page (Top Level)

Sub-Page

Multiple Pages

External Page (on the web)

Functionality

Global Footer

| 1.0.2 Member List | 1.0.4 Newsletter Sign-up | Privacy & Legal | FAQs | Contact Us | Sites |

<sites> | <sites>
<sites> | <sites>
<sites>

Lorem Ipsum Dolor Sit Amet   February 9, 2008   pg 3/9

Figure 11.14 *Advanced site map home page view*

Pages that you create after your first page should essentially map back to it. For every top-level page, you should have at least one page following that identifies all the pages, pagestacks, and external content that will be required for the website or application (**Figure 11.15**). If necessary, do not be afraid to connect subpages together. Site maps can grow to become more expansive than any single sheet of paper of standard size will allow. This is nothing to worry about, as long as your site map is well organized and the connections are clearly documented for your audience.

These examples are more than enough to get you started in the world of creating site maps. As you begin to make your way through a variety of projects and you find that your skills—and often your team or client needs—are growing, you will find that there are vastly different approaches and methods you can take toward delivering site maps.

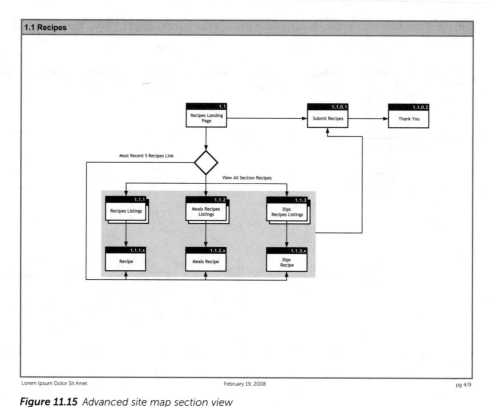

1.1 Recipes

Figure 11.15 *Advanced site map section view*

Breaking the Site Map Mold

You have now seen solid examples of site maps that should fit most of your needs in getting your primary tasks accomplished. Don't let those models prevent you from exploring ways that work better for you—and please share them with us! Different approaches can highlight information beyond basic site architecture. For example, consider the site map shown in **Figure 11.16**, which was kindly provided by Andrew Hinton, senior information architect at Macquarium.

This site map not only shows the various pages of the website, it also serves to provide insight into user paths and priorities. Andrew (www.inkblurt.com) says he created the site map after seeing an example from Wolf Noeding that sparked his creative flame. Andrew uses this site map to show various user scenarios and mental models related to the website. The larger circles on the map perform an additional function: They highlight top-level areas of the site that receive the most traffic.

Like all good user experience practitioners, Andrew borrowed—but also gave credit. There are limitless ways that you can expand your site maps as you begin to get more comfortable using the tools and identifying your work product—and client—needs. Let inspiration strike you where you find it! Don't be afraid to try something new, but take your time to make sure the time you spend is useful and valuable.

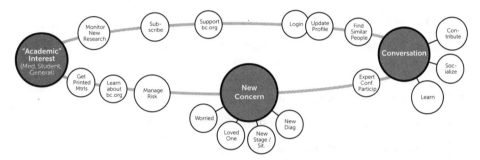

Figure 11.16 *Advanced site map. Courtesy of Andrew Hinton.*

Task Flows

Using many of the same basic elements as site maps, task flows are diagrams that identify a path or a process that users (and sometimes a system) will take as they progress through your website or application.

You can use task flows in a number of different ways. When used in conjunction with a site map they can show how a user arrives at a page with a specific set of information displayed. Sometimes they are used to show how a specific user type (a persona) would expect to traverse a website and what that persona would expect to see based on their personal mental model. You also can use task flows to identify complex processes that need to be clearly understood before the project is sent to the development team.

You might not use task flows on every project that you work on, and they may not always end up as work product that you present to your clients, but it is always a good idea to use them—even if just in a pencil-and-paper format for your own benefit.

A little clarity can go a long way.

In order to create a task flow, you need to have an understanding of the user's objective. In some cases you will receive a requirements document, and in other cases you may receive (or author) a use case. Although a use case consists of just a few sentences summarizing tasks and goals, it will allow you to synthesize the user's view into the experience.

The use case for the scenario shown in **Figure 11.17** might look like this:

▶ System displays project list

▶ User selects a project

▶ System displays basic project information, in Write mode

▶ User changes status of project to Closed

▶ System checks for pending tasks

    ▶ If there are pending tasks, system displays error notice

    ▶ If there are no pending tasks...

▶ System checks for pending payments

    ▶ If there are pending payments, system displays error notice

    ▶ If there are no pending payments...

▶ System displays summary page

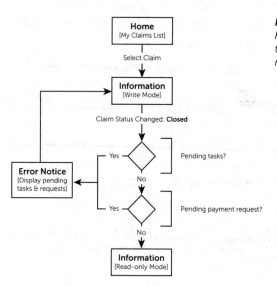

Figure 11.17 This task flow identifies how a system displays information to a user based on the responses to multiple conditions

The task flow in the figure depicts the sequence of information displayed to a user based on whether a variety of conditions from the use case are met. If either question in the center ("Pending tasks?" or "Pending payment request?") is answered with a yes, the system displays an error notice, potentially delivering additional information to help the user complete the required tasks prior to making forward progress. If both conditions are answered no, the system provides the user with a display that identifies success.

The task flow shown in **Figure 11.18** shows the paths that a user could take from a calendar application through a travel-shopping site. The task flow is very high level in that it identifies three very different paths that require testing by users to ensure that the detailed flow for each path meets user needs.

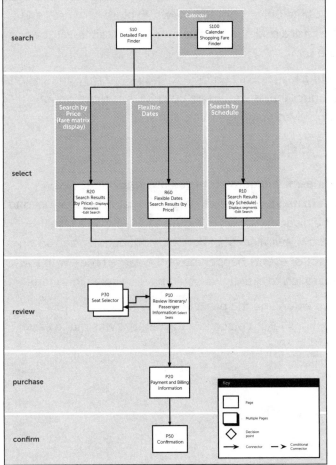

Figure 11.18 Task flow used to demonstrate the path of a user through the phases of a purchase process

Users of this application are able to enter a set of dates for their travel and then make purchases based on their own priorities. After users set their dates to search for travel, they can prioritize their results according to what is most important to them: price, flexibility of travel dates, or travel times (schedule).

The task flow identifies the high-level paths that a user could take in order to provide direction to the persons facilitating the testing. Detailed task flows could be created for each of the paths in the groupings and then provided to the development team to create the pages necessary for testing.

Taking Task Flows to the Next Level

As with all the topics in this book, don't feel as if what you are seeing here is the beginning and end of the universe of task flows. Explore new uses and expand your use of the basics outlined here as much as possible—as long as there is a good purpose for it.

As your skills with creating task flows continue to grow, you may find yourself creating a work product that is a bit more colorful, has more options, includes modified or improved language rules, and so on.

Swimlanes

James Melzer (www.jamesmelzer.com), UX Lead at EightShapes (www.eightshapes.com), has created a number of diagrams that extend far beyond the basic task flows. The diagram shown in **Figure 11.19** shows a task flow that was extended to show "swimlanes" of actions, notifications, and so on in a process that had a lot of events happening at the same time—with this project a traditional approach to task flows could have been a nightmare!

Instead, James explored extending the basic task flow to encompass all the various steps and actions taking place in a format that was much easier to understand.

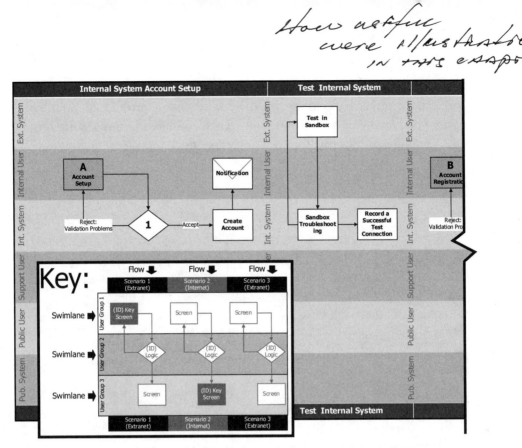

Figure 11.19 *This swimlanes diagram is an example of expanding task flows to illustrate complex scenarios with multiple actions in many places. Courtesy of James Melzer.*

James described the project and swimlanes as follows:

> The system lets people manage information about buildings they own. This extension would allow building services partners to provide data system-to-system on behalf of their customers, reducing the data entry needed from the owners. The project had three parts: partners configuring the presentation and operation of their data services, customers signing up and using the partner data services, and ongoing partner data management and troubleshooting on the back end.
>
> We were planning out a major extension to an existing system. We knew early on that nearly all the service scenarios involved multiple users and multiple systems. There were a number of notifications, and a lot of the processes were asynchronous. This diagram helped us identify, design, and explain the service scenarios needed for the project. In the full version of this work product, we actually had detailed wireframes arranged underneath the flows in this diagram. The whole thing covered a wall. Once we were fairly confident in the design concept, we chopped it up into a more traditional multipage specification.

Swimlanes are also useful when you need to cross out of the digital world and into the physical world for part of your process (**Figure 11.20**). In those cases, you can define actors and roles to help identify the steps in the process and the activities that they are engaging in.

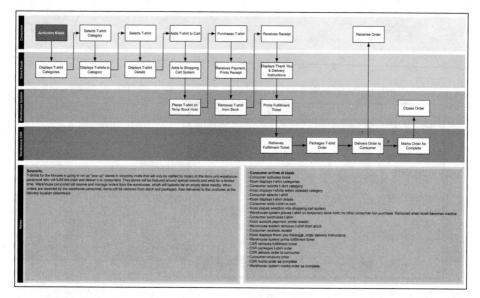

Figure 11.20 *This swimlanes diagram is an example of a swimlane that crosses digital and physical activities*

The important thing to remember here is to not limit yourself in your uses of task flows or site maps. Stretch the boundaries of the basics that you've been shown in this chapter. In the event you really need something to test your mettle, spend some time creating a task flow for how to tie your shoes.

Good luck!

12 Wireframes and Annotations

Design and Direction—
Before the Visual Design Begins

Wireframes and annotations are ways to identify the proposed content and structure, as well as functional behaviors, of a view of a web page or an application. When combined with site maps and task flows, these documents are also extremely useful for identifying prototyping scenarios and proofs of concept. Wireframes are typically presented in grayscale, bereft of graphical elements or finalized content; instead they use placeholder content to highlight representative locations that can be used as guidance in the visual design. Essentially, wireframes are used as a tool for communicating your designs.

Russ Unger

Basically a low-fidelity prototype of a web page or application screen, a *wireframe* is used to identify the elements that will be displayed on the page or screen, such as

- Navigation
- Content sections
- Imagery and/or media
- Form elements
- Calls to action (CTAs)

Wireframes are typically created in black and white or shades of gray, use placeholders for images, and do not get into specifics of fonts (although many apply font sizing to convey separations of copy types). They come in all shapes and sizes—from the very basic to so advanced that they nearly replicate full-screen design.

Wireframes are evolving; no longer are they merely provided to designers and developers as outlines for their tasks. Wireframes are now used to represent the site or application to clients, designers, developers, and any other team members who have a stake in it at its very core level. It is common to show them to clients to get validation on the "design thinking" before the visual design and development phases are started. Often the people who are creating the wireframes are working hand in hand with those who create the business requirements (in some cases, they are the same people).

It should also be noted that some of the best wireframes and annotations are the result of direct interaction and collaboration among the various work partners—from business analysts to developers and other designers. Some companies are shifting toward using their wireframes and annotations in place of business requirements documents (BRDs). Although the world is far from claiming that BRDs are extinct, the beginnings of this shift are enough to show just how important it is to be very thorough and thoughtful as you create your wireframes and annotations.

In many cases, users will be shown wireframes so they can validate the page elements or request modifications. Wireframes that are placed in front of users typically have a different name: prototypes. (For more information on prototyping, see Chapter 13.)

To help you identify the approach that works best for you, this chapter discusses the basics of creating wireframes and shows examples from designers in the field. Like the rest of this book, these examples are just the beginning—don't be afraid to explore and innovate on your own.

What Are Annotations?

Annotations are, quite simply, explanations and notes about an element or an interaction on a wireframe. They typically contain such information as

▶ Content identification or labeling

▶ Content source(s)

▶ Display rules

▶ Interaction rules

▶ Interaction destinations

▶ Process rules

▶ Error content/messaging

It's best to author annotations with very direct—if not terse—tone and clear explanations. Do not leave anything to chance in an annotation; there is a *very* big difference between *should* and *shall*.

> **Bad:** "Triggering this call to action (CTA) *should* result in the display of the home page."
>
> **Good:** "Triggering this call to action (CTA) *shall* result in the display of the home page."

OK, to be fair, the first example isn't exactly horrible, but the word *should* could leave room for confusion for a developer downstream in the process, who may not have the luxury of his favorite UX designer standing by to answer questions. Ensure that your annotation style is succinct and leaves zero ambiguity for anyone who may need to read—and rely upon—your instructions.

Who Uses Wireframes?

With their clear, concise annotations, wireframes are very nice, but who is really the audience for these outputs? Unfortunately, there is no simple answer to that. From project to project your audience may vary from a single person to any combination of several groups. **Table 12.1** outlines the potential audiences for your wireframes.

TABLE 12.1 Wireframe Audiences

AUDIENCE	PURPOSE
Project Management	Project managers may use wireframes as discussion points within the team to highlight strategy, technology needs, and a very high-level user experience.
Business Analysts	Business analysts may use wireframes to ensure that their requirements are being met and to validate that they have not missed requirements that need to be included.
Visual Designers	Visual designers may use wireframes as a blueprint for their output. Wireframes provide them with an accounting of page elements and behaviors that need to be included.
Content Creators	Copywriters, content strategists, editors, and other people responsible for copy may use wireframes to map to a content matrix and identify content needs throughout a project.
Search Engine Optimization (SEO) Specialists	SEO specialists can use wireframes to help identify appropriate naming schemes, copy needs, and enhancements to the overall SEO strategy. (For more information on SEO, see the online chapter, "User Experience Design and Search Engine Optimization," available on the companion website.)
Developers	Developers often use wireframes in conjunction with (and sometimes instead of) business requirements to understand the expected functions and behaviors of the design. In some cases, the wireframes may be used as the basis for a proof of concept.
Quality Assurance	A QA team can use wireframes as the basis for authoring its testing scripts. Once wireframes have been approved by the client, the variation should be minimal, and this allows the QA team to begin working on their tasks earlier.
Users	Users may see wireframes in very early stages, sometimes in the form of "paper prototypes," as a mechanism to test the design direction. (See Chapter 13.)
Clients	Clients are increasingly more involved in the review of wireframes to validate whether the business requirements, goals, and objectives are met and to provide approval to move forward into the visual design phase.

Creating Wireframes

To create a wireframe, you typically need a set of requirements. These can come in the form of a formal business requirements document from a client, a creative brief or project brief, meeting notes, a well-articulated site map or task flow, or even notes on a napkin that provide direction. One way or another, you need an understanding of what it is that you are trying to create for a user, what the connections are, and a general understanding of the technological limitations and expectations.

Note *For more information on defining business requirements, see Chapters 4 and 5. For suggestions on effective meeting notes, see the online bonus chapter, "A Brief Guide to Meetings," at www.projectuxd.com.*

After you compile the necessary information, take the time to carefully read through all the requirements, ask questions, and consider the answers to obtain any additional clarity, you're ready to begin creating your wireframes!

Tools of the Trade

There are many design tools that you can use to create site maps and task flows and in most cases, the good news is that you can use basically the same applications for wireframes and annotations. The bad news is that if this is your first experience in creating wireframes, you may feel just a little bit lost about where to begin.

Here are a few options:

▶ Microsoft Visio (http://office.microsoft.com/visio)

▶ Axure RP Pro (www.axure.com)

▶ OmniGraffle (www.omnigroup.com/applications/OmniGraffle)

▶ Balsamiq (http://balsamiq.com)

▶ Adobe Fireworks (www.adobe.com/products/fireworks)

▶ Adobe InDesign (www.adobe.com/products/indesign)

▶ Adobe Illustrator (www.adobe.com/products/illustrator)

▶ Apple Keynote (http://www.apple.com/iwork/keynote)

▶ Keynote Kung-fu (http://keynotekungfu.com)

▶ Microsoft PowerPoint (http://office.microsoft.com/powerpoint)

▶ OpenOffice Draw (www.openoffice.org)

▶ HTML & CSS

Many tools have stencils or libraries that you can pull design patterns from to help you build out specific elements of the page. As an example, the Yahoo! Design Pattern Library (http://developer.yahoo.com/ypatterns/) has many downloads available for Omnigraffle, Visio, Fireworks, Axure, InDesign, and more, which covers a good portion of the tools available to you.

You can find stencils galore online, and here are a few places to get you started:

▶ Welie.com (http://www.welie.com/patterns)

▶ UI-Patterns.com (http://ui-patterns.com)

▶ Patternry (http://patternry.com)

▶ Graffletopia (http://graffletopia.com)

▶ Axure Widget Libraries (http://www.axure.com/widgetlibraries)

▶ Loren Baxter's Better Defaults for Axure, A Widget Library (http://www.acleandesign.com/2009/04/better-defaults-for-axure-a-widget-library)

Ask the Expert: Leah Buley

Leah Buley is principal designer at Inuit. She highlights the importance of using pencil and paper (much like the authors) in her "How to Be a UX Team of One" presentation.

"When you first start sketching ideas for a wireframe, here's what often happens: You have one or two good ideas, and then you hit a wall. These ideas will probably come from something that you've seen and liked, or from something you've designed in the past. That's not an ending point; it's a good starting point.

The mind tends to race to what's familiar, but what's familiar may not always be the best solution to the problem. When you force yourself to seek more varied ideas, often by idea 4 or 5, you've come up with something new and interesting. I don't know why it happens that way. It just does.

Templates can be useful for guiding yourself through this process. You can use Adaptive Path's six-up template (**Figure 12.1**), which simply provides a space to do six little thumbnail sketches. The number of sketches isn't actually all that important. What is important is forcing yourself to move beyond the first few obvious ideas. Six is a magic number (for me) because the six-up template, with its six little boxes, encourages me to keep going until all the little thumbnails are filled in."

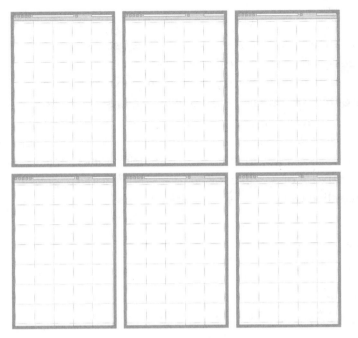

Figure 12.1 *Adaptive Path's six-up template*

But wait—there is still more good news. Nearly every seasoned user experience professional gets started with pencil and paper, so you should not feel as if you need to immediately choose a technology solution (although it is entirely possible that you'll need to translate from sketches to something digital rather quickly).

These are sound words to live by—especially if you are just getting familiar with the work you are doing in the world of UX design. As times passes, you will begin to identify an approach that works best for you, but there's not much better advice than Leah's. For additional insight into her approach, the entire "How to Be a UX Team of One" presentation is available online at http://www.slideshare.net/ugleah/how-to-be-a-ux-team-of-one.

Don't be afraid to get started with pencil and paper—just be sure to bring a lot of erasers. Mistakes are a part of the process, and you should expect that even after you have committed to a pencil sketch you will make modifications as you move to digital. In fact, if you are not already sketching first, sit down with a pencil and paper and sketch your ideas out before you open any digital tools to help you wireframe.

Few professions operate within the realm of iterations as frequently and consistently as UX designers. Very rarely, if ever, is design work accepted on the first pass, and sometimes you can only hope to be "wrong in the right direction." Because of this, start small: Take a single page or small portion of a section of a project, review it first with your internal team, and then with your client team to ensure that your understanding is on track. Getting your designs in line with the client's way of thinking about their business objectives up front saves you a lot of rework moving forward. The same approach can apply to design testing with users—seek validation early!

Start Simply: Design a Basic Wireframe

In this section, you will see how to create a wireframe at a very basic level. Often you may start with nothing more than a simple site map and some additional requirements, but with these you can build a wireframe for a website's home page.

Remember the basic site map from Chapter 9, which showed how a very simple website might be structured? **Figure 12.2** presents a refresher—as you can see there is a degree of navigational hierarchy shown. Every X.0 page identified is most likely a top-level, or primary, page. You can use this as a jumping off point for defining a portion of the business requirements and for a wireframe.

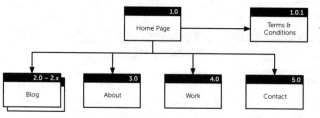

Figure 12.2 *A site map for a basic website with blog functionality*

Getting Started

It is not uncommon that you may be the author of your own business requirements document, and that can be a blessing and a curse. When you are the author of the requirements, essentially you have only yourself—or your client—with whom to discuss the meaning of anything vague or relatively undefined. Often it may feel as if you are making it up as you go—but don't let that deter you.

In many instances, your wireframes will help you identify gaps in the information you are working with. This can help you create the best solution—eventually. Remember, user experience practitioners work toward putting forth the best possible solution for the users, and your first versions of any project are always going to be used to solicit feedback and influence the next iteration of design. Your design does not have to be perfect, but you do want to make sure it looks clean and professional, and that in the worst case it's wrong in the right direction.

The requirements for this home page design are limited and very brief. Fortunately, the site map in Figure 12.2 provides enough information to formulate the navigation that could be used for the website:

▶ The home page (numbered 1.0) is the topmost level of navigation. Terms & Conditions (1.0.1) is most likely a common footer element, or at least it should not be considered part of the primary navigation.

▶ The other primary navigation elements are About (3.0), Work (4.0), Contact (5.0), and Blog (2.0–2.x)—which is depicted as a pagestack, so you can ascertain that it will be viewed as multiple dynamic pages and may have a "previous" and "next" form of navigation.

These primary navigation elements supply you with quite a bit of information to get started with—but that is nowhere near enough to effectively create a home page for a website. So, to help provide direction, the client supplied some additional information:

> The company is a boutique user experience design firm that has gained exposure due to its blogging and the range of projects that it has worked on. It is important that visitors to the website can quickly learn what the company/website is about through limited text and strong, evocative imagery that works in conjunction with user experience design. Additionally, it is important that the navigation is clear (would prefer reusable header and footer, if possible) and that there is a call to action to most recent blog postings so that visitors can

quickly read a summary of our latest take on current issues in the user experience world. If possible, it would be nice to be able to highlight recent work on the home page, but this is secondary, as much of our work is often in development or under strict nondisclosure.

The Wireframes and Annotations

There are a number of ways to interpret these requirements, and the first wireframe presentation to the client could be very similar to **Figure 12.3**.

WIREFRAME WITH ANNOTATIONS

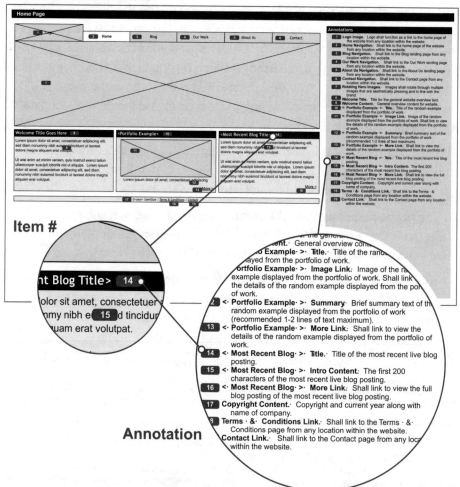

Figure 12.3 *Wireframes with annotations submitted for home page design*

The wireframe with annotations details every element on the page, as well as expected calls to action and the action results (such as loading a specific page). This particular example (**Figure 12.4**) works very well because of the limited number of elements and the limited amount of detail required.

Figure 12.4 Live home page design for www.userglue.com

As Figure 12.4 shows, the live version of this home page today is only slightly different than the original wireframe in Figure 12.3. Because timeline and content became issues, for instance, the Portfolio Examples section was removed. Also notice the difference in naming conventions for navigation and calls to action: The wireframe served as a guideline, it was not the final word. Your end result, too, will often have a variety of minor changes and updates compared to the content of your wireframe.

Fred Beecher, Lead User Experience Consultant at Evantage Consulting (http://evantageconsulting.com) provides an example of a wireframe with annotations from the field (**Figure 12.5**).

\\ FUNCTIONAL SPECIFICATION

Home

Here are some general notes about this page as a whole. This text can discuss the purpose of the page, audience, etc. Anything that applies to the page as a whole as opposed to information about specific UI elements. See the Annotations table for that information.

Additional content headings can also appear up here, such as Business Rules, Error Messages, etc.

Wireframe

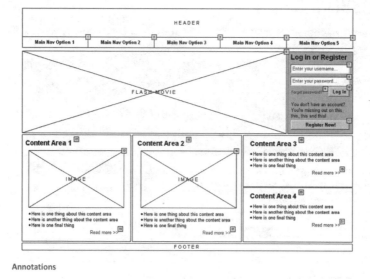

Annotations

Footnote	Label	Description	Control Type	Content Type	Possible Values	Business Rules	Link Destination
1	Main Nav 1	Clicking this link brings users to the XXX section hub page	Button (Navigation)	Text	Off; Hover; On		XXX section hub page
2	Main Nav 2	Clicking this link brings users to the XXX section hub page	Button (Navigation)	Text	Off; Hover; On		XXX section hub page
3	Main Nav 3	Clicking this link brings users to the XXX section hub page	Button (Navigation)	Text	Off; Hover; On		XXX section hub page

EVANTAGE
CONSULTING

5

Figure 12.5 A wireframe with annotations, created in Axure

Creating Wireframes:
A Sample Process

What do you need to get started on your first wireframe? You need to start by having as much information as possible in regards to your project. Hopefully, you will have access to information-packed artifacts such as

▶ Business requirements

▶ Design briefs, or creative briefs, or other named briefs that are relevant. For more information on design briefs, see *Communicating Design* by Dan Brown (New Riders, 2010)

▶ Stakeholder interviews

▶ Research performed

▶ Website analytics

▶ Personas that are rich with information about your users

▶ Site map

▶ User/Task flows or paths

▶ Content strategy documentation

▶ Statement of work

▶ ...anything else that you can find that is related to the project

Consume all of this. Voraciously. Get familiar with all the information that is available to you—hopefully you will have been involved throughout the project to this point and you will not have to engage in an exercise of cramming information into your brain.

Then you need some pencils and some paper. If you would like to use sketchboards for helping you in this process, Todd Zaki Warfel generously supplies them at http://zakiwarfel.com/archives/sketchboard-templates/.

And then you need to sketch.

What is This Sketching You Mention?

Bill Buxton said it best in *Sketching User Experiences: The Workbook* by Saul Greenberg, Sheelagh Carpendale, Nicolai Marquardt, and Bill Buxton (Morgan Kaufmann, 2011):

> Sketching is not about drawing. Rather, it is about design. Primarily, it is:
>
> ▶ A fundamental tool that helps designers express, develop and communicate design ideas;
>
> ▶ A critical part of a process that begins with idea generation, to design elaboration, to design choices, and ultimately to engineering.

This is very important. When you sketch before you get into a digital design tool of any sort, it allows you to rapidly explore myriad ideas, expand upon

Ask the Experts: Todd Zaki Warfel

Todd Zaki Warfel, author of Prototyping: A Practitioner's Guide *(Rosenfeld Media, 2009), endorses the 6-8-5 approach to sketching. This works well for groups, and you can apply the same type of rigor to your own individual sketching.*

The 6-8-5

Participants are divided up into small teams (typically 3–5). During the first round, they are asked to create 6-8 concept sketches on the 8 up sketch template. Participants are asked to work as individuals within their own teams during the first round. Collaboration and discussing the designs during the initial concept sketching. Following the initial sketching sprint, teams participate in a round robin style pitch and critique. Each member in the team gets 3 minutes to pitch their concept and how it satisfied the goals of the design challenge. The remaining team members get 2 minutes to critique the design and must collectively provide 2–3 ways the design achieved the goals as well as 1–2 ways the design either didn't meet the goals, or ask for further clarification in the next round.

After the team finishes the round-robin style pitch and critique, they come back together and pick from the best ideas as well as items that need further clarification. In the second and subsequent rounds, the team collaborates on the design within the given time constraint.

Oh, and then you give them the kicker. The time constraint is 5 minutes and it starts right now.

the ideas that seem to work the best for your project, and then simply throw away the ones that do not work (or keep them, take photos of them, and save them all away in a portfolio that allows you to highlight your process and thinking skills—hint, hint).

Sketching (**Figure 12.6**) also allows you to, through pitching and critiquing with various audiences from internal teams to clients and stakeholders to users, continue to increase the detail to which you are designing. Once you are at a comfortable point with your sketches, you can open up your favorite digital tool and start exploring those refinements.

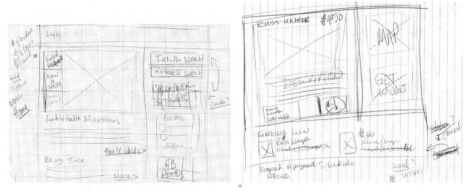

Figure 12.6 *Sketches. The unpretty kind. They do the trick.*

Also, you do not need to be an artist, or even very good at drawing, to sketch. The examples shown in Figure 12.6 are proof of this! If you can draw a circle, a square (or a square with an X through it to represent an image/media asset), a straight line and a triangle, you can draw most of what you would want in rough sketches.

If you want to get really creative with your sketching activities, plan meetings with your project colleagues, your clients, and even users if you have access to them, and get them to help you sketch what your project can look like.

Into the Digital: Wireframes

Now is the time to fire up the digital tool that you want to use to do your wireframes in. The options are many, so many in fact, that there are only a handful listed here, and there are probably more available each month. You have a lot of options; choose what fits into your budget and/or what you are comfortable with or have available to you. The end result is that you have something that you can use to communicate the designs to your audience(s).

Whatever tool you are using, you need to use it to bring your ideas and sketches to a bit more life. How to explain that, well, is not as easy to do in text. The variety of tools at your disposal makes it nearly impossible to complete in the context of a single chapter. Your goal, however, should be to use the sketches that you have created.

So, let's take a look at some pictures!

Remember our sketches from before? Okay, **Figure 12.7** shows them again.

When created in Balsamiq, however, they still have a slightly sketchy feel to them, but there is a dramatic difference in the presentation (**Figure 12.8**).

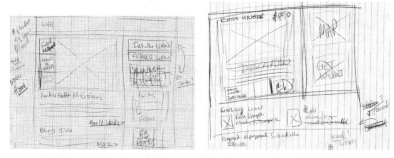

Figure 12.7 *Still the same sketches*

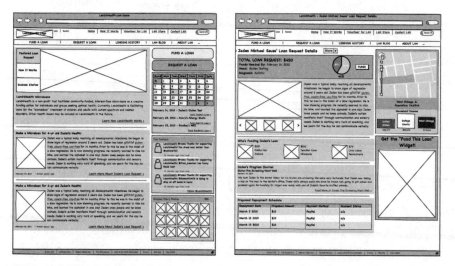

Figure 12.8 *The sketches turned into beautiful Balsamiq wireframes*

The digital tools allow you to get into specific details, better spacing, alignment and just add more clarity to what you were putting into your sketches. Unless you are a really great at sketching and drawing, it can be tough to create designs that express layouts effectively, or in specifically designated space sizes. Those who can do so, and do so well, are gifted and talented folks. Make friends with them.

Into the Digital: Visual Design

What does this all look like when it leaves your hands and gets into the hands of a visual designer? If you have been fortunate enough to collaborate with your content strategists, visual designers, and developers along the way, you probably will not see a grand departure, but you will see something that can be visually stunning and that continues to improve upon what you started way back in sketches, and then refined and improved upon in wireframes (**Figure 12.9**).

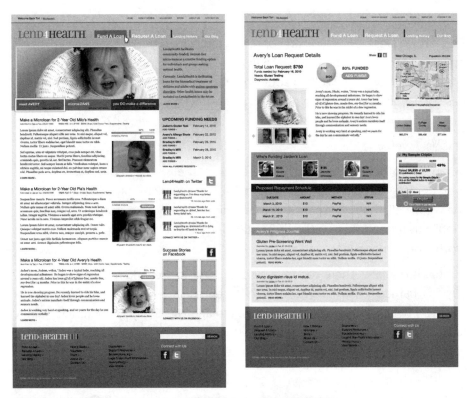

Figure 12.9 Wireframes turned into stunning design. Preciousssssss...

Ask the Experts: Brad Simpson

Brad Simpson, Principal at Bakery, LLC (http://done-n-done.com), finds that working closely with UX helps his visual design process.

I have worked in design for many years, and the more closely I work with the UX team—and the developers—over the course of a project the better the end result will be. It all has to make sense and every item has to have a purpose—working in collaboration with UX and the development team ensures that what I do lives up to the purpose and function intended. And by doing that, my part is better for it. Designers, embrace your Account, UX and Dev teams and the results will be amazing and every stakeholder will be proud.

Hey, What About This Responsive Design Stuff I Hear About?

Responsive Design is taking an approach that allows you to code a website once, but allows it to be flexible to fit the device it is being viewed on. The approach is new, the thinking about how to solve it is new, but the problem has sort of plagued the web design space for a long time—how do we make that which we design fit to whatever device that is viewing it?

This. Is. Awesome.

Ethan Marcotte has written an entire book on the topic titled *Responsive Web Design* (A Book Apart, 2011), and if you are working on projects for the web, well, those projects are in very high likelihood to eventually have mobile users, and that makes understanding Responsive Design entirely worth your time to learn more about.

But this is not free. There can be a bit of a "cost" to creating responsive designs, particularly when you involve stakeholders and clients that are not, well, you. That is, any time anyone needs to approve the way content is going to be displayed, there will probably need to be a paper trail that acknowledges and agrees to something that has been presented. So, while the code may be crafted in such a way that pages beautifully resize themselves for the devices that they are being viewed on, there is still a need to account for—and guide—how the design will update itself based upon the context of where it is being viewed. This means more wireframes for most of us.

The sketches and wireframes shown in **Figure 12.10** are representations of how the same design could be viewed in different browser sizes, possibly a tablet and a smartphone.

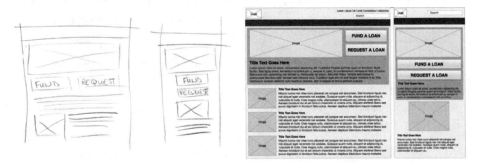

Figure 12.10 Sketches and wireframes of something slightly more responsive...

There are additional online resources to help you learn more about approaches to having your design accommodate responsive layouts:

▶ Responsive Web Design by Ethan Marcotte on A List Apart
  (http://www.alistapart.com/articles/responsive-web-design)

▶ Responsive Layout Wireframe at Wireframes Magazine
  (http://wireframes.linowski.ca/2011/09/responsive-layout-wireframe)

▶ The Goldilocks Approach to Responsive Web Design
  (http://goldilocksapproach.com)

As more new approaches to design and development materialize, it will become increasingly more important to understand the impact of those on your UX work. In many cases, simply being aware of the varying approaches can help you ask the right questions early in a project, which allows you to be better prepared as you do your work.

Wireframes Vs. Prototypes

When it comes to choosing whether or not to create wireframes or prototypes, you can find dissenting opinions across the UX communities. Either wireframes or prototypes can be successful for you, but how you choose which approach to take can depend upon a few things:

▶ What are you comfortable with using and knowledgeable in creating?

▶ What is your client comfortable with reviewing? Sophistication can vary among clients and setting expectations is important, regardless of which approach you take.

▶ What do you have the time, resources, and budget available to deliver upon?

Use whatever approach fits into this list. The mantra should be "what works for this situation right now?" and not what happens to work for someone else or is someone else's dogma.

Regardless of which approach you choose, you should still sketch first.

Which Design Is Right?

There is no right—or wrong—design, as long as the requirements are met. At times you may feel compelled to create multiple wireframes for a single page, to explore various approaches, to work through the details, and to present to potential users, teammates, and possibly your clients.

This is completely acceptable.

Remember that this is an exercise in iterations. The work that you present to a client is almost always guaranteed to not be considered "correct" or "final" on the first try. More often than not, you will find yourself working through at least one round of iterations and updates. Unfortunately, that can sometimes extend to multiple rounds—but that is the nature of projects, and it should ultimately lead to less exploration for your downstream work partners.

As you compare your wireframe and annotations to the two examples provided, examine the difference in approach and style of presentation. Compare these to the home page example earlier in the chapter and to the work that you did. Find the similarities and differences and create the approach that works best for you, unless there's an established template in place for you already.

In many cases, the hardest part about creating a wireframe is getting your pencil to your paper for the first time. Follow Leah Buley's advice and start sketching out multiple ideas—doodle and draw, explore different approaches, and test your designs with coworkers, peers, and family members until you feel confident that you can defend your design (without being defensive), and you will find yourself moving in the right direction.

A Final Note on Presenting Wireframes

Once you start creating wireframes and become more comfortable with the work product—and understand how valuable they are to your workflow—it's easy to forget that not everyone understands the amount of thought and time that goes into creating them. Often, clients and work partners may have been exposed to wireframes of a completely different quality level, complexity, or with a different style of annotations.

In fact, you may find that many of your work partners and clients have never seen a wireframe before (even if they say that they have). It's also not uncommon for clients and work partners to get confused about the differences between site maps and wireframes, and the purpose of each.

In other words, your first wireframe could potentially be your client's first wireframe as well! This makes it extremely important to accurately set the stage for what you are going to present. Before presenting the wireframes you need to clearly explain what they are, what they will look like in comparison to a final visual design, and what their purpose is.

Here's some additional advice for presenting wireframes:

▶ If possible, engage your client's team during discovery; try to get them involved in actively drawing on a whiteboard. Explain that they are contributing to the wireframing process and that the end result will look similar, but it will be produced in an electronic format. It is very important to explain that this is an activity that will lead to wireframes that may look completely different as you explore design options.

▶ Find strong metaphors to convey the differences between your wireframes and the final design of the project. A popular metaphor is

"Wireframes are to applications/websites what blueprints/floorplans are to a house." Wireframes allow changes to be implemented more easily and efficiently, and at a stage when changes are generally less expensive (prior to engaging the build teams and pouring the foundation).

▶ Tell your meeting attendees that the wireframes are *not* a final representation of the graphical treatment of the site. The wireframes are being presented to account for content, general layout, and interaction of the elements of the pages. Once wireframes have been approved, the building can begin. (Oh, and subtle changes may still occur!)

▶ Engage your visual designers—if there is time and budget—to provide design mock-ups to show the differences between your wireframes and a final design. If possible, show the client examples from other projects that demonstrate how wireframes and final designs are similar and different at the same time.

▶ Explain how other members of your project team will use the wireframes—it never hurts for a client to understand the importance of their review and approval of this milestone, as well as how wireframes inform the rest of the project.

Once your clients and work partners start to understand and appreciate the value of wireframes and where they live in the design process, it becomes easier to move your projects along.

Why?

Because wireframes help create visual clarity and direction throughout the rest of the project. In many cases, work partners and clients may even evangelize the usefulness of wireframes on your behalf. This allows you to spend more time focusing on user experience design and less time selling it!

13 Prototyping

Breathing (Some Sort of) Life into Your Designs

Prototyping is an effective way of testing and validating proposed functionality and designs prior to investing in development. Prototyping is also a great way to experiment and ideate with your team and/or your clients, especially when it comes to dealing with page view flows or complex interactions. You can use a number of tools and approaches—from the quick-and-dirty to the interactive and robust—to create prototypes. Your method will largely be determined by three factors: First, the purpose, or intent, of your prototype. What are you trying to accomplish through prototyping? Who is the intended audience? Second, the resources (tools, materials, and skill) that you have at your disposal to dedicate toward prototype development. And finally, your timeline— you've gotta get it done when it's gotta get done.

Jonathan Knoll & Russ Unger

In the context of user experience design, *prototyping* is the act of (and in many cases, the art of) creating, mimicking, or testing all or part of the functionality of an application or website with users. Prototypes can be created in an analog state (such as with whiteboards or pencil and paper) or in a digital state (with PowerPoint or Keynote, Acrobat, Visio, OmniGraffle, Axure, HTML, or other technology-based tools).

Prototyping should be an iterative process because prototypes are generally created to identify issues with—or to validate—the user experience. Once you gather feedback, you can make modifications to the prototype for additional testing. In other cases, a successful (enough) prototype can keep a project moving forward into other phases of the development lifecycle.

Remember that prototyping is a *process*—it's not an artifact. You might end up creating screens and (sometimes mock) functionality that you call a prototype, but these are *a part* of prototyping; they are not the end result. The outcome of the prototyping process is actionable internal or external feedback on concepts in order to enhance and improve the design.

This chapter, however, focuses on creation of the prototype only, leaving the details of testing to Chapter 14.

How Much Prototype Do I Need?

Any user experience design process should include some degree of prototyping—whether it is formal or informal, interactive or inactive. Prototyping does not have to be performed for an entire website or application. In fact, prototyping can be very effective when using a representative sampling of a system; in other words, you don't have to create a simulation of the entire system, you only need to simulate key parts and/or interactions. In most cases, you will want to test a handful of concepts and your prototype should include only those concepts.

You can engage in prototyping using any number of methods that are readily available to you: whiteboarding, pencil-and-paper sketching, storyboarding, cardboard cut-outs, and so on. In addition, a growing number of digital tools are available that allow you to create interactive prototypes and engage your test users in a more realistic environment.

The method of prototyping that you choose will largely depend upon the time and materials available to you, as well as your target audience and their sophistication level. The following sections cover some of the more popular methods available to meet many of your prototyping needs.

Paper Prototyping

Few activities can take you back to your early years quite like the hands-on, arts-and-crafts approach of paper prototyping. The only tools needed are pencils and pens, paper, scissors, and anything you can swipe from the art department or buy at a local office supply store.

Paper prototyping is flexible. As long as you have an eraser or more materials, you can create as many scenarios as you need. You can also revise rapidly from test to test—that is, if a potential user calls out a glaring error in something you have created, it is not a complex process to update the design before showing to the next potential user.

It's also cheap. Beyond the amount of time you invest in paper prototyping, you can generally create any scenario for much less than the cost of a couple of highbrow lattes. Paper, sticky notes, index cards, pencils, and the like should already be at your disposal, and if they aren't, you won't break the bank by stocking up.

The process is simple: Sketch the portion of the functionality you want to test. Present the functionality to the user(s). Document the feedback (it's paper, so flip your prototype over and start writing). Then move on to the next user, or make updates and start over.

Simple. Fun. Effective.

Used early in the process, paper prototyping can help uncover design-related issues before you've become heavily invested. Changes at this stage can be made quickly and efficiently, reducing your risk. This allows you to make efficient changes prior to investing too much in the design.

Using three sheets of different colored paper, each tab in **Figure 13.1** was sketched as it would display on the website, then they were stacked on top of each other. The Global Now tab is placed on top to display its content as if the user had just visited the home page for the first time. Each tab shows the navigation available to the users and allows them to select a different viewing option.

When a user selects a different tab, that particular tab is moved to the front of the stack to show the newly active tab's view of the content area, such as the My Itinerary tab displayed in **Figure 13.2**.

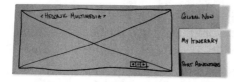
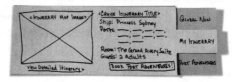

Figure 13.1 *Paper prototype of a vertical, tab-based navigation*

Figure 13.2 *Paper prototype of a vertical tab-based navigation with the My Itinerary tab activated*

Paper prototyping is about as low-budget as you can get and can be as simple as the exercise above. When you start exploring full systems, the hours you invest can become substantial (though your material costs increase only slightly). If you need to change the primary navigation on a hundred pages of paper prototypes, this method becomes costly. While paper prototyping is essentially low cost, it does not scale well for reuse when pieces need to be updated. At that point you should consider whether moving to digital tools would be more beneficial.

Digital Prototyping

If your prototyping needs are greater than paper can handle, you may find that a technology-based solution works better for you and your audience. These tools can enable you to showcase exactly how interactive portions of the site or application will appear to users.

Digital prototyping pulls from many other aspects of the design process. You'll be able to refer to your personas when presenting or testing your digital prototype, to your wireframes for blocking and visual treatment of the prototype, and to visual design assets (if they are available at this point in the process) for a realistic fit and finish to your prototype.

Wireframe vs. Realistic Prototypes

Just as with paper prototyping methods, your mileage may vary with digital prototypes. Depending on the tools, resources, and skills you have at your disposal, as well as the requirements you are dealing with, you may find that having your prototype look like wireframes is good enough for your project. In fact, it may be preferable. Wireframes can show the audience that the project is still a work in progress and not the final, production-ready site.

On the other hand, sometimes during design testing with users, you will find that the most important aspect of the prototype is how realistically it represents the final system.

The outcome of your digital prototype rests on three factors:

▶ **Who are you building this prototype for, and why?**

It is vital to the success of your prototype to know what you're doing with it before you get too deep into the project. Are you building a prototype for design testing with users? If so, what is important to focus on for the testing? Does it matter if the prototype is a black-and-white wireframe, or does it need to resemble a live website? Are you testing for discoverability of buttons and links?

Are you building the prototype for a business pitch that needs buy-in from a team of executives, managers, investors, or others who might be signing your paycheck at the end of the day? If so, what are you trying to communicate to them? What needs to *be* functional and what simply needs to *look* functional? These questions may help determine the requirements for your digital prototype.

▶ **What types of resources, tools, and skills do you have available?**

If you are not an HTML or Flash expert, and don't have the budget to engage someone who is, you can still build a very functional prototype by using a simple presentation tool like PowerPoint or Keynote or by using a wireframing tool like Visio or OmniGraffle. Even a simple PDF might work.

▶ **What does your timeline look like?**

Do you have the time to pull together a team and build an amazing, almost production-ready prototype that will show the users a crystal-clear vision of the production-ready site? Do you have a few hours to export your wireframes as HTML or to build a very simple Flash project to simply show the page flow and basic interactive elements within the project?

Both types of digital prototypes can be very useful. However, just as with any real project with a deadline looming, it's important to set expectations based on the time and materials available to you.

HTML vs. WYSIWYG Editors

HTML is the digital equivalent of a paper prototype. It is (sometimes) free and (somewhat) easy. If you aren't an HTML wizard or a front-end code expert, you can still be an HTML prototype wizard with just some basic knowledge of HTML.

There are essentially two ways to build an HTML prototype:

▶ Hand-coding the HTML

▶ Using a WYSIWYG editor, such as Adobe Dreamweaver, Realmac's Rapid-Weaver, or Microsoft Visual Studio. These tools have a code view as well as a layout view that allows you to visualize your code efforts without opening a browser.

In the recent past, those WYSIWYG editors were popular, but more web-based tools have begun to proliferate, such as: Handcraft (formerly Quplo), Justinmind, Balsamiq, IxEdit, Pencil, Mockflow, JustProto, InVision, and Protoshare.

Creating a Prototype with a WYSIWYG Editor

The great thing about using the layout view in a WYSIWYG HTML editor is that you can build a page layout with about the same amount of effort as it would take to lay out a page in Microsoft PowerPoint, Apple's Keynote, or any other simple graphical layout application (more on these later). And it's just as easy to add interactivity such as links, mouse events, and so on.

One of the most impressive aspects of Dreamweaver (**Figure 13.3**) is that it features what Adobe calls the Live View, which is based on the open source WebKit rendering engine. What does this mean? Quite simply, it means that what you see in Live View is exactly what you'll get in Apple's Safari and Google's Chrome browsers—assuming you've been meticulous with the details in your prototype. Dreamweaver is a very powerful prototyping tool, especially when used in conjunction with Adobe Fireworks.

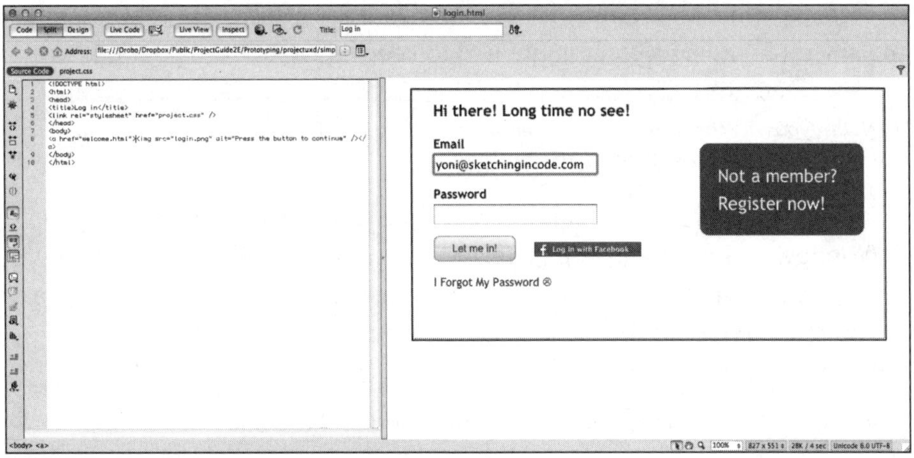

Figure 13.3 *A simple example prototype created in Dreamweaver*

Creating a Basic HTML Prototype

Possibly the least expensive way to build a simple, quick-and-dirty HTML prototype is to do it "by hand"—to type in the code manually in a text-editing tool.

One of the most common reasons for transitioning a design from wireframe to prototype is the requirement to show or test the proposed flow and navigation of the site. By taking blocks of elements or even full pages from your wireframe (or design mock-up) and setting them up as clickable images in your HTML prototype, you can very quickly and easily build a functioning prototype.

One simple prototyping method is to post clickable screenshots that can be viewed in a browser. A user can click to advance the view to a new screen. Wash, rinse, and then repeat. This is fairly straightforward and does not require a lot of "code knowledge" to pull it off in a fairly short amount of time.

In the following exercise, you must have wireframes or screens that you can export as an image file for a log-in page and destination (welcome) page at your disposal. You will need to have two files: `login.png` and `welcome.png,` which are the before and after states of a login process. If you do not currently have those ready, you can download sample images from http://www.projectuxd.com.

This entire exercise will be a lot easier if you create a folder and keep all of your files in its root. You can get a little more organized later in your code life by creating folder structures that can hold your scripts, style sheets, images, and any other artifacts you might need to keep separate from your pages.

Note *Typos are the most common mistakes made in HTML coding, so pay close attention to the accuracy of your typing.*

---

1. In your WYSIWYG HTML editor or a simple text editor, such as Notepad (Windows), TextMate (Mac), or TextWrangler (Mac), create a new document and save it as `login.html` in the same prototype folder. Make certain you select HTML as the file format in the event another file format has been set as the default.

2. In your new document, insert the following HTML code:

```
<!DOCTYPE html>
<html>
<head>
<title>Log in</title>
</head>
<body>
<a href="welcome.html"><img src="login.png" alt="Log in" /></a>
</body>
</html>
```

3. Save the document and then open the file in your web browser. You should see the log-in image you exported or downloaded, and the browser's title bar should display "Log in" (**Figure 13.4**).

4. The most important line of code in your document is:

```
<a href="welcome.html"><img src="login.png" alt="Log in" /></a>
```

This line adds your image to the page you have created and turns it into a link that loads the `welcome.html` page (which you'll create next).

In your text editor, save a copy of the `login.html` file, but save it as `welcome.html`.

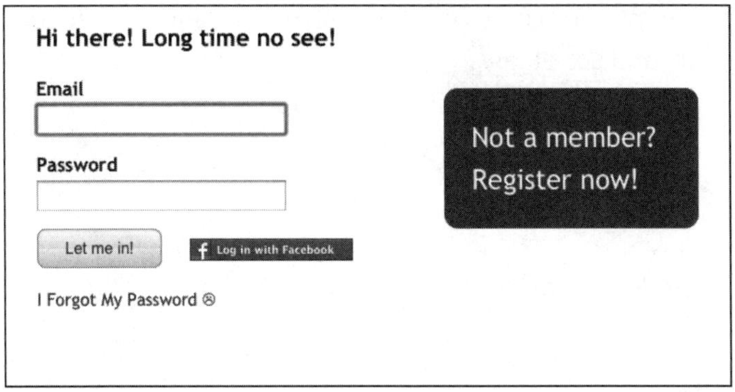

Figure 13.4
The login.html *live and in the browser*

In welcome.html, replace this line of code:

```
<a href="welcome.html"><img src="login.png" alt="Log in" /></a>
```

with:

```
<a href="login.html"><img src="welcome.png" alt="Start over" /></a>
```

5. Then save your file and re-open login.html in your browser. You know you want to, so do it: Click anywhere on the image in your browser. DO IT!

6. You now have built a simple prototype demonstrating a log-in process (**Figure 13.5**).

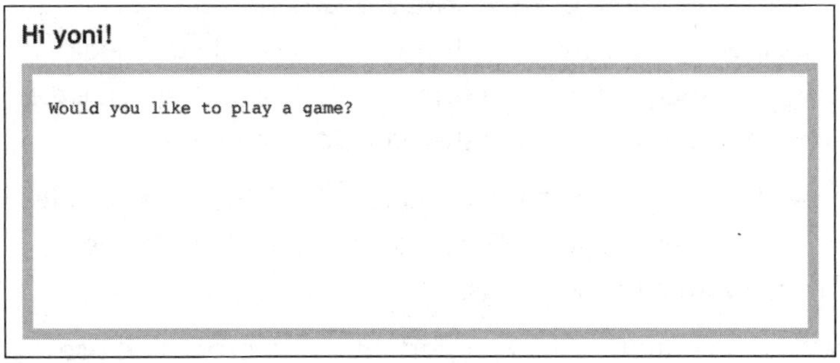

Figure 13.5
welcome.html *live and in the browser*

Breaking Down the Code

Now that you have created a basic prototype using a very limited amount of HTML, it's time to briefly walk through the code, or HTML markup, so you can have a better understanding of what you just created.

At the top of your document, the basics of any HTML document are placed: DOCTYPE, HTML, HEAD, TITLE, and BODY tags.

```
<!DOCTYPE html>
<html>
<head>
    <title>About</title>
</head>
<body>
</body>
</html>
```

These basic tags are required in any HTML document. The DOCTYPE simply tells the browser how it should read the markup (code) on the page. The DOCTYPE shown here indicates that the code below will conform to the HTML5 specification (mostly, though, this will just make developers happy that you care—it's not integral to most of what is happening under the covers).

The HTML tag is the root element of any HTML document—all other tags will be contained within it. The HEAD tag is a *container* for other tags that have information *for* or *about* the document. These tags tell your browser (as well as search engines!) what's coming. If your HTML document were a book, the HEAD tag would contain everything from the front cover up until the beginning of Chapter 1. The key player for your purposes, though, is the TITLE element, which lets you tell the browser what the name of the page is.

Finally, there is the BODY element. The BODY tag starts where the HEAD tag left off. In other words, the content of your HTML document—what the user sees—should be placed within the BODY tags.

It should not go without mentioning how important it is to properly close your HTML tags. Take another look at the HTML, HEAD, TITLE, and BODY tags. Most HTML elements have both start and end tags. The start tag (`<html>` or `<title>`) indicates the beginning of an element; the end tag (`</html>` or `</title>`) signifies the end of the element. Properly closing your elements is crucial to making sure browsers interpret your HTML document correctly.

Even a simple document can blow up—not display or function correctly—due to a missing closing tag. As you learn more about HTML markup, you'll find that a well-structured HTML document is also a way to communicate information architecture to your developers, especially if it takes advantage of all of HTML5's new semantic tags.

Getting back to the code, the IMG tag is used to add an image element to your document. It is all that you need to make sure that an image is displayed in a browser—assuming you have its src (path or URL) correct. In the following code example, it is assumed that the image file is in the root directory (the same directory as the HTML file referencing it):

```
<img src="login.png" alt="Press the button to continue" />
```

The ALT attribute is intended to provide the *alternative* text to display if the image cannot load. This isn't particularly important for most prototypes, so you can hijack the attribute and use it to provide simple instructions for your users when they hover their mouse over the image. What about an end tag? Since the contents of an image element are defined by the src and alt attributes, an IMG tag will not—and cannot—contain other tags or text, so it doesn't need an end tag. Other common tags which do not have an end tag include the INPUT tag (used to add various form elements to a document) and the BR tag (to force a line break).

Anchor elements—represented by an A tag—are used to essentially *link* to someplace *else*, which is indicated within the href portion of the tag:

```
<a href="welcome.html">Link text</a>
```

For the sake of remaining simple, the A tag in the example uses a *relative path*—"relative" because the files for this tutorial are all in the same (or root) folder. An absolute path looks like this:

```
<a href="http://www.sketchingincode.com/projectuxd/index.html">Link
text</a>
```

Anchor tags can also be used to link to a specific element within an HTML document. When they are used this way, there will be a hash (#) followed by the ID of the target element. The following link refers to an element on the index.html page with "basic" as its ID (the value of the id attribute):

```
<a href="http://www.sketchingincode.com/projectuxd/index.html#basic">
Link text</a>
```

Clicking on this link will take the user directly to the targeted element on the page. It might look something like this:

```
<p id="basic">some text</p>
```

Using the ID attribute in conjunction with hashed anchor elements also allows quick intra-page navigation, sometimes referred to as bookmarks.

As it happens, the HTML in our example is standards-compliant. As previously mentioned, typos are the most common mistakes when creating code. The ability to check your code using a markup validation service (see http://validator.w3.org) can save you a lot of time in the future.

That said, this is not especially beautiful code. But the purpose of this simple prototype example is to communicate your ideas to your audience—not to impress developers (not yet, at least).

This simple markup example linked multiple HTML pages by any click on the image. This is about as simple as it gets. But what if you want to get more granular with the clickable areas within the layout?

The answer: image maps.

With image maps, you can designate areas of an image to link to and display different pages when clicked. One of the easiest ways to create image maps is to use a WYSIWYG tool (such as Dreamweaver) to assign linkable sections of an image. You can do this without any real knowledge of how to create the HTML code, as most WYSIWYG tools allow you "draw" over the image to define the space that will contain the link.

> **Note** *For more information on how to create image maps, see the "How do I create an image map for my web page" tutorial by Dave Taylor at http://www.askdavetaylor.com/how_do_i_create_an_image_map_for_my_web_page.html.*

A Little More Than Basic

Even with image maps defining your clickable areas, a prototype can become unmanageable in a hurry if you're working with a lot of different states, user flows, or pages.

If you want to expand your basic prototyping skills so that you can display a page with form elements, include the ability to submit it, and then display a response to the form, well, it gets a bit more challenging. You probably would need to read some books or do a lot of online research to find some different examples to help you on your way. Sometimes, it's more difficult to search and find what you are looking for than it is to find someone else to do it for you. In any case, if you had a little JavaScript at your disposal and knew how it worked, you could probably pull off some impressive stuff—or at least add some interactions to your pages. If you're comfortable looking at HTML markup and you're interested in learning more about JavaScript, *DOM Scripting: Web Design with JavaScript and the Document Object Model* by Jeremy Keith (http://amzn.com/1590595335) is a great book to get started with. For an in-depth look at practical techniques—including some useful examples—try out John Resig's *Pro JavaScript Techniques* (http://amzn.com/1590597273).

This will *not* be a lesson in "all things JavaScript"; instead, we will use a popular JavaScript library that you have probably already heard of: jQuery (http://jquery.com).

If you are interested in a few slightly more advanced examples, Jonathan Knoll, Designer+Architect at InfinityPlusOne, has created them for you to learn from. Visit http://sketchingincode.com/projectuxd. The additional examples include a slightly advanced Log-in that allows you to communicate additional states of view without actually leaving a web page and a registration page that also lets you pass variables (as in a user name or email address) to a new page.

We've provided the code on a 5.25" floppy in the back of this book. Okay, since this is not a 1986 magazine on the Vic-20, we've actually supplied it all online for you. Bad jokes aside, you can find the code online at http://sketchingincode.com/projectuxd.

Example 1

This is a prototype that demonstrates a log-in experience. It is identical to the clickable image prototype provided previously, except this is entirely in code (the clickable images were left at home for this example). You will see a Log-in page (**Figure 13.6** on the next page).

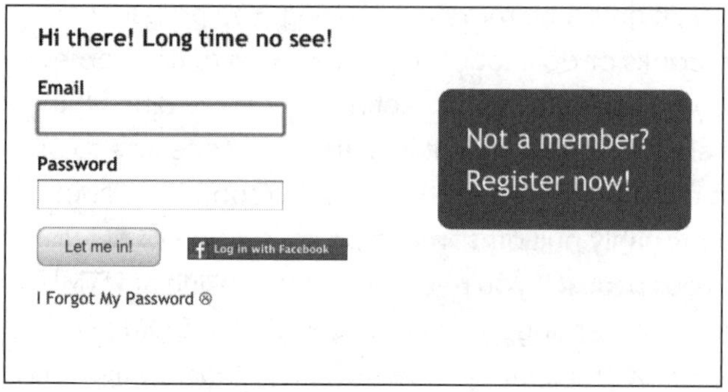

Figure 13.6
The log-in screen

Once you click through, the prototype loads a Welcome page that displays, "Hi yoni!," indicating that you have successfully signed into the website (**Figure 13.7**).

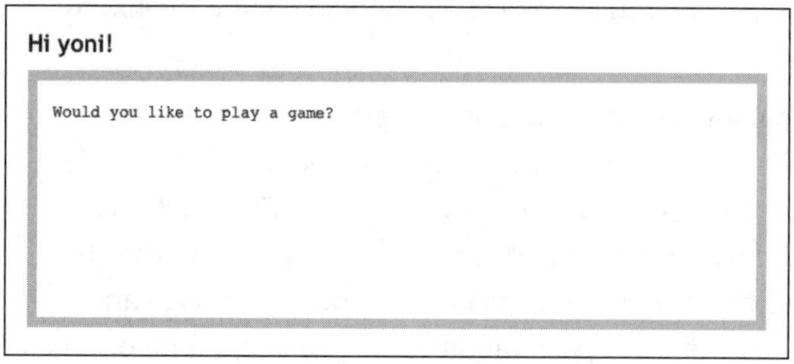

Figure 13.7
The Welcome screen

Example 2

This is a prototype that demonstrates a simple registration experience. This example uses jQuery to load a new image after clicking on the current image displayed on the page. You will see a Register page with nothing filled out (**Figure 13.8**).

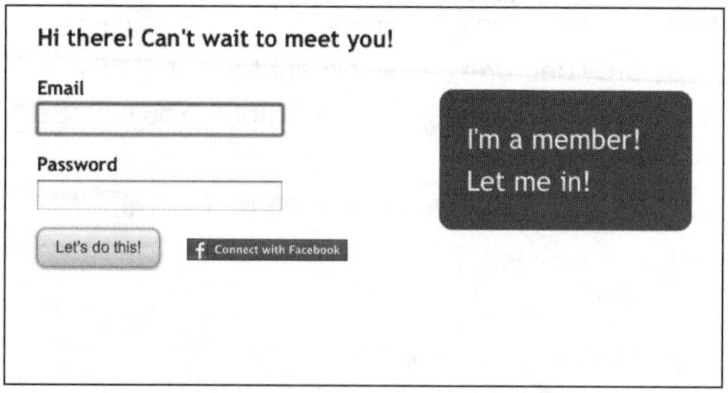

Figure 13.8
The Register screen

Upon clicking, a Register page with the email address entered into the email address field loads (**Figure 13.9**).

Click again to see the second step of the registration process (**Figure 13.10**).

Click a final time to load the Welcome page view (**Figure 13.11**).

For your benefit and exploration purposes, live examples of all of these prototypes—as well as all of the files that were used to create them—are available online for you to view and/or download at http://sketchingincode.com/projectuxd.

Sometimes you need more...

Image-based prototypes are great for contextualizing designs, demonstrating user flows and basic interactions, or for eliciting basic feedback. But sometimes you need more. In fact, one could argue that the Log-in example above is precisely the type of thing you should be testing with greater realism.

Users hate form fields, so any time you need to design and test a form, there's a good chance that your best bet is an HTML prototype with actual HTML form elements. This will allow you to test without providing too much guidance, and will allow you to observe unexpected behaviors.

To see and learn how to turn the previous prototype into a fully interactive prototype, go to http://sketchingincode.com/projectuxd.

HTML prototyping is just one approach to digital prototyping, and there a lot of ways to go about it. Many different frameworks and dynamic coding languages can be used to create very robust prototypes to meet almost any need. If HTML prototyping is an area you want to explore and expand upon, you might want to seek out tutorials and other resources for more of a deep dive in that area. To get started, you might want to research JavaScript, PHP (or other dynamic coding languages), jQuery (http://jquery.com) or the Yahoo! Interface Library (http://developer.yahoo.com/yui).

Note *For a deeper exploration into HTML, see* Introducing HTML 5 *by Bruce Lawson and Remy Sharp (New Riders, 2011). To learn more about Cascading Style Sheets, see* Stunning CSS3: A Project-Based Guide to the Latest in CSS *by Zoe Mickley Gillenwater (New Riders, 2011).*

Additional Tools for Prototyping

You've now explored hands-on options that can help you create prototypes in both analog and digital spaces. In addition to these methods, there are a number of other software tools that you can use to create prototypes that range from the basic "getting the job done" to ones that are more robust and filled with interaction and intelligence. The following list is far from inclusive, but it will provide you with a variety of options for creating the right prototype for your situation:

- ▶ PowerPoint & Keynote: Presentation software applications

- ▶ Keynote KungFu (http://keynotekungfu.com): Travis Isaacs has a great approach to visual prototyping

- ▶ Adobe Acrobat PDFs: Can be used to link pages of content based upon click interactions

- ▶ Visio & OmniGraffle: Pretty standard PC and Mac wireframing tools

- ▶ Axure RP: Wireframing with built-in methods for documentation and prototyping

- ▶ Adobe Fireworks: Fireworks has a standard set of UI elements that make prototyping relatively quick

- ▶ There is also a growing list of online tools for creating prototypes, such as InVision (http://invisionapp.com), Handcraft (http://handcraft.com), Justinmind Prototyper (http://justinmind.com/), mockingbird (http://gomockingbird.com) and many, many others

- ▶ Balsamiq Mockups: A very inexpensive tool that is designed with the non-designer in mind; rough and unpolished on purpose, with the intent of quickly getting a message across to your audience

- ▶ A developer: Someone who knows how to code better and faster than you and who will work with you to get to "something clickable" quickly

Working with a Developer

If you have the resources available to you, you may want to engage a developer to create a prototype for you based on your wireframes or designs. Note that the developer will need to have a firm understanding of what you are trying to accomplish, so this approach may require that you also create development specifications and requirements for the process to be efficient and effective.

If your prototype is being used for iterative testing, make sure that you communicate which parts of the prototype you are focusing on for testing and will therefore require changes to be implemented quickly. It is advisable to spend time with the developer during the development process and identify key areas of the code that should be flagged (with comments in the code) as susceptible to change. Be sure to remain engaged with your developer during the prototype development to keep the lines of communication open and ensure accuracy of the output.

Note For greater detail on a variety of prototyping approaches, see the book, A Practitioner's Guide to Prototyping, by Todd Zaki Warfel (Rosenfeld Media: http://www.rosenfeldmedia.com/books/prototyping).

Prototype Examples

The simple, easy-to-execute examples of prototyping in this chapter are far from a complete set of approaches that you should use for every situation. To highlight some real-world uses of prototyping, Keith Tatum and Jon Hadden generously shared from their experiences.

Keith Tatum, Creative Director, Retail Direct Client Team at Resource Interactive, created the paper prototype in **Figure 13.12** to explain the left-hand navigation links and identify the navigation hierarchies and categorizations to his collaboration partners at Align Interactive (www.aligninteractive.com). In addition, the paper prototyping process allowed him to bypass the wireframe phase and move into visual design and layout (**Figure 13.13**).

Keith took advantage of his team's common understanding of the design and development tasks to quickly create a design within two workdays. This allowed the team to proceed with development quickly upon approval of the visual design concept (**Figure 13.14**).

Jon Hadden (www.jonhadden.com), Senior User Experience Designer at space150, created a prototype of the calendaring functionality for a tool he is building called Project Manager. Project Manager is a collaborative, web-based application for managing projects. It began as OmniGraffle wireframes and was then built as a high-fidelity XHTML prototype to help determine if the functionality was both usable and affordable.

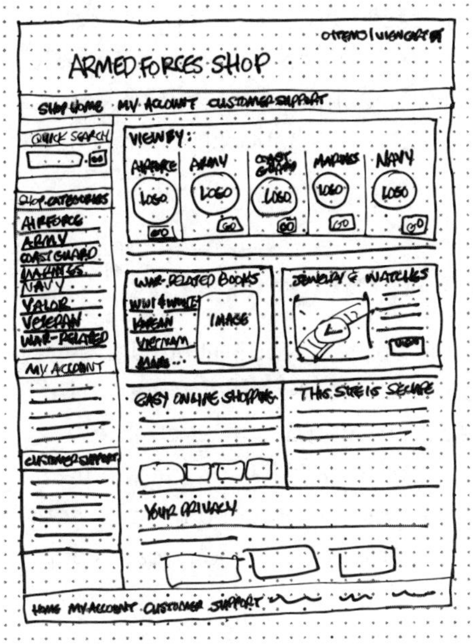

Figure 13.12 *Paper prototype used to explain navigation concepts to development team*

Figure 13.13 *Live website design based on paper prototype*

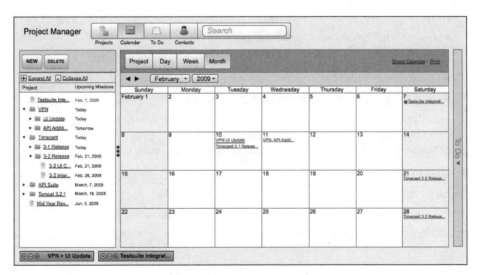

Figure 13.14 *Functional prototype of a calendar tool, mocked up using high-fidelity XHTML, CSS, and JavaScript. Courtesy of Jon Hadden.*

Affordability is an important point: In some cases, portions of an application or project can be put to the prototype test to see if the functionality is cost effective. If the cost of creating functionality becomes a concern and prototype development exceeds time-and-materials expectations, you may need to evaluate the viability of your project.

What Happens After Prototyping?

Once you have completed your prototyping process, you will need to synthesize your results and turn them into something actionable. If you were paper prototyping, you might need to begin creating digital wireframes based on the feedback you received. If you are already in a digital wireframe mode, you may need to update your wireframes and proceed through your project process. Or, you may need to take your feedback and update your prototype for another round of reviews.

Todd Zaki Warfel, president of Messagefirst (www.messagefirst.com), shared the following:

> Prototypes are a way to achieve one or more of the following goals:
>
> ▶ Work your way through a design
> ▶ Create a common communication platform
> ▶ Sell your design ideas internally (e.g., to your boss, other designers, etc.)
> ▶ Test technical feasibility
> ▶ Test design concepts with end users/customers
>
> Prototyping serves as a feedback mechanism. Through prototyping, you can determine whether to continue with a particular design direction or explore a different one, prior to moving on to the next phases of your project.

Remember: Regardless of where you are in the process, prototyping is just a piece of the process, and as with any other piece, you need to be aware of when you have reached the point of maximum effectiveness and are ready to move on to the next stage of the user experience process.

14 Design Testing with Users
Break Away from What You Think You Know—And Find Out How They Think

In Chapter 6 we covered several UX design techniques that can help you understand your user groups—their needs, attitudes, and preferences as they relate to the overall subject matter represented by your site.

This chapter discusses techniques that will help you gather user information about particular designs or elements of designs. We'll focus on exploratory techniques often used early in the design phase and on testing to validate design decisions, which can be used at many points in your project. First, let's talk about exploring design concepts with your users.

Carolyn Chandler

*C*oncept is generally the word used to describe an abstract idea, such as happiness, collaboration, or efficiency. In the field of UX design, *concept* is also used to refer to design elements that are meant to represent one or more abstract ideas to the project team or a potential user. In this sense of the word, a conceptual design element can be visual (for example, a photo of a machine to represent the concept of efficiency) or it can be text-based (for example, a short collection of sentences written to express a company's focus on efficiency, using words such as *timely* and *responsive*). *Concept* can also mean the exploration of wireframes, visual design mock-ups, or rough prototypes that are meant to express the general messaging on the site (see Chapter 13 for more on prototyping).

Concept exploration typically happens early in the design process, after you've defined your user groups but before you've gotten into the detail of each page or screen. The research can provide inspiration for designers and reduce some of the risk of bringing a new product to market, because you'll be able to hear (and then plan for) the kinds of reactions you may get from potential users.

The primary purpose of concept exploration is to understand the kinds of responses and ideas that are elicited from your user groups when faced with a set of design elements.

Concept exploration may consist of one-on-one discussions or may take place in a group but include some individual activities aimed at gathering and discussing a variety of viewpoints. The latter can be set up like a focus group, with a portion of the time dedicated to concept-testing activities, followed by a group discussion (see Chapter 6 for more on focus groups).

Let's look at an example of concept exploration that was performed for a nonprofit microfinance organization.

Microfinance is the funding of very small loans for entrepreneurs in impoverished countries. These loans can allow the borrowers to build businesses and as a result improve the lives of their families and communities. The loan funds come from individuals who come together to lend or donate small amounts to make up a larger loan (for example, $25 each to fund a loan of

$800 needed by a store owner in Kenya). The entrepreneurs pay back the loan as the business grows.

The funding model is very powerful, but the organization sometimes found it challenging to explain the concept in simple terms.

In addition to having the challenge of describing microfinance, the organization was also unsure about how to handle messaging and design with regard to religion. This particular microfinance organization was inspired by the faith of the founders and employees. Many in the organization wanted to make this inspiration apparent in the design of the site, but they were unsure about how to hit the right balance: If the presentation of religious messages was too strong, it could alienate potential givers who were not members of that faith. Too subtle, and the organization would not be truly representing its values.

Potential Pitfalls of Concept Exploration

Henry Ford once said, "If I asked my customers what they wanted, they would have asked for a faster horse." Although you may get some great ideas out of exploring concepts with potential users, you don't want to rely on them to stand in for designers. After all, the most memorable designs are often very different from what has gone before, and research participants may not be comfortable with a large degree of change.

Participant responses will be rooted in their current understanding. What you're collecting are reactions, not predictions of what they will or will not want in the future. Also keep in mind that many other factors outside of the design itself will influence future behavior (such as positive word of mouth).

Avoid asking participants to make direct choices (like "Which concept is better, A or B?"); instead listen to how they use their own words to describe the concepts presented. The results should be thought of as input into the design process, not a mandate to designers.

For an excellent overview of the potential pitfalls of testing design concepts and for recommendations on how to use the technique well, take a look at this article on the AIGA website: "Design Meets Research," by Debbie Millman and Mike Bainbridge: http://www.aiga.org/content.cfm/design-meets-research

The UX designers on the project decided to explore the possible ways that imagery and text could be used to both explain the microfinance model and represent the religious inspiration of the organization without alienating potential donors. To do this, they chose photos and words that could be used to explain concepts related to the model (such as *self-reliant* and *investment*), and others that represented various degrees of religious messaging (for example, *faith* and *spirituality*).

Focus groups were then planned with participants who fell into the site's target user groups. Two user groups were included: those who indicated that they donate as an expression of their religious beliefs, and those who did not.

For each group, the facilitator explained the donation model (saying nothing about religion). Then each participant was given a sheet of poster board, a set of photos, and a set of words to use, plus additional blank cards for filling in their own words if they chose. They were asked to create a collage that displayed the images and words they would use to explain the model to their friends and family. When they were finished, the participants came together again to present their collages, explaining why they chose certain images and text and why they chose not to include others. **Figure 14.1** shows an example of a collage created in this exercise.

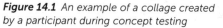
Figure 14.1 *An example of a collage created by a participant during concept testing*

The project team gained valuable insight from these collages and the discussion that followed. Insights included

▶ Participants shied away from imagery that represented success in "Western" terms (for example, business suits and briefcases). They wanted to improve the lives of entrepreneurs without changing their culture.

▶ All user groups agreed that the focus of the site should be on the goal of the organization (providing entrepreneurs with the funding to grow and prosper) rather than the motivation behind it (religious inspiration). Participants believed it was important that the organization remain true to who they were but that those messages could be provided in an area set aside for describing the organization itself (such as an About Us area).

The attitudes and interests that surfaced helped the team decide on a direction for site messaging—and provided a good example of the value of concept testing!

Exploring Visual Design Mock-Ups

At some point in the project, you may have mock-ups that represent the potential design of pages of the site. If you decide to explore designs with participants, it's best to have two or more variations available for them to compare and contrast. With just one, you're more likely to get the "nice" bias: people don't want to sound overly critical of the mock-up because they don't want to hurt the designer's feelings. However, with two or more mock-ups, they will generally feel more comfortable being critical because they're more focused on comparing designs than directly critiquing them.

You can give the participants each design separately (either on a monitor or as a paper printout) and ask a set of questions. For example, you might ask participants to look at each design for a minute and then choose at least three terms from a list that best describe the design. They could circle their choices on a sheet with 20 words such as *boring, trendy, conservative, loud, safe*, and so on in random order.

Responses to open-ended questions could also be gathered. For example, you could give participants five blank lines to write down their general impressions on the design.

Some of the information you might gather includes

▶ Common brand associations made by your participants: "Pseudo Corporation is the Rolls Royce of widget makers: It looks great but you probably can't afford it."

- ▶ Design and lifestyle fit: "I don't think I'd let my son go to this site. He's only 8, and these images look too adult for him."

- ▶ Effectiveness of a particular mock-up in explaining a new concept: "Oh, I get it—this site is like a wedding registry, but you're registering for charity donations instead of dishware."

- ▶ Ways that participants define some of the key terms you're using: "When I see the word *solution* on this site, it makes me think I'm going to find all the products and the services I need to track my shipments."

- ▶ Questions or concerns about how a particular set of tools would be used or the impact of introducing them (the following section illustrates several examples of participant concerns).

Designers can use these responses to judge if the reactions they are getting are along the lines of what they intended or if they may need to try another approach.

Keep in mind that participants (and project stakeholders, for that matter) often cherry-pick different elements from different designs: "I like this part of concept A, and I like this part of concept B." This is a natural reaction, but it shouldn't be taken too literally. You don't want an unnatural melding of two different design directions. If the visual designer does feel that the popular elements blend well together, then go for it. But leave room for her to tell you it's less "chocolate-and-peanut butter" than "chocolate-and-pickle."

Overall, there are no hard-and-fast rules for the activities included in concept tests or the types of elements you can test. Rather, the key is to make sure that you set the right expectations with the project team about the kind of information that will be coming out of the tests and how that information will be used to inform design decisions without stifling creativity.

Choosing a Design Testing Approach

Once you've moved beyond the conceptual exploration and have a proposed direction, it's time to consider testing your design decisions with users.

The testing approach you take will affect the kinds of skills you need, the type of access to users that is necessary, and the space and software required to conduct your research. Include more than one approach if you have the time and budget—each will have its own strengths and weaknesses, and combining two approaches helps you create a full picture. Here are some of the decisions you'll need to make in order to finish with the right kind of data for the problems you're trying to solve.

Qualitative Research vs. Quantitative Research

Research approaches are often described as being either quantitative or qualitative. *Quantitative* research is focused on numerical data and is meant to provide *high-confidence*, *repeatable results* among your target user groups. It relies on your inclusion of a set of users from among that group (called the *sample size*) that is large enough so that findings from it can be used to make inferences about the way the user group as a whole will respond, within a certain range of error. Overall, it's a more scientific approach to research, with a formality to the test design and analysis. The focus is on *assessing* the current design—in particular, against other iterations of the site, against competitors, or against a set of benchmarks.

Performing quantitative research means involving a higher number of participants to account for variations you'll find from individual to individual, like speed of typing, familiarity with similar sites, and so on. Surveys are an example of a method of information gathering that can be expanded to a larger audience, resulting in quantitative data—if you ask the right questions, that is (see Chapter 6 for more on surveys). If quantitative information is important to you, you may also want to consider automated research tools, covered later in this section.

Qualitative research, on the other hand, is not as focused on confidence levels and repeatability, but rather on gaining *context* and *insight* regarding user behavior. It relies on the designer's interpretation of findings, intuition, and common sense. (Contextual inquiry, discussed in Chapter 6, is an example of qualitative research.) A qualitative approach allows an openness to the testing that's conducive to exploring ideas and gaining insights; the discussion with the user is as important as her performance, if not more so. The focus is on *improving* the current design—gaining insight and reactions to what is presented in order to generate ideas.

In-Person Research vs. Remote Research

The research methods covered in this book can all be conducted in person, but some can also be conducted successfully from the comfort of your own home or office. This is called *remote research,* and it's become increasingly effective with the availability of new tools, equipment, and techniques.

Here are some of the factors to weigh when deciding whether to perform research in person or whether to perform it remotely.

▶ **Context of environment**. By conducting research remotely—rather than having the user come to your location or (even better) having you go to their location—you will lose some of the overall context of their environment. Even if you ask them to set up multiple webcams to see their space, there's a discovery when you're in-person that's hard to replicate when you're working remotely (for example, gaining insight by seeing how they're filing particular forms on their desk).

▶ **Context of need.** There's a benefit to using remote research regarding context here. If you're testing a website that's already available and in use, you can gain important contextual information by immediately recruiting users who have come to the site for their own natural reasons. Tools like Ethnio intercept users who have come to your site and ask if they're interested in participating in research. Those who qualify (based on any screening process that might be in effect) are then directed to a facilitator who asks them to participate in an interview or usability test. This is called *time-aware research* and has the great benefit of including actual users who are performing a natural task, which provides highly valuable information on the context of their need. In-person research often doesn't have this useful "just-in-time" element (although contextual inquiry can provide this—see Chapter 6 for more on that method).

▶ **Access.** Here's an area where remote research often proves the best approach. Scheduling in-person research just tends to require more time, both for the facilitator and the participant. Because remote research leaves out travel time, scheduling snafus, and other issues that could cause a missed appointment, it's a lower-commitment way to reach a large number of participants. If your target users are in other countries, or if they have frenetic schedules, remote research can give you better access and encourage a higher participation rate.

▶ **Cost.** Remote research is often thought of as being less expensive than in-person research. This isn't always the case, as remote research tools and equipment cost money, and you still need to plan for the cost of research planning, test design, recruiting, compensation, and analysis (covered later in this chapter). However, remote research does cut out travel costs and time wasted when schedules combust.

Time-Aware Research

In the book *Remote Research*, Nate Bolt and Tony Tulathimutte describe one of the greatest benefits of some remote research approaches—the ability to intercept users as they are performing a task on a site or application. The authors call this "time-aware research."

Try as you might, in-person research will introduce an element of the unnatural. After all, you're either asking someone to leave their typical context (home, work, the train) and to recreate their needs in an unfamiliar space, or you're entering their domain—often when they're in the middle of something else—and asking them to think of a task scenario for testing. Just-in-time interceptions of users make it much easier for them to describe the need that brought them to your site.

For more on time-aware research and other remote techniques, pick up *Remote Research: Real Users, Real Time, Real Research* by Nate Bolt and Tony Tulathimutte (Rosenfeld Media, 2010).

Remote Research Considerations

If you do decide to conduct your research remotely, here are some steps to include in your planning.

▶ **Choose your tools carefully.** The tool you pick should clearly help you achieve your overall research objectives. See the sidebar later in this chapter entitled "A Sampling of Remote Research Tools" for some ideas on tools and their use. Whichever tool you consider, be sure to run through a test scenario with it before committing to it.

▶ **Consider what hardware and software your users are likely to have.** If you want to watch users complete a task remotely, you need to make sure they have dedicated access to a computer as well as an application that allows them to share their screen (note, however, that this could present a security risk, so don't assume they'll have the know-how, ability, or permission to install applications or plug-ins and share their screens). If this is going to be a challenge or frustration for your user groups, you may need to vary your approach (for example, use a survey that can be completed without special software or use an in-person approach instead).

▶ **Test your setup before sessions begin.** There can be a lot of moving parts with remote tools, especially if you're trying to screen users with one tool and conduct the research with others. Add in recording software and equipment, and it can be easy to have missing parts, disrupting your research.

▶ **Have IT troubleshooting expertise at the ready.** Even best-laid plans can go awry, and if you're conducting moderated testing, you may find yourself tap-dancing with an amusing story while on the phone with a user. It's helpful to have someone there to find the missing plug or "turn on the internets."

Moderated Techniques vs. Automated Techniques

Most of the techniques covered at this point have been *moderated*, in which a facilitator (also called a moderator) talks directly to users and guides them through the research. For qualitative approaches in general, this gives the facilitator the chance to assess the attitudes and emotional responses of participants, varying their questions in order to dig into areas of interest. Moderated approaches can be time-consuming and limited in scope, however, because the number of sessions is limited to the hours available from the facilitator.

Surfing

Kyle Soucy provides an excellent overview of the benefits and drawbacks of using automated tools in his article, "Unmoderated, Remote Usability Testing: Good or Evil?" at http://www.uxmatters.com/mt/archives/2010/01/unmoderated-remote-usability-testing-good-or-evil.php

The number of effective *automated* tools for gathering research has exploded over recent years, providing a way for participants to complete research tasks online and have their responses and behaviors captured by the tool for later analysis. Automated tests are set up by the researcher beforehand, and results are analyzed after a set period of time (or after a target number of users have responded). Generally these techniques lead to a larger sample of data showing user success rates and behavior for specific questions and tasks. Chapter 6 introduced some automated tools, such as those used in card sorting or for conducting surveys, and there are many more now available for other uses. To figure out which one is right for you, ask these basic questions and evaluate tools based on your answers:

▶ **What are you essentially trying to discover?** If you're looking for a visual representation of the behaviors that can be discovered with web analytics, use a tool like ClickTale on live versions of your site. If you're trying to build out the information architecture of your site, OptimalSort can help you create a remote card sorting test. If you have an information architecture that you want to test interactively, you can use Treejack to simulate the browsing of a set of categories and subcategories. If you want to simulate an online task and need to upload images like sketches, wireframes, and screenshots, tools like Usabilla, Loop11, and UserTesting.com will help you set up visual tasks.

▶ **What forms of data do you need captured?** UserFly captures cursor movements. ClickTale shows heat maps around frequently clicked elements of the page. UserTesting.com includes recordings of user feedback. Determine what is essential and use that information to choose the best tool for you. When in doubt, consider what will get you the best answers to your burning questions and consider what type of data will be most effective with the team members and executive sponsors who will view the results.

▶ **How would you like to recruit users?** Some tools provide the ability to intercept users while others include a panel of potential users as part of the cost of using the tool. For the low-cost options, you'll probably need to recruit users yourself.

▶ **How will participants get to your test?** If you're trying to automate screening of your participants and you have multiple versions of the test, you may need to set up your own online screeners to direct participants appropriately. Some tools help you screen users, but in many cases you'll need to pair an automated tool with a survey tool like Wufoo or SurveyMonkey.

▶ **Who's doing the analysis?** Some tools come with a package that includes a report. Others provide basic analytics and leave the heavy lifting of analysis for you. Either way, you'll need someone to verify that the results are aligned with the questions you were trying to get answered.

Setting up automated research can take more effort than moderated research in the planning stages, because you have to be even more careful about how you ask questions—especially if you're focused on quantitative data and want to be able to compare a large sample size of people who answered exactly the same questions (see Chapter 6 for more on avoiding leading questions). You'll also want to set up a sample test when evaluating tools, to ensure you can really ask your target questions in the right way within the chosen tool.

Once the information starts coming in, it's generally easy to see patterns in the numbers using automated approaches; also, adding additional participants has much less overhead than moderated approaches do. However, you should always try to include qualitative questions in your test in order to better understand the meaning behind the results.

Automated tests generally work best for simple, linear tasks where you can ask specific questions and easily understand whether a user has succeeded or failed at a task (or in the case of analytics-based tools, where you can see signs of issues such as drop-offs). These tests work best in conjunction with other approaches, like interviews, which provide more information on motivations. However, on their own, they can still help the team understand problem areas quickly, so it's helpful to consider them in the lead-up to detailed research planning.

Errata ?

A Sampling of Remote Research Tools

As previously mentioned, there are an enormous number of remote research tools available. You can see a comparison of some tools at the following sites:

▶ http://www.the10most.com/entrepreneurs/online-usability-testing-10-great-tools-to-make-your-web-site-easier-to-use.html

▶ http://www.usefulusability.com/24-usability-testing-tools/

The following tools convert data from web analytics into visual representations like video and/or heat maps of click paths. They can be used to find potential issues with your design or to test two different live versions of a design (called A/B tests):

▶ ClickTale (http://www.clicktale.com)

▶ Crazy Egg (http://www.crazyegg.com)

▶ UserFly (http://userfly.com)

The following tools can be used to set up a usability test, with multi-step tasks and related questions:

▶ Chalkmark (http://www.optimalworkshop.com/chalkmark.htm)

▶ Loop11 (http://www.loop11.com)

▶ UserZoom (http://www.userzoom.com)

▶ UserTesting.com (http://usertesting.com)

▶ Usabilla (http://usabilla.com)

If your focus is on testing the navigational structure or category structure of your site and you don't have (or want to use) page designs, try the following tools:

▶ OptimalSort (http://www.optimalworkshop.com/optimalsort.htm)

▶ Treejack (http://www.optimalworkshop.com/treejack.htm)

If you need to include survey questions as part of your research, the following tools will help (see Chapter 6 for more on survey design):

▶ Google Docs (https://docs.google.com). This free option allows you to create a simple web form off the online spreadsheet

▶ SurveyMonkey (http://www.surveymonkey.com)

▶ Wufoo (http://wufoo.com)

Usability Testing

As mentioned in the previous section, there are many elements of your design you can test with users. However, if your goal is to understand and improve on a user's ability to successfully complete key actions in your product—like, say, adding a product to a shopping cart and then checking out—you'll want to focus on usability testing.

Usability testing is one of the most frequently used UX design testing methods. It's also the most well known among those who aren't UX designers themselves, so your business stakeholders and project team may already be familiar with it. The concept itself is elegantly simple: create a prioritized set of tasks for your site, ask some users to perform them, and note where they have issues and successes.

Usability Testing vs. User Acceptance Testing

Some people in your organization may have the misconception that usability testing only happens near the end of development or beginning of deployment, when there's a functioning version of the site or application—perhaps something in beta mode. This impression may also be related to the common practice of conducting user acceptance testing (UAT) at this later point. The similarity of the names can cause the two to be confused.

For applications that go through a formal QA process, UAT is one of the later stages of testing, and is rarely conducted on actual users. The main purpose of UAT is often to serve as a final check on whether the application has met the functional requirements set out by stakeholders; it can also catch any errors or bugs participants report.

Although UAT can bring out usability issues, it should not be relied on as the only method for catching them on a project. Because it occurs so late in the process, changes based on feedback from UAT are much more costly. It's far better to catch major issues earlier in the process, before much time is spent in development. Usability testing is designed to provide more true-to-life performance information earlier in the process.

The following sections discuss these common steps involved in usability testing:

- ▶ Planning the research
- ▶ Recruiting and logistics
- ▶ Writing discussion guides
- ▶ Facilitating
- ▶ Analyzing and presenting results
- ▶ Creating recommendations

Before you get started, consider your project objectives. They'll help you maintain focus throughout but will be especially helpful in the early stages as you choose an approach and plan the test.

So is usability testing a quantitative method or a qualitative method? That's one of the longest running discussions in the field of UX design.

Either approach is possible and each can produce useful results. Proponents of a more quantitative approach say:

- ▶ Quantitative research allows for setting of measurable benchmarks that can be tested against in later iterations, showing progress toward a goal (for example, reducing the time it takes to check out by 20 percent or catching 80 percent of the usability issues in a site). This also makes it a good approach when you want to perform a formal comparison of two sites or evaluate a particular site.

- ▶ It provides results that can be validated statistically, which can be important when recommendations need to be defended to stakeholders who trust data-driven decisions.

- ▶ It reduces the likelihood of an individual UX designer's bias affecting the results.

- ▶ It provides a higher degree of confidence that the results are reflective of the entire user base.

- ▶ It offers a clear, numerical method of validating a finding (for example, how many users encountered the same issue).

Proponents of qualitative usability testing say:

- ▶ Qualitative research builds experience and empathy in the designer, promoting creative solutions focused on the user.

- ▶ It relies heavily on the UX designer's intuition to make reasonable recommendations, which is a large part of why she's on the team.

- For usability testing in particular, a qualitative approach is often less costly than a quantitative one, because fewer users are required and because qualitative research does not require a knowledge of formal scientific design and analysis (such as statistics).

- It's very easy to analyze the results of quantitative studies incorrectly, thereby lying (however unintentionally) with data. So a quantitative approach—if it's not run correctly—can actually introduce more risk than a qualitative test.

- Although findings are not validated numerically, they can be validated by a designer, who will make the call about the issue's likely impact using his informed rationale and then build the case with user stories.

Qualitative usability testing is the more accessible approach for those who haven't had training in formal scientific methods, and provides a rich source of data for informing design. For these reasons, we'll be focusing on the design of qualitative testing for the rest of this chapter.

How Many Users Are "Enough"?

Asking "How many users are enough?" in a group of UX designers is like bringing up religion at a political rally—it's a subject of hot debate.

It's also a question that can't be avoided, because you'll need a framework to start from in order to plan your research. It's tied to the approach you use: quantitative or qualitative.

To give the short answer, here are the guidelines that seem to have gotten the most consensus in the UX field, provided by Jakob Nielsen:

For a quantitative usability test, plan for a higher number of participants: 20 participants per round of research (see http://www.useit.com/alertbox/quantitative_testing.html).

For a qualitative usability test, five to eight users per group for each round of research is usually sufficient. Ideally, more than one round of research is conducted to uncover issues that may have been "hiding" under other issues or unintentionally introduced in the new design (see http://www.useit.com/alertbox/20000319.html).

Planning the Research

When designing a usability test, there are a few questions you should answer early on to provide focus and scope. This could be provided as a document written for and discussed with the project team and key stakeholders, often called a *user research plan*. The plan should outline your approach as chosen above.

Why Are You Testing?

Write a clear statement outlining the objectives of the test, based on one or more of the goals of the overall project. See Chapter 2 for examples of design goals and how they vary based on project type.

Who Are You Testing?

Once you've created your user model (see Chapters 6 and 7) you can use it as the basis for your decisions on which users to test. If you haven't already, meet with the project team and relevant stakeholders to prioritize the user groups. This information will feed into your screener (discussed under "Recruiting and Logistics").

This point is also where you should choose the user groups to be represented and the number of users to include in each group.

What Are You Testing?

The question of what you are testing includes two interrelated questions: What method will you use to represent the site or application, and what tasks do you plan to include?

If you have an existing application for redesign, you may choose to run the whole test on the current version first to find major usability issues to address.

If you're working with a new design, you can use sketches or paper prototypes (for example, a packet of printed wireframes) to represent new interface elements like pages. These low-fidelity representations of the UI allow you to quickly generate and discuss ideas among the project team, and iterate on them quickly with participants (see Chapters 12 and 13 for more on sketches and wireframing).

When you're working with a new design that includes highly interactive elements, it may be better to create a prototype that simulates the navigation flow of the design realistically but can still be created quickly, before full-scale development begins (see Chapter 13 for more on prototyping).

The pages you include will be closely tied to the tasks that you pick. If you plan on using prototypes to test with users, you'll need to plan for the main pages of the task as well as intermediate pages and alternate paths. You may not need to detail each one, but you'll need to plan for a response if a user goes in that direction. Sometimes this can be as simple as a page that states a certain path is not available and requests the user to return to the previous page to try again.

The specifics of your tasks will go into the discussion guide (discussed below), but because the scope can vary greatly depending on the type of tasks you include, it's helpful to have the list outlined during planning.

 Deep Diving

For more on iterative designing and testing with sketches, as well as truly inspirational insights into creativity in the design process, read *Sketching User Experiences: Getting the Design Right and the Right Design,* by Bill Buxton (Morgan Kaufmann, 2007).

For more about techniques in paper prototyping, check out *Paper Prototyping: The Fast and Easy Way to Design and Refine User Interfaces,* by Carolyn Snyder (Morgan Kaufmann, 2003).

If the list is too long and you're not sure how to prioritize, here are some possible priorities to consider:

▶ Areas where the design breaks some established conventions. Are you calling it a "goody bag" instead of a "shopping cart"? It's probably a good idea to see if that's clear to your users.

▶ Areas where design decisions are politically charged. You may have a strong feeling that a particular design direction is the right one, but you know there are a lot of disagreements among stakeholders or other members of the project team. Seeing is believing.

- Areas where usability issues can have critical consequences, such as lost sales or, in the worst case, lost lives (healthcare applications involving medication dosage are a good example of this).

Next, you'll determine the information you want to gather while a user is trying to perform each task.

What Information Are You Gathering?

We're focusing on qualitative usability tests, which tend to have a smaller set of measurements. For the most part you want to understand the issues users may encounter, the different levels of frustration they may experience, and the severity of a particular problem. For example, maybe there's an intermittent problem (not experienced by all users) that results in the irretrievable loss of a posted story. That should definitely be a high-concern problem in your report!

To get some perspective across the users you are testing, or across rounds of testing, there are some measurements to consider gathering as part of your test. Again, if you're conducting a qualitative test with a smaller number of users, don't take these numbers too far (calculating an average number doesn't make a lot of sense if you're only testing five users), but the following measures can help you understand the severity of some of the issues users are encountering.

Success: The degree to which a user was able to complete a task. If you're looking across users, you could also refer to "success rate"—the number of users who are able to complete the task successfully. It sounds simple, but this means you need to define the meaning of *success*!

For less formal tests you may say a task is successful if the user achieves the end state (for example, an editor successfully approves a story). You can track success more formally by noting the different levels of intervention needed by the facilitator:

Level 1 Prompt: The test facilitator responds to a participant's question but doesn't provide any additional detail. For example, a participant asks, "I think it would be this button, should I click on it?" and the facilitator responds, "Go ahead and try it." A Level 1 prompt alone doesn't mean a failed task, but it is good to note because the participant is probably experiencing some uncertainty at that point. (Although if this is the first task, it could also just be that he is unfamiliar with usability tests).

If a user needs no prompting to complete the task, or needs only one or two Level 1 prompts, you may consider that step a success—unless you feel the amount of time it took the user was well beyond the level of patience likely for your users.

Level 2 Prompt: The test facilitator sees a participant is struggling and gives a hint in response to a question. This level doesn't include giving the answer directly, but the response may affect the user's approach. For example, the facilitator might say, "Is there anything else on this page that you think may relate to this task?" Here you could set a limit on how many Level 2 prompts may be given before the task is marked as failed (for example, at the second prompt) or as "succeeded with difficulty."

Level 3 Prompt: The participant has given up in frustration or has struggled to the point where he would likely have given up if faced with the task in real life. In this case, the facilitator gives a direct answer to part of the task—for example, saying, "To approve this story, you would click on the Submit button." If a participant requires a Level 3 prompt, the task is typically marked as failed.

User satisfaction: Sure, he completed the task successfully, but how did he feel about it? It can be helpful to include a few follow-up questions after each task (with the timer off) so you can understand how happy or frustrated your users are afterwards. If you get someone who doesn't like to talk, this may be the main window you'll have into their soul.

Table 14.1 shows examples of some of the post-task questions you could include.

TABLE 14.1 User Satisfaction Questions

QUESTION	STRONGLY DISAGREE	DISAGREE	NEITHER AGREE NOR DISAGREE	AGREE	STRONGLY AGREE
The task took longer to finish than I expected	1	2	3	4	5
The task was easy to complete	1	2	3	4	5
I felt frustrated when trying to complete this task	1	2	3	4	5

User Satisfaction Questions

User statements: This isn't a metric, but what users volunteer is a key set of details to collect. Adding user quotes to a report is a powerful way to bring the human element to the results so that stakeholders aren't just interpreting data but are understanding perceptions that lead to insights. During the test you may just mark statements as either questions or comments; we'll be splitting those out in the report (see the later section "Generating Insights").

Recruiting and Logistics

Now that you have the outline of the research and you know how many participants you need from each group, it's time to get some tests scheduled!

Generating a List

When you created your research plan, you outlined the types of users you were looking to include. Use that outline to generate a list of potential participants. Look for sources that provide names, email addresses, and phone numbers, such as:

▶ Registered users of a related company site

▶ Customer contact information

▶ Sites or groups relevant to your topic of research. Postings about your research can be broad, such as to Craigslist, or targeted, such as to discussion groups centered around your company's industry.

▶ E-mails to acquaintances with a connection to the subject of the test. You want to ask them to forward the invitation to others who may be interested, since using subjects whom you know personally could bias the results. This kind of word of mouth is a great way to find pockets of potential participants, but keep in mind that these candidates still need to be screened. (If you or others on the team know people well, it can be tempting to let them slip through.)

▶ Requests in the form of short surveys that prequalify participants, either in ad space on relevant sites or on the company site. Ethnio (http://ethn.io/) is a live web recruiting tool that inserts screeners into websites to convert visitors to potential research participants, for example.

- ▶ Postings or prequalification questionnaires in public places where potential participants may be found. For sites with a strong association to a physical place, you could do the majority of your screening and scheduling on site as well.

- ▶ Third-party recruiting firms, who may also run your screener for you and help with scheduling. This can be an expensive option, but if you're looking for a specific participant type that's hard to recruit or you need to recruit a lot of people, you can save a lot of time by outsourcing this part of the process. Some firms specialize in certain fields as well (such as medical) and can give you pointers on how to encourage a high participation rate.

Be prepared to get creative here. Use your empathetic skills to think like your target users—where can you find them and what may motivate them to join? This last question leads us to the next topic.

Choosing the Compensation

What will motivate members of your user group to participate in the research? It may or may not be money, but participants want something of value for their time.

If you're working on a site for internal users, you'll need to demonstrate that value to the managers who need to approve the use of company time for participation in research. In this case, you might focus on how a better system directly relates to benefits for his or her group.

If you're working with potential external users, here are some variables to keep in mind when determining how you'll compensate:

How general or specific is the audience? For a widely used e-commerce site your audience is likely to be general and you can often offer a lower rate of compensation in the form of a check or gift card. For an application used by lawyers, your compensation will need to be high value, and it is often better to use something other than money as compensation (for example, access to a premium service). In those cases a check may actually seem like an insult—someone who bills $250 an hour isn't likely to participate for money. If you're working with customers of big-ticket items, treat them as a specific audience and compensate them well.

How much interest is the topic likely to generate? Some participants will join because they want to see what's coming in the area you're testing. If it's a high-interest area, you may not need to provide much extra compensation at all—the reward is having access to something no one else can see yet. But be realistic here: *You* may be that enthusiastic about the topic, but will your users be?

Will people participate mainly because they want to contribute something to the cause? Some groups will be motivated by altruistic purposes, and may be turned off by the offer of money to participate. If you're testing something that betters the community (online or off) you may get more participation—and happier participants—if the experience is about coming together rather than getting paid. In this case you can show your appreciation with public acknowledgment and by letting them know, once the site is complete, the contribution they were able to make by participating.

How inconvenient will participation be? If participants need to travel to your site, be prepared to provide greater compensation. If they're participating in remote testing from the comfort of their own home or office, less is required. Time also comes into this equation, of course, and people will expect to be compensated more highly for 2 hours than for 30 minutes.

Possible Forms of Compensation

Your situation will vary, but here are some things you could offer:

▶ $30 for a half-hour remote test with a general user group

▶ $80–$120 for an hour-long, in-person test with a general user group

▶ $180–$250 for an hour-long test with a specific user group that you determine will respond well to monetary compensation

▶ Free service for three months; free products made by the company (ideally ones that are not yet available to everyone); membership to an exclusive group for six months and the like, for a specific user group that is unlikely to be impressed with a check, for instance, lawyers, doctors, and sales executives

Here again is where it helps to be creative and to focus on your personas. What will motivate your user group?

Screening

A *screener* is a type of questionnaire you can use with potential participants before you schedule them. It ensures they fit within your definition of a representative user. Questions are meant to

▶ Ensure the respondent is either a current user of the features you're testing or a likely future user

▶ Determine his fit into one or more of your user group(s)

▶ Help you get a good mix of participants within that user group

▶ Exclude particular respondents who may have experience that could skew your results

▶ Gather key details you need to know about before a participant arrives (optional)

Your screener should include an introductory script that your recruiter can read over the phone, along with directions on when to qualify the participant (if they fit) or terminate the call (if they don't).

The end users of your screener will be the people recruiting your participants—or the potential participant if you're using an online form to screen. Either can work, but generally it's best to gather a list of those interested using a form or e-mails and then screen them by phone. Why? Because, unfortunately, it's usually easier for people to misrepresent themselves on paper than when answering someone directly, and it's not unusual for someone to try to join a study even if they don't qualify for it. Especially if compensation is involved!

Your screener should also weed out those who have knowledge that may affect your results. For example, a common question to ask is if the respondent works in the field of market research, because they are probably too familiar with research in general and as a result aren't as likely to give you genuine reactions. You may also want to screen out those who work for competitors if there are concerns about sharing design information.

Following are some examples of questions you might see on a screener for a business-to-business web ordering application. In this case, we're targeting a user group that is comfortable with using and purchasing via the web and is likely to do so on their own as well. Note that some questions are meant to screen participants in or out, while others (like Question 4) are more geared toward placing qualified participants into the correct user group.

1. What age range do you fall into? [mix of ages above 18]

   Under 18 . . . . TERMINATE

   18–24

   25–34

   35–44

   45–54

   55 or above

2. How often do you use the Internet at home?

   Never . . . . TERMINATE

   Less than once a month . . . . TERMINATE

   A few times a month

   At least once a week

   Several times a week

   Once a day or more

3. When was the last time you made a personal purchase of a product online?

   Within the past month

   1–3 months ago

   3–6 months ago

   6–12 months ago . . . . TERMINATE

   Over 12 months ago . . . . TERMINATE

   I've never made a personal purchase online . . TERMINATE

4. When was the last time you visited pseudocorporation.com? [Group A are infrequent or nonusers; Group B are frequent users]

   I've never visited the site . . . . CHECK for GROUP A

   Within the past month . . . . CHECK for GROUP B

   1–3 months ago . . . . CHECK for GROUP B

   3–6 months ago . . . . CHECK for GROUP B

   6–12 months ago . . . . CHECK for A or B

   Over 12 months ago . . . . CHECK for GROUP A

Planning for Space and Equipment

By this point you know whether you're testing remotely or in person and the amount of time you need for each participant. Here are some of the other decisions you should finalize:

Where you're testing: In a rented space with an observation room, in a conference room at the company site, or on location where potential users will be? Plan for a quiet place that can fit two or three people comfortably along with the computer setup you'll be testing on. If you're testing remotely, you'll still need a quiet, dedicated room with great audio and a reliable internet connection.

What staff you'll need besides the facilitator: You can save time and increase accuracy by having a note-taker log information during the test, for example. Other possibilities include a greeter for in-person research (to meet incoming participants, hand out questionnaires while people are waiting, and escort participants into and out of the test room) and someone to provide IT support should something come up during the test.

How you'll be recording the test: You can use a variety of methods, but software such as TechSmith's Morae and Camtasia Studio make screen recording easy, and Morae has additional webcam video and audio integration features.

Writing Discussion Guides

Finally, you'll need to assemble the materials you need for the test itself. You have your general tasks listed in the research plan; now you need to finalize the actual text and instructions for the task. You'll have at least two packets here—one for the test facilitator and one for the participant (with enough copies for each test to include one of each).

Begin with an introductory script that the facilitator can read to the participant. Lots of good examples are available at http://usability.gov/templates.

Your instructions should include all the specific information that the participant needs to successfully complete the task or tasks you're testing.

If your tasks require a lot of data entry and personalization, set some information up ahead of time and give your participants predetermined data to use. For example, if a login is involved, you will probably have all participants use the same set of login credentials. Make sure the instructions for the task include all of this information clearly so that it's easy to fill in.

Here's an example of how a task for a content editor becomes more specific in the discussion guide. The original task in the plan is

"Find an article that's ready for editing."

In the discussion guide this becomes the following:

INTRODUCTION

Your manager has asked you to take on a new role: editing and approving articles posted by writers contributing to the company website. Once you approve an article it will be posted to the site in the News area.

You and three other editors will be approving the items to make sure they fit with the company's message. You've been given the following login information for the editing tool:

Username: **grobertson**

Password: **come2gether**

Please read each task out loud, and then complete it using the editing tool.

Task 1

Log into the tool and open an article that's ready for editing.

As you can see above, we've altered the task to end with a clear final state—an open article. This kind of tweaking will be common as you move to this level of detail and plan for measuring success. You can also follow each task with the user satisfaction questions discussed in the planning section. In general it's best to give each task its own page so the user isn't tempted to look ahead.

In summary, your test materials should include the following:

▶ Consent form for videotaping

▶ Discussion guide for the facilitator, with introductory script

▶ Discussion guide for the participant, with detailed tasks and user satisfaction questions

▶ A format for note taking. This can vary from a logging tool built into testing software to a spreadsheet for typing in responses to a printed template for checking off key information (such as types of prompts required). Spending a little extra time before the test in setting this up will ensure you get consistent results and save you a lot of time in reviewing recordings.

▶ Optionally, a questionnaire. Sometimes participants come early and have a little wait time—this is an excellent opportunity to gather a little extra information. If you've designed a survey previously, why not reuse it here?

▶ The method of compensation, to be given to the participant at the end of the test (money in an envelope, a widely accepted gift card such as a Visa gift card, etc). If you've chosen compensation such as free services, where nothing is handed out after the test, reassure the participant that they'll be receiving follow-up no later than the next day.

If you're using paper prototyping, you'll also have those materials to work with. Make sure you have the sets prepared before your first test.

Facilitating

The job of the facilitator is to introduce the participant to the process, answer their initial questions, and then glean what insights you can while still trying to allow the participant to act as naturally as possible.

Be sure to ask users to think out loud during the test, as if they were talking to themselves (and gently remind them to do so if they start to work silently).

The "think aloud" technique is the way you gain the most insight into users' behavior. You'll learn a lot about their problem solving and thought processes if you hear about them during the task itself, versus asking participants to recreate them later when their recollection may not be as accurate.

Also, be careful not to give the participant the "right" answer too quickly! One of the hardest parts of conducting a usability test is watching your carefully selected participant struggle mightily with a task and just letting them struggle.

After all, you're probably in this field because you're an empathetic individual. You want to help people. So it can feel a little sadistic to watch someone get increasingly frustrated, have them turn to you for help, and then respond, "What would you do if you were trying this on your own?"

Whenever a participant asks you a question as he works, hold back a few beats before answering. Participants are most likely to ask questions right at the beginning of the test, especially if they feel awkward about working with you sitting next to them. Once they realize you're there for observation more than for conversation, they'll often start to focus on the task more than your presence.

Here are some examples of participant questions and suggested responses:

Participant:	"It looks like it may be this tab, should I go here?"
Facilitator:	"Go ahead and try it."
Participant:	"Am I supposed to go here?"
Facilitator:	"Is that what you think you'd do at this point?"
Participant:	"Is this the way to submit comments?"
Facilitator:	Silence. Has a friendly and relaxed look on her face as she smiles at the participant, then looks at his screen expectantly.

So when do you intervene?

If the user has already given more effort than you think he realistically would when working on his own, and you feel you've learned why he ended up down the wrong path, it's time to move on—especially if you have more tasks to get through and you don't want him to carry his frustration through to the rest of the test.

In Chapter 6 we mentioned the importance of avoiding leading questions in user interviews. The same applies here as well. If you feel you're too close to the design and that criticism might make you respond defensively, consider coaching someone else to facilitate while you take notes.

Analyzing and Presenting Results

You've finished all the tests and now have a mountain of data to wade through. But there are some key findings that you already think are relevant, and your project team is dying to know how it went.

You may want to schedule a casual verbal overview of your top-of-mind takeaways for the team. It can help you verbalize some of the trends you noticed and help set the stage for your later report. Be sure to communicate that these are initial impressions and you'll need time to analyze your data in more detail. You don't necessarily want to jump into recommendations here before you have a full picture of where any problems may lie.

Once you have time to sit down with the data, review it with a couple of things in mind:

The amount of time you have for analysis. It's easy to get lost in the details and try to include everything. As always, keep an eye on your test and objectives as you tease out the important findings. If you have ten hours of test recording and five days to write the full report, you probably don't want to take the time to watch the video of every test. Rely on your note taker and go back to the videos mainly to make sure the key quotes you remember are recorded correctly.

How your results will be used. This is an important detail that can often be underestimated. You may create a beautiful 20-page report, but only one of those pages is likely to get a lot of mileage: the executive summary.

If your business stakeholders are going to want to see the details, the report itself can be the main way to communicate results. If you think you'll need two levels of detail—one for stakeholders and another for the project team—consider creating a presentation version of the report as well, which hits on key findings in a more visible, digestible, and prioritized way. Those who are interested in more detail can then refer to the full report.

Prioritizing Issues

At the end of the test you'll potentially have a long list of usability issues to understand and prioritize. Here are some characteristics that will help you determine how severe an error is:

Consequences. The negative results of encountering the issue. For example, if a participant loses data because of a usability issue, that warrants a High rating. Let's say she spends ten minutes filling out a complex form and accidentally chooses a link taking her to another page. If she hits a browser's Back button, is her data gone?

Recoverability. The degree to which the participant can recover after encountering the issue—for example, is he able to easily get back via an alternate path?

Frequency of occurrence. Because you're not working with a large number of people this doesn't stand alone as a mark of severity. But if five people make the same mistake and it leads them down a less optimal path, that's a good sign you should consider making it a higher priority.

Rational cause. If the issue wasn't encountered frequently but it was made by someone who fit within your user group, she made it for a rational reason, and there was a clear cause for the error, that issue should be considered as you make your recommendations.

Generating Insights

Aside from the issues you've gathered, you'll have a wealth of statements made by users that can bring out valuable insights for the project team. As described in Chapter 6, an affinity diagramming exercise is an excellent way to gather these statements and collaboratively identify patterns.

Here are some of the ways you could categorize user statements (see the "Contextual Inquiry" section in Chapter 6 for more detail):

▶ Goals

▶ Mental models

▶ Ideas and feature requests

▶ Frustrations

▶ Workarounds

▶ Value statements

▶ Delights (don't leave these out—you don't want to lose the good stuff!)

▶ Expectations (especially when they are missed)

Both in insights and in recommendations be sure to include the positive findings as well. Usability test reports are often seen as being too negative, mainly because the researcher prioritizes discussion of the things that need to be fixed over the things that are going well. Taking time to discuss the good things will make the overall report experience better for everyone. It also helps the design team get engaged with the results—and excited to make the design even better.

Creating Recommendations

Even before you start analysis you probably already have some good ideas in your head for fixing the issues encountered in the test. Sketch them out along the way as you identify issues and insights, so you don't lose them. Just be careful a single idea doesn't take over too early and sway your view of other potential approaches that may resolve more issues.

A good recommendation should

▶ Resolve more than one issue, if possible. You may want to group issues together under one larger recommendation, depending on how detailed and specific you get with your issue descriptions.

▶ Be actionable and simple—avoiding prematurely detailed designs.

▶ Use verbiage that is straightforward but doesn't condescend. Receiving criticism is a difficult thing, especially for those who were directly involved in the design tested. Don't underplay issues, but keep in mind that your words need to come across as constructive and respectful.

Remember that recommendations need to be targeted to their end users just as much as the system does. As you finalize your report, circle back and ask yourself if the original objectives were met and how to best provide your results to the variety of people who will be using them: stakeholders, designers, and developers.

Speaking of developers, it's time to bring them into the forefront again. In the next chapter, we'll be covering the things to keep in mind as you transition from design into development, and beyond.

15 Transition: From Design to Development and Beyond

Where Do We Go from Here?

The Define and Design phases of your project are over.
Now what? A good user experience design process never
ends. After you've been through so much defining and
designing, how do you remain engaged to ensure that
the final project deliverable is the user experience you've
designed—and where do you go from there?

Russ Unger

Almost Done

While this is nearly the end of the book, it is not, however, the end of the user experience design process—although it might seem like it on the surface. Once you've been through all of the previous phases of a project, you might think your work is done and you don't have anything more to contribute. In many cases, UX design efforts end up as tasks on someone's project plan somewhere, and after your work product is handed over to the rest of the team, you invariably get shuffled to another project. Time to close that door and start on something new, right? Very wrong!

You still can do a lot to ensure that the best possible user experience design is produced.

Visual Design, Development, and Quality Assurance

In some cases, working with a design or development team that receives your project-based work product is seamless. Sometimes, downstream work partners rely on you to answer questions, provide input, and help them with some of the design concepts they are working on. (This may even sound a lot like prototyping to you!) In these work environments user experience design is already being embraced, and the team probably has had the foresight to give you the time to perform these consultative tasks.

In many organizations, however, the roles of user experience designers, information architects, interaction designers, and so on are still very new. How to manage these roles can be unclear, and the decision about how engaged you should be may fall upon someone who does not fully understand user experience design. It may be up to you to find ways to continually remain engaged.

Here are some suggestions:

1. Buy them a copy of this book, please.

2. Don't be shy.

3. Read through the rest of this chapter and look for opportunities in which you can be engaged and useful.

4. Ask to be engaged and be ready to defend your request.

There are other cases where you may find that the visual design or development team is the king of the company and their projects, and you may find it challenging to remain engaged. You may find yourself trying to break down walls just to be able to review the work and ensure compliancy. This is not always the case, but it does happen.

Ask the Experts: Christopher Fahey

Christopher Fahey, founding partner at Behavior Design (www.behaviordesign.com), is no stranger to overcoming this challenge. He offers this advice:

Some organizations are tightly compartmentalized. In order to keep engaged in the development of the project after the initial design phases are complete, you will need to be proactive and demand the opportunity to give feedback and correction to the visual design and development teams. They often simply won't even think to ask you to be there.

Ideally, you will do this during the planning and budgeting stages of the project. If not, you may have to literally volunteer your services to ensure that the design doesn't degrade during subsequent development.

One trick is to simply ask to be added, even informally, to the Quality Assurance team (assuming you have one—if not, definitely ask this of the visual designers and developers!) and to be given access and passwords to any development locations and bug tracking tools. Then you are able to add your critiques and deviations to the same bug-fixing queue the developers are looking at every day.

Of course, many projects won't have the luxury of a quality assurance team. In a perfect world, every project would have such a team; however, in reality QA is not always available. Sometimes, developers are performing QA themselves, as they develop. In addition to making you cringe, knowing this should make you try even harder to work with developers.

It is especially true in many small companies: QA is a luxury. QA is "performed by everyone, but especially the developer," says Troy Lucht, Founder of Olive Tree Promise (http://olivetreepromise.com/).

> Everyone tries to—and wants to—pitch in, but without resources dedicated to authoring test scripts, it can be impossible to inform people as to what they should test when development is often performed until the last possible minute. In many cases, our in-house designer is the person who knows the application as well as I do, so he is able to provide more informed feedback. Adding a user experience designer to the mix would really round things out for our small team.

The Art of Negotiation

The art of negotiation may become a critical aspect of your role as a user experience designer. Downstream work partners, such as visual designers and developers, may take liberties with their changes to your work without realizing how it affects key parts of the user experience. In the event that someone tells you something "can't" be done, you must be prepared to come up with a Plan B. Good negotiation skills will help you defend your design decision (which should be based on the research that you've done) and convince others that the user experience *can* be done. Alternatively, those skills will help you work with your partners to create a satisfactory Plan B approach that meets as many of everyone's needs as possible.

For additional insights on negotiating, check out *Getting to Yes: Negotiating Agreement Without Giving In,* by Roger Fisher, William L. Ury, and Bruce Patton (Penguin, 2011) and *Selling to the VP of No,* by Dave Gray (XPLANE Corp., 2003).

Although your user experience design work product may not include creating test scripts, in some cases you can test against the wireframes and annotations you created to ensure that all elements are accounted for and all the defined calls to action are functioning correctly. This situation is not perfect, but it is an approach that can be useful when QA does not exist.

The key takeaway here is that user experience design does not end just because you have turned over your work product and performed a knowledge transfer. Your role may temporarily assume more of a consulting nature, but you are far from done.

Design Testing with Users (Again)

Didn't we already do user testing?

Hopefully, you can answer yes to this question, but it does not always happen. Unfortunately, neither does this particular step of testing, which is designated for testing the final, designed and developed site with real users prior to launching.

This allows you to take one final look at the website and find the last-minute bugs and errors that you might have overlooked during QA testing. Once you identify your target set of users, you can test the website against any scenarios that appear to be high risk or that may have had issues in previous iterations of the site. This round of testing can provide you with the information necessary to determine whether or not your site is ready to launch. If there are significant issues uncovered during this round of testing, it may be important to make updates and test again.

10, 9, 8, 7, 6, 5, 4, 3, 2, 1 ... Launch!

"If you build it, they will come..."

That theory gets mentioned a lot—and disproved nearly as often. You can build the most beautiful, satisfying, usable application possible, launch it into the world, and find out two months later that almost no one is adopting it.

What gives?

User adoption is the degree to which the user base you're targeting ends up using the site or application. Some adoption issues can be avoided if you follow good practices in search engine optimization (see the online chapter, "User Experience Design and Search Engine Optimization," available on the companion website) to make sure your users can find the new site.

User adoption also means good user experience design doesn't stop once the project is over—or that it's limited to the project you're working on.

You can help the marketing, customer support, public relations, and training teams ensure a smooth deployment and user base that's excited about the site or project by helping them with three factors that often affect user adoption:

- Personal advantage
- Support
- Network opinion

Let's take a closer look at each of these in turn.

Personal Advantage

One of the most important questions to answer for the users will be "What's in it for me?"

As great as your site may be, if you can't quickly explain the unique benefit it brings to a particular type of user (or one of the personas you have identified), you may struggle to engage users.

Some advantages are direct: "By using this camera feature, you can post photos to your online account with one click of a button."

Some are indirect: "By using this timesheet tool, the company can more easily track the time you're spending on each project."

You've spent valuable time gaining insights into your users; now use that insight to help the marketing department tailor its messages.

Support

When your users need help with the site, how do they get it? Beyond the contextual assistance that your excellent user experience design efforts will strive to provide, the answer to this question also includes training and customer support.

Do you feel your users may respond better to classroom training instead of online training? Will some of your users bypass training and expect to have all they need within the site itself? Is live chat an important option to your users for customer support, or will they be satisfied with telephone and e-mail support?

Support efforts are tricky, and understanding the users allows you to be effective in helping your customer support and training departments.

Network Opinion

Word of mouth is the most important influencer around. What kind of reputation does your client's company and its current website have within the target user groups?

Even if the answer here is positive, that doesn't mean that no effort is required—maintenance is always important when it comes to reputation. Don't use a positive response as an excuse to skip to the next section: The effort involved in maintenance does not have to be substantial, but the effort required to rebound from a reputation nosedive can be staggering. A little TLC can go a long way, so keep reading.

If the answer is negative, then serious effort must be made to improve perceptions. You may need to reach out to the user community and identify who the influencers are, how they prefer to communicate, and how they influence their audience—and then engage them. There are many ways to engage your users via social networking and influence the opinions held about your client, company, and website. Help your client identify opportunities to engage these communities and attempt to steer them in a positive direction.

If all three of these factors are in place and you still notice a low degree of usage, consider how and what your competitors are doing to meet users' needs. How can you differentiate the product or site?

Postlaunch Activities

These are interesting times that we're living in: So many companies are launching with themselves—or their products—in a "beta" state. A *beta launch* typically means that real, unfiltered users are the audience for live testing of the website to help identify bugs, errors, crashes, or any other problems. At one time betas were typically offered up only to developers, but it has now become a common practice to open betas up to the user community as a whole.

During a beta phase, it is imperative that communication methods are set up to record and report any issues that users may have. Any type of system malfunction that occurs must be recorded and made available to the project team. There must also be a mechanism in place to let users report issues they encounter to the appropriate members of the project team. If this kind of communication doesn't happen—if the user experience designers, visual designers, and developers don't know what's going on during the often rigorous and fast-paced beta phase—the website may be updated and redeployed to users without much of the strategy implemented.

Postlaunch Analytics

After you've launched your site, one of the first things you should do is begin to accumulate data on site usage. The best source for this is your site's log file. Unfortunately, user experience designers probably aren't at the top of the list to receive or review this information, so seek out whoever is in charge of hosting the site and apply those negotiating skills of yours.

Website analytics can give you some insight into the visitors to your site. Among other aspects, you can get an understanding of

- Who new site visitors are
- Who repeat site visitors are
- Number of page views
- Page view duration
- Page depth
- Where visitors exit the site (which pages)
- Session duration
- Advertising impressions
- Search terms used, results, and re-searches

This information can help you understand where users are having problems by highlighting trouble spots on the site. Although analytics may come across as dry and numbers heavy, the data and insights will help you put together appropriate questions when you do your postlaunch testing.

Note *For more information on website analytics, Avinash Kaushik's* Web Analytics: An Hour a Day *(Sybex, 2007) is a good place to start.*

Postlaunch Design Testing with Users (Again, Again)

After you accumulate data from your website analytics and gather information from customer support or other departments interacting with users, you can begin to compile a list of questions to use in another round of design testing with users. In other words, use the data you have collected to create a new set of questions to ask users of the site, and use the skills you learned in Chapter 14.

One of the benefits of this round of testing is that you have an opportunity to test the same batch of users that you worked with previously to determine if their opinions have changed after launch and more usage of the website. This can be quite helpful: If you retest the same batch of users (or a portion thereof) you can re-ask some of the original questions (opinions about functionality, ability to achieve specific tasks, and so forth) and analyze the variance in responses over time.

This potential for variance can help you uncover new areas for improvement in the site, as well as gain some insights into the users' learning curve, based on previous rounds. As an added benefit, analyzing the differences in responses may also help you identify new questions that were not considered previously.

16 A Brief Guide to Meetings

Be Aware of the Basics of Holding Good Meetings

Meetings are often the bane of any project's existence. They can make or break your project—and it's important to understand some of the basics of planning appropriate meetings and how to keep them on track.

You hardly need to be an expert at Robert's Rules of Order in order to hold an effective meeting—and those rules are rarely—if ever—used in today's project world. While you can learn many of the basics of conducting project-based meetings by observing, you can also pick up a lot of bad habits and poorly implemented shortcuts that way.

This brief chapter will provide you with a clear approach to effectively holding meetings.

Russ Unger

Cost of compression
any kind?

It's always important to consider whether the cost of a meeting is justifiable before you even consider scheduling one. Every one-hour meeting you schedule doesn't simply cost *you* one hour of time, it also costs you one hour *per each employee* in the room.

That means that if you have eight people in a meeting for one hour, and each person has a business cost of $100 per hour, you've just spent $800 on a meeting—the equivalent of a single workday. Keep in mind that this does not account for travel time or loss of other work that could be accomplished, so the $800 is definitely a low estimate.

That's a lot of time and money for a simple 1-hour meeting. It's even more expensive when you factor in any tardiness, lack of focus, wrong people in the meeting, or other distractions.

To plan for meeting success, you have to determine that having a meeting is the right thing to do in the first place. Diane Brewster-Norman, one of the creators of the Franklin-Covey Meeting Advantage workshops (www.franklincovey.com/tc/publicworkshops/communication/meeting) has identified five key questions to ask before calling a meeting:

▶ Does the total cost of the meeting justify the advantages of holding it?

▶ Are the people who can make decisions available to attend? (Is the timing right?)

▶ Is the purpose of the meeting clear?

▶ Is the necessary information available?

▶ Have alternatives to holding a meeting been considered?

If you answer yes to these, you have the need for a meeting. If you have determined that you cannot otherwise get the information or the approvals you need to continue making progress on your project, then by all means, schedule a meeting!

But first, make sure that you can't get the same results by picking up the phone, sending e-mails or instant messages, or trying other avenues. Use the approach that's the most efficient and effective way to get the results or information you need. For that matter, you should do your best to avoid using e-mail as a crutch to avoid face-to-face or asynchronous one-to-one meetings.

Last but not least, when scheduling your meetings, always try to get the early time slots when you know people are in the office. While it is slightly unrealistic to think that all your key players will be in the office at 8 a.m., you should have a general sense for when people arrive and are ready to start their workday. Do your best to book the earliest time that everyone you require is available. If that time slot is unavailable, the middle of the morning and the middle of the afternoon are generally good options to try. Note that these options are generally in the "middle"—try to avoid holding your meetings at a time that would disrupt people's usual start-of-the-workday and right after-lunch habits. Those are the times that people may have the most difficulty committing to.

No matter what you do, make sure that you take every step necessary to avoid being the person who schedules a meeting for the first thing in the morning on a Monday or the end of the day on Friday (or any workday, if possible). No one really likes that person.

The Agenda

Just as every project should have a good supporting project plan, a good meeting should have an agenda prepared beforehand. The agenda keeps your meeting on track; it provides attendees with the purpose of the meeting and an outline of the topics for discussion.

An agenda also forces the meeting organizer—you—to spend some quality time thinking through the goals and objectives of the meeting, as well as who should be in attendance. A little planning goes a long way toward the success of your meeting, sets the expectations and responsibilities of the attendees, helps you obtain your goals for your meeting, and gives you one last chance to consider alternative approaches to accomplish the agenda.

As shown in the sample in **Figure 16.1**, an agenda should always have the following information:

▶ Meeting title or type

▶ Meeting date, time, and duration

▶ Physical location

▶ Dial-in information (if required)

- ► Online conference information (if required)
- ► Attendees list
- ► Meeting purpose
- ► Who is responsible for what and how long they have to accomplish it

Meeting Agenda

PROJECT STATUS	MEETING LOCATION
November 12, 2012 10:00 – 11:00 A.M.	The Bean Conference Room Dial-in Information: 800-123-4567 Attendee Code: 1234567# Online Conference Location: http://meeting.yourcompany.com/

Attendees:

Russ Unger, Carolyn Chandler, Brad Simpson, Christine Mortensen, Jonathan Ashton, Chris Miller

Meeting Purpose:

- ► Review the current status on Research, Graphic Design and SEO
- ► Discuss outstanding issues
- ► Prioritize and plan next steps

PRESENTER	TOPIC	TIME
Russ	Welcome	5 minutes
Carolyn	Research Update	10 minutes
Brad & Christine	Graphic Design Update	15 minutes
Jonathan	SEO Update	15 minutes
Chris	Parking Lot	10 minutes
Russ	Next Steps	5 minutes

Figure 16.1 *A basic meeting agenda sample*

At the very least, your agenda should provide enough information so that all attendees have a clear understanding of what the purpose of the meeting is and what is expected from them. Keep your purpose direct and to the point, and always try to use actionable words that clearly describe what the expectations are.

Meeting Rules

Even after you have meticulously ensured that it is appropriate to hold a meeting and have created a stunning agenda, all it takes are a couple of slight missteps to make the entire session unproductive. Despite your best efforts, meetings can pretty easily jump off the rails and take on a life of their own.

To alleviate some of the stresses that go along with being the person in charge of the meeting, establish some ground rules for the attendees that set expectations early on.

Basic Meeting Rules

The following ground rules for your meetings will provide clear direction to attendees and help support you as you strive to keep the meeting on track:

▶ Send any required reading materials with sufficient advance notice. Send a reminder of the obligation within 24 hours of the meeting. If you are able to do so, deliver a hard copy of materials to attendees as far in advance of the meeting as possible. This may seem silly, but it will help attendees to show up prepared.

▶ Always start and end your meetings on time. Better yet, try to end 60-minute meetings between 5 and 10 minutes early and 30-minute meetings about 5 minutes early to allow your attendees time to pack up their belongings and have time to travel to what is most likely their next meeting.

▶ Keep your meetings as short as possible. Ideal meetings are 30 minutes, and maximum meeting times should be no more than 2 hours. Anything longer is most likely trying to cover too many topics, and 2 hours is well beyond anyone's attention span anyway.

- If your meeting requires a majority decision, invite an odd number of people. If your meeting requires consensus, invite an even number of people.

- Keep discussions focused on the agenda items.

- Be a good listener. Do not interrupt when others are talking, and do not assume that you know what they are going to say.

- Go "topless." Unless they are required for the meeting, leave all laptops, phones, and other distracting devices out of the meeting space. At the very least, make sure all such devices are turned off or muted.

- Show up for the meeting prepared. As the person who sets up the meeting, make sure you supply printed copies of any necessary materials and/ or instruct attendees to bring their own.

Note *People often skim through or overlook meeting notice details, so be prepared by either sending out a reminder or supplying required materials.*

- Document *every* meeting and assign a note taker for your meetings. If no note taker is assigned, surprise, you're it!

- Make the meeting rules available to everyone for the first meeting. Depending upon the group of people, it may be helpful to append these rules to your agenda template (**Figure 16.2**).

- Close your meetings by identifying the next steps and assigning responsibilities and deadlines for tasks.

- Distribute your meeting notes no more than 24 hours after the meeting.

Although these ground rules can be helpful, they are only useful as long as the attendees are willing to support them—and you. In a perfect world, the meeting rules would simply be followed and all of your meetings would be successful. The real world isn't perfect: People always have different agendas, other obligations, and sometimes they rely on technology or other people to keep them up to date with their calendars.

As long as you do everything you can to try to keep the meeting you've scheduled on track, your attendees will eventually follow your lead and help you have successful meetings. But be forewarned: The path to hell is paved with good intentions. If you should become the person who deviates from the agenda and guidelines that *you* set, your respect could go flying out the window.

Meeting Agenda

PROJECT STATUS	MEETING LOCATION
November 12, 2012 10:00 – 11:00 A.M.	The Bean Conference Room Dial-in Information: 800-123-4567 Attendee Code: 1234567# Online Conference Location: http://meeting.yourcompany.com/

Attendees:

Russ Unger, Carolyn Chandler, Brad Simpson, Christine Mortensen, Jonathan Ashton, Chris Miller

Meeting Purpose:

▶ Review the current status on Research, Graphic Design and SEO

▶ Discuss outstanding issues

▶ Prioritize and plan next steps

PRESENTER	TOPIC	TIME
Russ	Welcome	5 minutes
Carolyn	Research Update	10 minutes
Brad & Christine	Graphic Design Update	15 minutes
Jonathan	SEO Update	15 minutes
Chris	Parking Lot	10 minutes
Russ	Next Steps	5 minutes

In order to keep the meeting on-track and as effective as possible, please do your part by observing the following meeting rules:

▶ Arrive on time (or send a proxy who can make decisions in your absence)

▶ Stay on topic; reserve side conversations for after this meeting

▶ Allow the person with the floor to finish speaking before responding

▶ Leave laptops and other devices behind or shut them off

▶ Bring all required materials to the meeting

▶ Carolyn will be the note taker—please turn in your notes to her if necessary

▶ Meeting notes will be sent to attendees within 24 hours

Figure 16.2 *A basic meeting agenda with meeting rules*

After the Meeting

Once your meeting is over, it's time to get back to work!

Almost.

Actually, it's time for you to sit down and put all your notes together to send back to the meeting attendees—assuming, of course, that you are the note taker. Regardless, the responsibility is on you to ensure that everyone has an opportunity to review the notes and provide additional input or feedback. This allows everyone to continue making progress in a unified fashion, based on the outcome of the meeting.

Good meeting notes will provide everyone with a clear accounting of what occurred in the meeting and what their objectives and responsibilities are moving forward (**Figure 16.3**). Your meeting notes should clearly indicate action items and who is responsible for completing those tasks, as well as any decision points that needed to be resolved. Treat your meeting notes as a paper trail, and file them away with your other project documentation, along with any modifications or conversations about those notes.

Last but not least, do not put off sending out your meeting notes any more than 24 hours. If too much time passes, it's not nearly as easy to decipher your own notes, and people's recollections can fade. A delay can open the door to varying opinions and potentially create additional work by triggering more discussions of topics covered in the meeting.

Meeting Agenda

PROJECT STATUS	MEETING LOCATION
November 12, 2012 10:00 – 11:00 A.M.	The Bean Conference Room

Attendees:

Russ Unger, Carolyn Chandler, Brad Simpson, Christine Mortensen, Jonathan Ashton, Chris Miller

TOPIC	NOTES
Welcome	Review current status from disciplines Discuss outstanding issues Prioritize and plan next steps
Research Update	Research in progress, 50% complete In-person research underway Scheduling facilities in the Midwest for next week
Graphic Design Update	Defined color scheme Iconography created and ready for review
SEO Update	Keyword study complete Content analysis 25% complete
Parking Lot	Chapter outline complete & sent to publisher Assigned chapter due dates Implementing publisher templates for chapters
Next Steps	**Russ:** Next status meeting scheduled for November 19 at 10 A.M. **Carolyn:** Complete next 25% of research in Midwest **Brad & Christine:** Graphic Design to comp book covers **Jonathan:** Complete next 25% of content analysis **Russ & Carolyn:** Keep writing—faster! Chapters due 12/12 **Chris:** Chapters reviewed within 24 hours of receipt

Figure 16.3 *An example of basic meeting notes*

Dealing with Nonconformers

Although you will invariably do your best to be a great meeting planner, agenda creator, and note-taker and -sender, some people will simply fail to comply with your requests to follow the meeting rules that you establish. Unfortunately, some of them will be your coworkers and friends; others will undoubtedly be even worse offenders: your clients.

It seems pointless to write a chapter on dealing with meetings without mentioning how to deal with the people who don't conform to the meeting rules. How do you prevent someone from breaking the rules you put into place? How do you politely suggest that someone put away their mobile device and stop sending instant messages or e-mails while you are trying to hold an effective meeting?

An unscientific poll of Twitter users uncovered a variety of approaches. Hopefully, some of these will help you identify a solution for dealing your nonconformers:

> "Have a respectful, frank, professional conversation with the client that if they accept a meeting, that the clock starts when the meeting starts."

> "The last coworker to the meeting has to be the note taker."

> "Inform coworkers not to waste anyone's time by being tardy."

> "One company used to make the late people wear a VIP button that had lots of ribbons. That conveyed to people that you must be a VIP to make all of these other people wait on you."

> "Start the meeting on time. If people are late tell them they can read the notes that will be sent around after the meeting."

> "Bring coffee, tea, donuts, cookies, etc. to your meetings and people will begin to show up early or on time. They'll also be a bit more attentive and helpful."

> "As the meeting organizer, make sure that you are not only on time, but a little early to every meeting. People will know you by that behavior and begin to follow suit."

While some of those are humorous, dealing with people who do not or will not take your meetings seriously is a sensitive issue. A respectful approach to meetings generally starts from the top down within an organization. If you are having a difficult time getting attendees to observe the meeting rules, start by having a discussion with your immediate superior to ask for support.

(If your immediate supervisor is part of the problem, you may need a different book for support!)

In all seriousness, start with respectful, open lines of communication and ask for support. If you still run into problems, assess the company culture you're dealing with and determine whether this is a problem that you simply have to live with or if you can go up the chain of command to ask for support. These situations are sensitive to deal with—be sure to proceed with caution, courtesy, and respect.

A Final Note on Meetings

This chapter has provided a brief introduction to planning and holding effective meetings as well as proper meeting follow-up. Meetings are necessary to keep a project moving. Part of your task will be to find the most effective way to run them with your team.

Countless approaches to meetings exist; this chapter presented only a sampling. Some companies hold meetings standing up to help move them along quickly and keep attendees alert and undistracted by technology. Some groups attempt to schedule all their meetings on a single day to attempt to increase productivity. Some create nifty catch phrases, such as "topless meetings," to gain attention for their meeting philosophies. Some hold "minimeetings," in which only a couple of people discuss a limited number of issues, to minimize the signal-to-noise ratio.

Whatever the approach, there is no denying that meetings simply do have to happen. Regardless of whether you bring distant teams together via technology or sit down in a coffee shop with a peer, once you start discussing a project, you are having a meeting—even if it's unscheduled.

You might as well spend a little effort and show up prepared, even if it's just with a punch list of questions you need to get answered. You could even call that list an agenda, if you were so inclined.

Over time, you will evolve your style and approach, and determine the method that works for you. Whether or not you call it a *meeting* is your choice.

All Done, Right?

Nope.

Just Like Starting Over...

Through your collection of analytical data and design testing with research data, you can begin to compile a list of enhancements and improvements that would be beneficial for the website. Once you have fully compiled these, you can put together a new proposal (Chapter 3) based upon your recommendations. This proposal could lead you to a brand new project, which could send you all the way back to defining a new set of project objectives (Chapter 4) and business requirements (Chapter 5). You can then move forward into additional research (Chapter 6), creating personas (Chapter 7) for newly identified targets, enhancing your SEO (in the online chapter, "User Experience Design and Search Engine Optimization," available on the companion website), updating or creating new site maps and task flows (Chapter 11), updating or creating new wireframes and annotations (Chapter 12), launching into additional rounds of prototyping (Chapter 13), and more design testing with users (Chapter 14).

You get the idea.

Projects should not die. They should be the springboard into new projects that are geared toward continually improving the user experience design.

INDEX

A

accessibility 187
acknowledgement for projects 63–64
action
- economy of motion and user 200–202
- elicited by marketing campaigns 15–16
- object's properties communicating 198
- responses to user 202–204
- understanding site's potential for 196–197

active observation 115
activities in project 164, 181–183
additional project costs and fees 60–61
advanced site maps 228–230
affinity diagramming
- applying to card sorting 116–117
- solving design conflicts with 179–180

affordance 198
age of personas 136
agendas for meetings 323–325, 327
agile approaches 75–80
AIGA 61
Amazon.com 197–198, 202
American Customer Satisfaction Index (ACSI) 119
analytics tools 33
analyzing usability test results 308–310
Anderson, Stephan P. 215
Angeles, Michael 221
annotations
- defined 239
- uses for 237, 246–248

Aquent 61
arrows 223–224
Art of Game Design, The (Schell) 209
associations 197–198
assumptions in proposals 57–58
audience
- developing persona for target 140–141
- knowing site's 189
- testing sites for 300
- wireframe 239–240

audits
- qualitative 153
- quantitative 152–153

B

baby-naming websites 135
Bainbridge, Mike 281
balancing
- advocate input 173–175
- design elements 6–7, 193–196

Baty, Steve 111
Beecher, Fred 247
Beyer, Hugh 117
biographies 136
Bloomstein, Margot 147
body language 123
Bolt, Nate 287
Boston Globe, The website 194–195
brand presence websites
- common types of 13
- defined 11
- design goals for 13–14
- focus of 11–12

brands
- about 12
- role of brand strategists and stewards 35–36, 41

Brown, Dan 249
Brown, Sunni 142
Build-Measure-Learn loop 77–78
Buley, Leah 242–243
business advocates
- balancing input of 173, 175
- clarifying objectives of 70
- listening to 97
- role of 169

business analysts 36–37
business requirements 83–100
- adding user requirements to 102
- coalescing 98–100
- developing 83–86
- developing wireframes and 238
- gathering with heuristic analysis 89
- meeting to gather 94–95
- site type and development of 11
- stakeholder input on 90–97
- taking time to visualize 165–166
- turning objectives into 83–86

business stakeholders. *See* stakeholders
Buxton, Bill 250, 296

C

card sorting
- applying affinity diagramming to 116–117
- defined 109, 124–125
- process of 125–126
- variations on 126–127

Carpendale, Sheelagh 250
chartjunk 192
Cialdini, Robert B. 215
Cipov, Matt M. 193
Cisco 25
clients
- presenting wireframes to 257–258
- providing contracts and proposals for 50–51

closed sorts 127

collaboration
    coordinating work among designers   183
    developing custom design principles with
       216
    effect of project approach on   81
    planning project   181
Communicating Design (Brown)   249
communication problems   178–179
companies. *See also* business requirements
    assessing competition   72
    building brands   12
    clarifying project objectives   68–71
    contracts and proposals for   50–51
    examining history of   43–44
    hierarchy within   45–46
    network building within   41–42
    quality assurance teaks within   313–314
competition   72
concept exploration   280–283
conditions   224
conflicts
    with business requirements   99–100
    managing during prioritization   177–180
connectors   223–224, 225
consensus   178–179
consumers. *See* users
content. *See also* content source websites;
    content strategy
    adhering to content strategy   149
    developing   37–38
    minimum required for personas
       134–136
    optional persona   137–138
    role of copywriter in   38–39
    scope of   146
content audit   152–153
content flow   156
content matrix   154, 227
content source websites
    card sorting for   124–125
    common uses for   16
    defined   11
    design goals of   17–18
    focus of   16–17
    further information on   17–18
content strategists
    finding   149
    Laura Creekmore   64–65, 146–147, 160
    Matthew Grocki   146–147, 148, 149
    role of   37–38, 41
    Sarah Krznarich   151, 161
    Tim Frick   158–159, 162
    tools used by   152–156
content strategy   145–182.
    See also content strategists
    about   145–146
    adhering to   149
    copywriting vs.   150–151
    defining role of   150–152

developing   162
    finding artifact needed for   156
    finding content strategists   149
    further information on   156–157
    information architecture vs.   150
    need for   146–147
    tools for   152–156
    when needed   147–148
Content Strategy at Work (Bloomstein)   147
Content Strategy for the Web (Halvorson)   146
content templates   154–155
context for mobile devices   27
contextual inquiry   108, 114–117
continuing education in UX design   7
conversion   16
copywriters   38–39
copywriting   150–151
Coroflot   61
corporate culture
    examining project history and   43–44
    hierarchy in   45–46
    logistics within   46
    power distance in   45–46
    understanding   42
costs
    additional project   60–61
    estimating project   61–62
    meeting   322
Creekmore, Laura   64–65, 146–147, 160
cross-over projects   11
Csikszentmihalyi, Mihaly   207–208, 212
Cunningham, Christopher   212
customers. *See* user groups; users

D
data-driven personas   139
data from usability testing   109, 127, 297–298
decision points   223
Define phase   73–74, 164
deliverables   58–59
demographics   104, 136
design goals
    brand presence websites   13–14
    content source websites   17–18
    e-commerce websites   20
    e-learning application   20
    marketing campaign websites   15–16
    site type and   10
    social networking application   21
    task-based application websites   19
    using prototyping for   278
Design of Everyday Things, The (Norman)   198
design principles   185–218
    about   186
    benefit of   185
    creating own   215–218
    interaction   196–204
    Lean UX   76–77
    mobile site and application   26–27

UX experts
    Brad Simpson   254
    Christopher Fahey   313
    Jeff Gothelf   78–79
    Laura Creekmore   64–65, 146–147, 160
    Matthew Grocki   146–147, 148, 149
    Sarah Krznarich   151, 161
    Tim Frick   158–159, 162
    Todd Zaki Warfel   132, 249, 250, 278
UX organizations   8

V

value proposition   15
variation in design   187–188
Vinh, Khoi   196
visual design   186–196
    about   186
    correlating page number to site map   227
    economy in elements   191–192
    exploring mock-ups of   283–284
    further information on   193, 196
    hierarchy and dominance   189–191
    miscues in   200
    proportion and balance in   193–196
    unity and variety in   187–188
visual designers
    passing wireframes to   253
    role of   39–41
    working from wireframes   258
Visual Display of Quantitative Information,
    The (Tufte)   193
Visual Vocabulary for Information
    Architecture   222–224

W

Warfel, Todd Zaki   132, 249, 250, 278
waterfall approach   74
Web Accessibility Initiative (WAI)   187
Website Analysis and MeasureMent Inventory
    (WAMMI)   119
websites. *See also* mobile sites and applications;
    wireframes
    accessibility of   187
    analytics for postlaunch   318
    attractiveness of   205–207
    baby-naming   135
    brand presence   11–14
    common site map mistakes   224–228
    content source   11, 16–18
    creating wireframes from site maps   244
    e-commerce   19–20
    economy of motion for   200–202
    element hierarchy and dominance for
        189–191, 199
    flow and game design for   207–212
    gamification of   210–211

interaction design for   196–204
maintaining   59, 319–320
marketing campaign   14–16
microsites   14–15
mobile-optimized vs. multiple mobile
    apps   26
paper prototypes of   261–262, 276–277
planning mobile-optimized sites   23–26
postlaunch activities for   317–319
remote research tools for   291
responses to user action   202–204
responsive design for   23–24, 254–255
SEO value of content   160
sketching experience of   250–251
social networking applications   21
tab associations for   197–198
task-based application   11, 18–19
types of   10–11
unity and variety in design   187–188
usability heuristics for   87
visual design for   186–196
visual miscues on   200
WebTrends analytic tools   33
Weinschenk, Susan   215
wireframes   237–258
    annotations on   239, 246–248
    converting sketches to digital   251–253
    correlating site map number to   227
    creating   240–241
    defined   238
    developing iterations in   256–257
    getting started on   245–246
    passing to visual designer   253
    presenting to clients   257–258
    project information needed for   249
    prototypes vs.   238, 256
    responsive design using   254–255
    sketching user experience   250–251
    tools for creating   241–243
    uses of   237, 239–240
    working from site maps   244
work for hire   59
writing
    annotations   239
    copywriters' role in   38–39
    proposals   50–51
    usability test discussion guides   304–306
    user stories   81
Wroblewski, Luke   22

Y

YooHoo & Friends   203
Young, Indi   117

Z

Zichermann, Gabe   212

psychology   205–215
visual design   186–196
design testing   279–310.
    See also usability testing
    choosing approach for   284–290
    concept exploration   280–283
    exploring visual design mock-ups   283–284
    final round of   315
    in-person vs. remote research   286–287
    moderated vs. automated techniques for   288–290
    postlaunch   319
    qualitative vs. quantitative research   285
    role of usability testing in   292–294
    usability recommendations from   310
designers
    balancing designs   6–7
    brand strategists and stewards   35–36, 41
    building support network for   40–42
    business analysts   36–37
    coalescing business requirements   98–100
    conducting heuristic analysis   88–89
    content strategists   37–38, 41
    copywriters   38–39
    developing contextual inquiry   108, 114–117
    effect of Lean UX on   79
    front-end developer   40
    gaging prototype needs   260–261
    information architects   30–31, 34
    interaction designer   31–32, 34
    interviewing users   107, 111–114, 304
    involving focus groups   109, 121–124
    managing meetings   330–331
    presenting wireframes to clients   257–258
    priority setting by   170
    roles for UX   30–42, 92
    sharing work between   183
    understanding company culture   42–46
    user researcher   32–34
    using surveys   108, 118–120
    visual designers   39–41
    where to find   7–8
Develop phase   74, 164
development advocates
    balancing input of   173–175
    priorities of   175–177
    role of   169
digital prototypes
    creating in WSIWYG editor   264–265
    development factors for   263–264
    HTML   264–274
Discipline of Content Strategy, The (Halvorson)   146
documentation
    agile approach to   78–79
    detail and formality in   81–82
    planning project   164, 181–183

DOM Scripting (Keith)   271
dominance in visual design   189–191

E
e-commerce websites   19–20
e-learning applications   20
economy of motion   200–202
ecosystem of projects   10
editorial calendars   155
editorial workflow   156
elements
    adding competitive   211
    aligning site map   225–226
    arrows   223–224
    balancing design   6–7, 193–196
    conditions   224
    connectors   223–224, 225
    decision points   223
    economy in   191–192
    hierarchy and dominance of   189–191, 199
    page   222
    pagestack   222–223
    site map and task flow   222–224
emotional design   206–207
Emotional Design (Norman)   206
Empathy Map   141–143
Epinions   213
error messages   203–204
estimates
    project cost   61–62
    time for documentation   182
Evans, Poppy   196
Exploring the Elements of Design (Evans and Thomas)   196

F
FaceOff   210
facilitating usability testing   306–308
Fahey, Christopher   313
Favreau, Jean Marc   50
features. *See* ideating and visualizing features; prioritizing features
Feeding America website   188
Fitts' Law   200
flow and game design   207–212
Flow (Csikszentmihalyi)   207–208, 212
focus groups   109, 121–124
Frick, Tim   147, 158–159, 162
front-end developer   40

G
games   207–212
Gamestorming (Gray, Brown, and Macanufo)   142
gamification   210–211
Gamification by Design (Zichermann and Cunningham)   212
Garrett, Jesse James   222–224

gestures   28–29
Gmail   204
goals. *See* design goals
Google analytics tools   33
Gothelf, Jeff   78–79
governance plan   155
Gray, Dave   142
Greenburg, Saul   250
grids for proportion   23, 195–196
Grocki, Matthew   146–147, 148, 149
groups sorts   127

H

Hadden, Jon   276
Halvorson, Kristina   146, 153
hardware
    remote research   287–288
    usability testing   304
Health Month   211
healthychildren.org website   190
Hess, Whitney   80, 217
heuristic analysis
    benefits of   87
    conducting   88–89
    defined   86
    gathering requirements with   89
heuristics   86, 87
hierarchy
    corporate   45–46
    page element   189–191, 199
Hinton, Andrew   230–231
Hoekman, Robert, Jr.   7
Hofstede, Geert   45
Holtzblatt, Karen   117
home page
    created   248
    designing   245
    wireframe and annotations for   246
HTML prototypes   264–274
    breaking down code for   267–270
    coding log-in process for   266–267
    sketching in jQuery   270–274
    testing forms with   274
    ways to build   264–265

I

ideating and visualizing features
    importance of   165
    skills and techniques for   165–166
    storyboarding for   166–169
image maps   270
in-person design testing   286–287
Influence (Cialdini)   215
information architects   30–31, 34
information architecture   150
Information Architecture Institute   61
Ingram, Richard   156
interaction design principles   196–204

associations and affordance in   197–200
    core of   196–197
    economy of motion   200–202
    further information on   198
    responses to actions   202–204
interaction designer   31–32, 34
iterations
    defined   75
    developing MVP with each   77
    frequency of UX   244
    in modified approaches   80–81
    needed for prototyping   259–260
    planning project   181
    wireframe   256–257

J

jQuery   271

K

Keith, Jeremy   271
Knemeyer, Dirk   12
Knoll, Jonathan   271
Koster, Raph   210
Krznarich, Sarah   151, 161

L

Lean Startup, The (Ries)   76
Lean UX
    deliverables in   78–79
    further information on   80
    origins of   76
    principles of   76–77
licensed work   59–60
location of personas   136
log-in process
    coding HTML prototype for   266–267
    prototyping views for   271–273
LUXr   80

M

Macanufo, James   142
maintaining websites   59, 319–332
Marcotte, Ethan   23–24, 254
marketing campaign websites
    common features of   14
    defined   11
    design goals for   15–16
    focus of   14–15
    further information on   16
Marquardt, Nicolai   250
meetings
    agendas for   323–325, 327
    approaches to   331
    cost of holding   322
    managing   330–331
    notes from   328–329
    requirement-gathering   94–95
    rules for   325–327

running effectively   90, 96–97
scheduling   323
Melzer, James   234–235
mental models   117
message architecture   154
Messagefirst   132, 139–141
methodologies   73–82
    agile approaches   75–80
    defined   73
    further information on   81
    impact on project design   81–82
    milestones for stakeholders   82
    modified waterfall approach   80–81, 164
    steps in common   73–74
    waterfall approach   74
microsites   14, 15
Millman, Debbie   281
Minimum Viable Product (MVP)   77
mobile sites and applications   21–29
    advantages of   26
    characteristics of   24–26
    design principles for   26–27
    examples of Cisco's   25
    further information on   24, 27–28
    proportion for   194–195
    responsive design of   23–24, 254–255
    smartphone gestures   28–29
    when to use   22–23
modified waterfall approach
    about   80–81
    overlapping phases in   164

N

names for personas   135
nested menus   202
New York Times, The   214
Nielsen, Jakob   87
Norman, Don   198, 206
notes from meetings   328–329
numbering site maps   226–228

O

occupation of personas   136
OmniGraffle templates   221
Omniture analytic tools   33
100 Things Every Designer Needs to Know
    About People (Weinschenk)   215
Ordering Disorder (Vinh)   196
organizations for UX design   7–8

P

page elements   222
page inventory   152–153
page templates   154–155
pages
    alignment and spacing on site maps   225
    numbering on site maps   226–228
pagestack element   222–223
paper prototypes   261–262, 276–277

Paper Prototyping (Snyder)   296
passive observation   115
performance
    expectations of site   202–203
    flow states and site   208–209
personas   129–144
    benefits of   129–131
    content for   131, 134–136, 137–138
    creating   131, 133, 143–144
    data-driven   139
    defined   130
    developing   128, 141–143
    example of   132
    target audience group   140–141
    types of   130
photos for personas   134–135
planning
    project's activities and documentation
        164, 181–183
    remote research   287–288
    space and equipment for usability testing
        304
    usability testing   295–299
    user research   110
postlaunch activities   317–319
power distance   45–46
principles. *See* design principles
prioritizing features
    balancing input from advocates   173–175
    considerations for   178
    further information on   180
    managing conflict while   177–180
    prioritization worksheet   172
    team's roles in   169–173
    UX designer's role in   170
Pro JavaScript Techniques (Resig)   271
project glossary   96–97
project manager   44, 170
Project Manager prototype   276–277
project objectives   68–73
    developing into business requirements
        83–86
    prioritizing   71
    site type and project   11
    solidifying   68–71
    SWOT sessions defining   71–73
project overviews   54
project sponsor   91
project teams. *See* teams
projects. *See also* prioritizing features; project
    objectives; proposals
    about   10, 47
    acknowledgement and sign-off for   63–64
    additional costs of   60–61
    building networks within company   41–42
    common site map mistakes   224–228
    conflict over features in   179–180
    corporate history of   43–44
    cost estimates of   61–62

projects (*continued*)
  creating design principles for   215–218
  cross-over   11, 19–21
  designer's roles on   30–42
  developing common language for   96–97
  e-commerce websites   19–20
  ecosystem of   10
  gathering requirements for   83–86
  heuristic analysis of   86–89
  identifying site type for   10–11
  lack of alignment on   178–179
  making wireframes for   249
  methodologies for   73–82
  mobile site and application   21–29
  payment schedules for   62–63
  prioritizing requirements for   164
  proposals defining approach of   55–56
  solidifying objectives of   68–71
  statement of work for   49, 65–66
  working within corporate hierarchy   45–46
proportion and balance   193–196
proposals   49–66
  acknowledgement and sign-off   63–64
  additional costs and fees   60–61
  assumptions in   57–58
  challenges of   49
  components of   51–52
  defining project approach   55–56
  enumerating deliverables for   58–59
  outlining scope of work   57
  ownership and rights   59–60
  payment schedules   62–63
  project estimates   61–62
  project overview for   54
  revision history for   53–54
  statement of work   49, 65–66
  title page for   52–53
  writing   50–51
prototype developers   275–276
prototypes   259–278.
    See also digital prototypes;
    HTML prototypes
  digital   262–274
  examples of   276–278
  gaging needs for   260–261
  iterative process for   259–260
  log-in process   271–273
  paper   261–262, 276–277
  tools for   274–275
  using for design goals   278
  wireframes vs.   238, 256
  working with developers   275–276
psychology design principles   205–215
  about   186
  attractive design   205–207
  flow and game design   207–212
  focusing on positive responses   204
  further information on   215
  providing social proof   212–214

Q

qualitative approaches
  qualitative audits   153
  research   285
  usability testing   293–294
quantitative approaches
  quantitative audits   152–153
  research   285
  testing   293–294

R

rapid development approach   75–80
recording usability test results   304
Reisg, John   271
remote research
  automated tools and   288–290
  benefits of   287
  design testing as   286–287
  planning for   287–288
  tools for   287, 291
Remote Research (Bolt and Talthimutte)   287
remote sorts   127
requirements-gathering meetings   94–97
research. *See* user research
responsive design   23–24, 254–255
Responsive Web Design (Marcotte)   23–24, 254
revision history for proposals   53–54
Ries, Eric   76–77
roles
  outlining project   90–92
  screeners   302–303
rules for meetings   325–327

S

Saffer, Dan   28, 217
Schell, Jesse   209
scope of work   57
Seductive Interaction Design (Anderson)   215
Seiden, Josh   130
sign-off for projects   63–64
simple site maps   228
Simpson, Brad   254
site maps
  aligning elements of   225–226
  basic elements in   222–224
  common mistakes in   224–228
  creative   230–231
  defined   219–220
  developing advanced   228–230
  illustrated   220
  numbering on   226–228
  simple   228
  text on   226
sketching
  converting to digital wireframe   251–253
  responsive design   255
  sketchboard templates   249
  user experience   250–251

Sketching User Experiences (Greenburg, Carpendale, Marquardt, and Buxton) 250, 296
Slavin, Tim 155
smartphones. *See also* mobile sites and applications
    gestures for 28–29
    sales of 21
Snyder, Carolyn 296
social interaction 5
social networking applications 21
social proof 212–214
software
    required for remote research 287–288
    site map and task flow 221–224
    wireframe design 241–242
Software Usability Measurement Inventory (SUMI) 119
Soucy, Kyle 288
space and equipment for usability testing 304
Spool, Jared 144, 180, 217
sprints. *See* iterations
staffing usability tests 304
stakeholders
    defined 91
    developing project requirements with 84–86
    finding right 92–93
    gathering ideas from 90–97
    listening to 97
    milestone approval from 82
    prioritizing user group attributes 105–107
statement of work (SOW) 49, 65–66
status icons 192
stencils 242
storyboarding 166–169
    brainstorming team for 166–167
    developing storyboard 167–169
    preparing for 166
    questions for 167
structuring websites. *See also* prototypes; wireframes
    site maps 219–220, 222–231
    task flows 219–220, 222–224, 227, 232–236
support for users 316
surveys
    software for 119, 291
    using 108, 118–120
swimlanes 234–236
SWOT analysis 71–73

T

tablets
    developing mobile-optimized 25
    portrait and landscape mode for 193–194
tags in HTML documents 268–269
target audience personas 140–141

task-based application websites
    common uses of 18
    defined 11
    design goals for 19
task flows
    basic elements for 222–224
    defined 219–220
    examples of 232–233
    illustrated 220, 232–233
    numbering 227
    swimlanes 234–236
    uses for 231, 234
Tatum, Keith 276
teams
    collaboration among 81
    common terminology among 96–97
    conflict in 177–180
    design principles focusing 216
    developing storyboards 166–169
    kickoff meetings for 68
    lack of alignment in 178–179
    positive tension among 173–175
    prioritization by 170–173
    prioritizing features 164, 169–173
    project roles for 30–42
    responsibilities and roles of 90–92
    sketching user experience 250
    using Lean UX approach 79
    working with prototype developers 275–276
templates
    content 154–155
    Empathy Map 142
    OmniGraffle 221
    sketchboard 249
    wireframe 242–243
test participants
    compensating 110, 300–301
    interviewing 107, 111–114, 304
    number of 294
    screening 302–303
testing. *See* design testing; remote research; usability testing
Texas Instruments microsite 15
text on site maps 226
Theory of Fun, A (Koster) 210
Thomas, Mark A. 196
time
    documentation 182
    required for digital prototypes 263
    visualizing business requirements 165–166
title page for proposals 52–53
Tognazzini, Bruce 88
tools
    analytics 33
    body language as 123
    prototyping 274–275
    remote research 287, 291

tools (*continued*)
    software for UX design   221
    surveying   119–120
    used by content strategists   152–156
    wireframe   241–243
touch gestures   28–29
troubleshooting remote research sessions   288
trust   206
Tufte, Edward   192, 193
Tulathimutte, Tony   287

U

unified design   187–188
usability testing
    analyzing results of   308–310
    attractive products and   206
    compensation for   110, 300–301
    data gathered in   109, 127, 297–298
    discussion guides for   304–306
    facilitating   306–308
    focus groups and   121
    further information on   296
    number of participants in   294
    planning research for   295–299
    prototypes for   278
    qualitative vs. quantitative methods in   293–294
    recommendations from   310
    recruiting users for   299–300
    screening participants in   302–303
    space and equipment for   304
    steps in   293
    terminating interviews for   304
    tools for   291
    user acceptance testing vs.   292
    visual design   190
Usability.gov website   305
user acceptance testing   292
user advocates   169, 173–175
user experiences. *See also* UX design
    importance of tangible and online   4–5
    sketching   250–251
user groups
    defining   102–107
    example user model   106–107
    listing attributes of   103–105
    prioritizing attributes of   105–107
user interviews   107, 111–114, 304
user models   106, 107
user requirements
    adding to business requirements   102
    prioritizing for project   164
    visualizing features for   166–169
user research. *See also* usability testing
    about   101
    card sorting   109, 116–117, 124–127
    choosing techniques for   102, 107–109
    contextual inquiry   108, 114–117

    defining groups for   102–107
    designing from user models   107
    developing persona from   131
    focus groups   109, 121–124
    further information on   111
    incorporating in site design   11
    listing group attributes   103–105
    planning   110
    prioritizing group attributes for   105–107
    reviewing   128
    selecting types of   110–111
    steps in   102
    surveys   108   118–120
    tools for surveying   119–120
    usability testing   109, 127
    user interviews   107, 111–114, 304
user research plan   295–298
user researcher   32–34
user stories   81
userglue website   247
users
    compensating for usability testing   110, 300–301
    conflicts between requirements and needs of   99–100
    customer experience of brand   12
    defining documentation's   182
    economy of motion and action by   200–202
    flow states of   207–208
    knowing audience   189
    listing advantages for   316
    number in usability testing   294
    recruiting for usability testing   299–300
    screening usability testing   302–303
    site responses to action   202–204
    surveying satisfaction of   298–299
    tailoring microsites to experience of   15
UX design. *See also* design goals; design principles; software
    basing only on user models   107
    building support network for   40–42
    conducting heuristic analysis of   86–89
    continuing education in   7
    defined   3, 6
    ensuring production of quality   312–314
    evaluating user adoption of   315–317
    final design testing in   315
    focusing on digital experience design   5
    importance of tangible experiences   4
    making case for   33
    methodology's impact on project   81–82
    organizations for   7–8
    planning mobile-optimized sites   23–26, 317–319
    postlaunch activities in   317–319
    steps in design launch   315–317
    storyboarding for   166–169
    SWOT analysis in   71–73